Sport and Society

Issues in Society

Series editor: Tim May

Sport and Society
History, Power and Culture

GRAHAM SCAMBLER

Open University Press

Open University Press
McGraw-Hill Education
McGraw-Hill House
Shoppenhangers Road
Maidenhead
Berkshire
England
SL6 2QL

email: enquiries@openup.co.uk
world wide web: www.openup.co.uk

and Two Penn Plaza, New York, NY 10121–2289, USA

First published 2005

A catalogue record of this book is available from the British Library

ISBN-13 978 0335 21070 1 (pb) 978 0335 21071 8 (hb)
ISBN-10 0 335 21070 8 (pb) 0 335 210716 (hb)

Library of Congress Cataloguing-in-Publication Data
CIP data applied for

Typeset by YHT Ltd, London
Printed in Poland, EU by OZGraf. S.A.
www.polskabook.pl

Contents

Series Editor's Preface

The social sciences contribute to a greater understanding of the working of societies and dynamics of social life. They are often, however, not given due credit for this role and much writing has been devoted to why this should be the case. At the same time, we are living in an age in which the role of science in society is being re-evaluated. This has led to both a defence of science as the disinterested pursuit of knowledge and an attack on science as nothing more than an institutionalized assertion of faith with no greater claim to validity than mythology and folklore. These debates tend to generate more heat than light.

In the meantime the social sciences, in order to remain vibrant and relevant, will reflect the changing nature of these public debates. In so doing they provide mirrors upon which we gaze in order to understand not only what we have been and what we are now, but to inform ideas about what we might become. This is not simply about understanding the reasons people give for their actions in terms of the contexts in which they act, as well as analysing the relations of cause and effect in the social, political and economic spheres, but about the hopes, wishes and aspirations that people, in their different cultural ways, hold.

In any society that claims to have democratic aspirations, these hopes and wishes are not for the social scientist to prescribe. For this to happen it would mean that the social sciences were able to predict human behaviour with certainty. This would require one theory and one method applicable to all times and places. The physical sciences do not live up to such stringent criteria, whilst the conditions in societies which provided for this outcome would be intolerable. Why? Because a necessary condition of human freedom is the ability to have acted otherwise and to imagine and practice different ways of organizing societies and living together.

It does not follow from the above that social scientists do not have a valued role to play, as is often assumed in ideological attacks upon their place and role within society. After all, in focusing upon what we have been and what we are now, what we might become is inevitably illuminated. Therefore, whilst it may not be the province of the social scientists to predict our futures, they are, given not only their understandings, but equal positions as citizens, entitled to engage in public debates concerning future prospects.

This international series was devised with this general ethos in mind. It seeks to offer students of the social sciences, at all levels, a forum in which ideas are interrogated in terms of their importance for understanding key social issues. This is achieved through a connection between styles, structure and content that is found to be both illuminating and challenging in terms of its evaluation of topical social issues, as well as representing an original contribution to the subject under discussion.

Given this underlying philosophy, the series contains books on topics which are driven by substantive interests. This is not simply a reactive endeavour in terms of reflecting dominant social and political pre-occupations, it is also pro-active in terms of an examination of issues which relate to and inform the dynamics of social life and the structures of society that are often not part of public discourse. What is distinctive about the series is an interrogation of the assumed characteristics of our current epoch in relation to its consequences for the organization of society and social life, as well as its appropriate mode of study.

Each contribution contains, for the purposes of general orientation, as opposed to rigid structure, three parts. First, an interrogation of the topic which is conducted in a manner that renders explicit core assumptions surrounding the issues and/or an examination of the consequences of historical trends for contemporary social practices. Second, a section which aims to 'bring alive' ideas and practices by considering the ways in which they directly inform the dynamics of social relations. A third section then moves on to make an original contribution to the topic. This encompasses possible future forms and content, likely directions for the study of the phenomenon in question, or an original analysis of the topic itself. Of course, it might be a combination of all three.

With the above in mind, I am very pleased to include Graham Scambler's new book in the series. There was time in which the Protestant ethic perhaps got the better of social scientists via their relative silence on the issue of sport in society. Sport was concerned with the aesthetic area of social life and was clearly distinct from work. It brought with it connotations of leisure and even the pursuit of pleasure for its own sake, rather than the worldly calling of good works in the name of possible election after life.

As Graham Scambler charts, whilst reward, performance and exceptionalism were always a part of sport, what has changed is its association with cultural icons, such as Muhammad Ali, whose presence was mediated across the world through new forms of global communication. This, together with a growing interest in the leisure society that is part of the conspicuous consumption that surrounds daily life in advanced capitalism and sport being seen as a site of investment for financial return, transformed the sporting landscape.

These transformations signalled a move from the sport of capitalism to capitalism in sport. Sport was money and sporting heroes could be used to sell goods manufactured on one side of the world where wages were low, to another side whose concept of value was increasingly embodied in wearing clothing that advertised the company that manufactured them in the first place. Consumption and production were linked in a supply chain that stretched across the world mediated through the culture of sporting legends.

With large multi-national corporations making such investments in sport, there is also a cultural investment, with a long history, that is made by those who are the faithful fans of its sites of activity. Yet there is no necessary relation between their sense of belonging and identity and the extent to which sporting clubs are seen as sites of investment by those with other interests. Deploying the arguments of Jürgen Habermas, Graham Scambler argues that power and money have become the steering mechanisms that link athletic activity to capitalist systems.

His argument then turns to the relationship between sport, exercise and obesity. The former can often lead to injuries and has also been the subject of much media attention in relation to illegal drug use. International athletes are routinely subject to ever greater pressures in order just to compete, let alone win. The fitness 'industry' has also moved into a cultural terrain in which the desire for the healthy body is routinely informed by idealized images to which few conform. Yet this becomes an individualized process of choice. Apparently unconnected, for example, is the selling of school playing fields and government targeting of teachers and parents as responsible for inculcating the benefits of exercise and diet into young people who, in turn, are surrounded by adverts and opportunities to consume unhealthy foods.

Graham Scambler does not suggest that sport is determined by the forces he charts. Yet there is an increased tendency for capitalism to move into more terrains of sporting activity, alongside a culture of individualized blame against those who are the antithesis of the healthy individual, as if sport (rather than exercise) and health were inextricably linked. In the final part of the book he then suggests a jigsaw model of sociological enquiry that seeks to counter existing relations between sport and society in order that sport can be brought back to the public realm of deliberation from which it has been extracted. For all those interested in this potential and the future of sport, this sets a challenge that is worthy of a different form of investment than is currently dominant.

Acknowledgements

This book owes a great deal to colleagues, friends and family. As a fairly recent recruit to the sociology of sport I have found numerous colleagues' studies and expositions both enlightening and enjoyable. To Tim May, the series editor, go special thanks for his close reading of the initial draft and subsequent deft and wise counsel. Thanks go also to a group of friends with whom I have played badminton weekly for a quarter of a century, consumed countless beers and debated every sport known to humankind. They are Ken Reeves, Mike Roshier, Bill Tallis and, first reserve, Roger Kerswell. I may just possibly have learned something from these people. As ever, Annette Scambler's industry and support enabled me to keep going and see the project to its conclusion. As all the above would undoubtedly insist, the book's theses and conclusions are my fault.

The volume is dedicated to Angela Kerswell, who died in 2004 and whose irrepressible enthusiasm for life is missed.

Introduction

It is a routine refrain in sociology and many other disciplines that the market for textbooks so beloved of contemporary publishers appears all but exhausted. There already exists, for example, a multiplicity of excellent student texts on the sociology of sport, many but not all arising out of North America and Europe. Perhaps the publication in the symbolic year of 2000 of the *Handbook of Sports Studies*, edited by Coakley and Dunning, represents a culmination of this expansion. So why then another introduction to the sociology of sport? A first point in defence is that this volume is not a conventional textbook. While it offers fairly wide-ranging coverage of the now considerable body of theory and research on sports phenomena, albeit with clear foci on Western 'history, power and culture' and in later chapters on disorganized capitalism, and hopefully in a way accessible to undergraduate students, it is characterized by a strong critical impulse. Exegesis is typically accompanied by rebuttals and qualifications, offspring of a commitment, logical and moral, to a reflexive critical sociology of sport. And second, *Sport and Society* aspires to make a contribution in its own right to the manner in which, and the agenda with which, reflexive critical sociologists of sport conduct their investigations. This is not a claim to significant originality: undeniably, the book owes much to the pioneers and present practitioners of sport sociology. However, the attempt to learn from and apply the critical realist philosophy of Roy Bhaskar and the critical social theory of Jürgen Habermas, deploying what I call the *jigsaw model*, does amount to some kind of innovation. The result is a tentative and provisional but also distinctive frame within which the changing social relations of sport might appropriately be considered. It is a frame turning on the proposition that the day-to-day pursuit of exercise and sport in the lifeworld is being – increasingly rapidly – 'colonized' by an excessive and unaccountable system rationalization, that is, manipulated by the subsystems of the economy (through money) and the state (through power). Real and reinvigorated relations of social class are posited as crucial to this process of progressive colonization.

In Chapter 1 in Part One, premodern sport is discussed via the founding and institutionalization of the ancient Games at Olympia. This establishes parameters or points of comparison for modern sport. For example, the attributes of athletic competition at Olympia seem closer to those of the open or professional (post)modern Olympiad than they do to de Coubertin's amateur ideals enshrined in the reconstructed Games of 1896. Chapter 2 charts the genesis of what most commentators define as modern sport in England in the eighteenth and nineteenth centuries. Public school and Oxbridge in origin and ethos, this period progressively witnessed the rationalization and codification of a remarkable range of pastimes and sports, setting the rules that have often survived more or less unchanged through to the thoroughly globalized present. Chapter 3 describes de Coubertin's personal crusade to re-invent the Olympics, drawing on this English amateur ethos, and traces and assesses its progeny through the twentieth century up to and including the Sydney Games of 2000.

Part Two focuses on some paradigmatic and some novel phenomena of the sporting present. Chapter 4 distinguishes between exercise and sport and examines their respective linkages to health, considers rates of participation, and incorporates brief topical assessments of state policies on exercise and sport, of growing rates of obesity and of the role of drug use in society and sport. Special attention is paid to the logics of the regime of capital accumulation of the economy and of the mode of regulation of the state, and their respective social relations of class and command. In Chapter 5 it is suggested that while Elias is justified in discerning a 'civilizing process' in occidental pastimes, there is reason to suspect a 'de-civilizing spurt' coinciding with disorganized capitalism. Attention is given to the putative generalized re-emergence of violence in sporting activity and, more specifically, to the recasting of combat sports like boxing as forms of entertainment. The discussion is extended to encompass the involvement of women in violent and combat activities. Chapter 6 analyses the colonization of modern sport through an examination of the development and hyper-commodification of association football in England, culminating in the currently precarious dynamics of the Premiership. This prompts a series of reflections on modern and postmodern sports iconography, incorporating sociological portraits of Muhammad Ali and David Beckham.

The third Part more directly addresses the theoretical underpinnings of the sociology of sport. Chapter 7 provides outlines and comments on the key paradigms or research programmes that have informed the sociology of sport and sports studies, namely, functionalism, conflict theory, interpretive sociology, feminism, figurational sociology and post-structuralism/postmodernism. It ends with an exhortation to synthesis rather than mere eclecticism. In Chapter 8 a framework within which the contemporary issues of the sociology of sport considered in Part Two might be re-assessed is articulated. This lays out the salience of Bhaskar's critical realism, Habermas' critical theory and what will be termed the jigsaw model for a reflexive critical sociology of sport. The final chapter concludes with an overview of sport in disorganized capitalism and a tentative agenda for future research.

This is not a conventional textbook of the sociology of sport. There are plenty of those available in what seems an ever-expanding marketplace, many of them impressive and comprehensive. Rather, an attempt is made here to cover and to do a modicum of justice to the principal paradigms of the sociology of sport while simultaneously proffering a distinctive theoretical stance. In sport, as in other spheres, the lifeworld, it is maintained, has ceded ground to, and been colonized by, the subsystems of the economy and state. Further, in the present era of disorganized capitalism the reinvigorated class relations of the economy have tended to subdue the command relations of the state, allowing for an unprecedented hyper-commodification of sporting activity. It is this proposition that underpins many of the analyses that follow. If the text provokes colleagues and students critically to re-examine the views to which they presently incline, whatever these might be, it will have served its purpose.

PART ONE

History and Sport

1

The Ancient Games

When and how did sport begin? Some have claimed that all the most noble of human accomplishments, from poetry to sport, have their genesis in the impulse to *play*. And if it is accepted that other creatures share this impulse – and most animals, like children, delight in running, chasing, tumbling, wrestling, and so on – then on this view sport may even be held to antedate humans (Huizinga, 1938). Others link sport with *work* rather than play. The German Marxist Lukas has argued that sport actually distinguishes humans from other species (see Mandell, 1984). He argues that spear throwing was probably the first sport. To become proficient with spears required sustained practice and the mastery of types of judgement very different from those needed by forefathers hunting without the benefit of tools. Unlike their predecessors, whose play, relaxation and exercise differed little from that of other creatures, spear throwers introduced sport as a preparation for work. Their sporting or athletic activity was a reflection of their need to survive and progress. Reference to spear throwing suggests yet another linkage, between sport and *combat*. Maybe, it has been contended, sport was above all else an early, organized mode of training for warfare.

The trouble with theories like these about the origins of sport is twofold. First, they are, and are likely to remain, highly speculative. There are next to no systematic data available on forms of life in prehistory. All that can be said, based on archaeological artefacts and ethnographic evidence, is that there were probably many and varied sporting and athletic festivals before the founding of the great empires from which are dated the beginnings of civilized settlement. There is some evidence for believing, for example, that as early as 4000 BC horse racing occurred at Mycenae; that by 3000 BC chariot racing, archery, stick fighting and other 'paramilitary' athletic training took place in Mesopotamia; and that horse and chariot races and combat contests were held in the Indus River region by 2300 BC (Cashmore, 2000: 82). Similarly, indications survive of ball games played by native Americans, of wrestling matches among Amazonians and Papuans, and of high-jumping by the African Bantu; all of these seem to have attracted bands of spectators. It seems far-fetched to presume, as theoreticians often do, that sport had a unique and functional point of origin.

> Some forms – archery and chariot races, for example – developed out of martial practices. Other sports evolved from necessary endeavours; hunting and horse racing are classic examples. Still other forms emerged as individuals contested for place in a society, or, as did ball games, in the course of religious rituals or festivals. Indeed, given the significance of religions in these early societies, many sports occurred in the context of festivals that honoured the gods and became ritualised themselves. (Struna, 2000: 188)

But this is not to say very much.

The second problem is one of definition. While it is possible to use the term sport in an ecumenical, transhistorical sense, as for example the historian Baker (1982) does when he deploys it to describe any socially organized physical game or contest, such definitions are likely to be bland and unhelpful. Moreover it is a mistake to assume that the concepts of sport or athletic competition familiar to us in the West at the beginning of the twenty-first century can be readily applied to activities in prehistory or in later premodern social formations. While there are certainly continuities with the past, there are also radical discontinuities. Sporting activity derives its meanings from, and can therefore only be fully grasped in terms of, the culture of which it is part. That this is so will become clearer when we compare the ancient games at Olympia with the modern 'Olympic Games'. It is in acknowledgement of the cultural specificity of families of concepts about sport that some analysts have argued that sport *as we understand it* has its roots not in prehistory but in England around the time of industrialization. The logic of this position will be examined in Chapter 2 and elaborated in reflections on the modern and postmodern Olympic movements in Chapter 3. The subject-matter of these early, largely descriptive chapters – documenting three key *long moments* in the evolution of sporting activity – will be mined as a resource throughout the remainder of the volume.

Whatever the theoretical interpretation of the origins of sporting endeavour, there is no doubting the historic significance of the ancient Games at Olympia, the focus of this opening chapter. Furthermore, enough is known about both the Games and the politico-cultural institutions they reflected to permit a reasonable reconstruction of the ground rules of competition. It is likely that the first Games were held in 776 BC. Remarkably, they were then repeated every fourth summer until at least AD 261, over a thousand years without a single cancellation. The Greek world was, of course, far from static during this period and it is important to realize something of the scale and nature of the changes it underwent. The brief account that follows provides a backcloth to the analysis of the Games themselves.

Change in the World of Hellas

When the Olympic Games were first established the Greeks were confined to the southern tip of the Balkans, the Aegean islands and the Aegean coast of Asia Minor. There followed a long period of expansion, with small groups leaving their poor rural communities, generally dominated by aristocratic landowning families, to travel west to Sicily and southern Italy, along the Mediterranean coast, and to Cyrene in Northern Africa. Others moved north-east along the shores of the Black Sea. After the conquests of Alexander in the fourth century BC there were further excursions into Egypt, Syria and Babylonia. Despite founding discrete communities over vast new territories, these immigrants retained their identities as Greeks. They continued to share the same language, gods and customs and to take part in the Olympic Games on an equal footing. This cultural continuity, manifested in a strong Greek or Hellenic consciousness, did not however lead to political unification. ' "Hellas" was thus not a country or a state but an abstraction, like Christendom in the Middle Ages or Islam today. The games were pan-hellenic ("all Greek") rather than, strictly speaking, international' (Finley and Pleket, 1976: 7).

This gradual process of migration and colonization gave crucial impetus to economic and political change. Trade between old and new communities grew rapidly, as did the opening up of overseas markets. Thriving and increasingly prosperous urban communities developed in all parts of Hellas, from Athens to its remotest outposts. And economic change was accompanied by political change. No longer could the monopoly of political power by a few landowning families be taken for granted. In the more advanced urban communities in particular, protracted and sometimes bitter struggles for political rights and political power were underway as early as the seventh century BC.

The period from the mid-sixth to the mid-fifth century BC is often referred to as the 'Age of the Tyrants', tyranny in this context meaning autocratic rule by a single man or family. The tyrants were usually drawn from the aristocracy. None of them established a monarchy, although a few families, like that of Othagoras of Sicyon, retained power for decades. Most commonly the sons of tyrants, possessing 'neither the efficiency nor charisma of their fathers', forfeited power after a bout of oppressive and unpopular rule (Carlton, 1977: 73). On the Greek mainland, tyranny was relatively short-lived and was typically succeeded either by some form of oligarchic rule, as in Corinth, or by some form of democratic rule, as in

Athens. With the notable exception of the Athenian democracy, founded in 508 BC, regimes were remarkably unstable.

Whatever its form of government – tyranny, oligarchy or democracy – each established community or *polis* ('city-state') was in principle an autonomous entity, comprising the city itself and its rural hinterland. But the reality was often different. Sparta, an exemplary case for those favouring a link between early sport and preparations for warfare, seized the district of Messenia as early as the eighth century BC, and during the sixth century brought most of the rest of the Peloponnese, excepting Argos, into a league which she dominated. In the fifth century BC, Athens created a tribute-paying, maritime empire that incorporated, in its prime, most of the Aegean islands, the coastal cities of Asia Minor and some others.

Another feature all communities shared, regardless of their form of government, was a profound social inequality. Finley (1983) has offered a conservative estimate that there were about 60,000 slaves in Athens at the end of the fifth century BC. Overall it seems that slaves made up about 30–35 per cent of the populations of major Greek communities. There were also clear divisions among the citizens themselves, for example between the wealthy and those living a life of subsistence, between urban dwellers and peasants, and between members of the old established aristocratic families and the *nouveaux riches*. Finally, it is clear that Greek communities were intensely patriarchal: most of the slaves were in fact women.

Finley and Pleket argue that in considering the shifting historical context of the Olympic Games it is useful to think in terms of three stages. From 776 BC until late in the fourth century BC they were part of the Hellas characterized by the city-state. The second stage was marked by the Hellenization of the Macedonians, culminating in the creation of the League of Hellenes in 338 BC under the Macedonian King, Philip II. His son and successor, Alexander, reigned for 13 years, during which time his conquests extended Greek/Macedonian influence far and wide; it was during this period that migrants reached parts of India, as well as Egypt, Syria and Babylonia. New territorial states were established, frequently under autocratic monarchies. The Greeks and Macedonians formed a closed ruling class in the areas they conquered, founded Greek cities – such as Alexandria and Antioch – and retained their Greek culture. Their conquered subjects persisted in their own languages and forms of life, although gradually the elite among them were accepted into Helles, and therefore also into the Olympic Games.

The final stage began with the Roman conquest, commencing with the capture of Sicily towards the end of the third century BC. In 146 BC the old Greek mainland became a Roman province; and following the defeat of Anthony and Cleopatra at Actium in 31 BC the whole of the Roman republic was transformed into an autocratic monarchy under Augustus. The Romans lacked both the will and the means to impose a uniform culture across their empire, with the result that it remained divided between the Latin west and Greek east (including Sicily). Games like those held at Olympia remained largely confined to the east. For all that the Greek cities had lost their political status and autonomy, their cultural salience for their citizens was barely diminished. 'An Olympic victor in the third century AD still identified himself with his city, as had his pre-decessors a thousand years before, and his city with him' (Finley and Pleket, 1976: 11). It is unknown when the last of the ancient Games was held at Olympia, although they clearly lasted until at least AD 261. Given their religious significance it seems unlikely that they long survived the impact of Christianity, and especially the Christian emperor Theodosius I's edict in AD 393 that all pagan cults and centres be closed down.

The Olympic Programme: Religion and Sport

The games held at Olympia were the oldest of the four pan-Hellenic festivals which constituted the *periodos* or 'circuit' games. The other three were the Pythian Festival at Delphi (in honour of Apollo), the Isthmian Festival at Corinth (in honour of Poseidon) and the Nemean Festival at Nemea (in honour of Zeus). The Pythian Games, 'reorganized' in 582 BC, took place every four years in even years between the Olympic Games; the biennial Isthmian Games, also reorganized in 582 BC, occurred in Olympic and Pythian years; and the biennial Nemean Games, reorganized in 573 BC, took place in the years in between. The games came to Olympia in 776 BC because it was already a recognized sacred site: it had become a shrine of the god Zeus in about 1000 BC. In the words of the German historian Deubner (1936: 5):

> The Olympic Games were sacred games, staged in a sacred place and at a sacred festival; they were a religious act in honour of the deity. Those who took part did so in order to serve the god and the prizes which they won came from god. For when the wreath woven from the branch of sacred olive was placed on the victor's head it trans-mitted to him the life-giving properties with which that tree was charged. The Olympic Games had their roots in religion.

The most ancient monument to the worship of Zeus was the great ash altar in the centre of the sacred grove, probably dating back to the tenth century BC. One late Greek writer described it as a steep mound over 20 feet high, consisting entirely of the charred bones and ashes of ten centuries of animal sacrifice. Athletes and others engaged in worship were permitted to mount the broad platform near the base, but only the priests and diviners could ascend to offer sacrifice at the summit (Robertson, 1988). The great sacrifice to Zeus took place on the morning of the third or middle day of the festival, that is, immediately after the full moon. It culminated in the slaughter of 100 oxen, the thighs of which were burned at the top of the

Figure 1.1

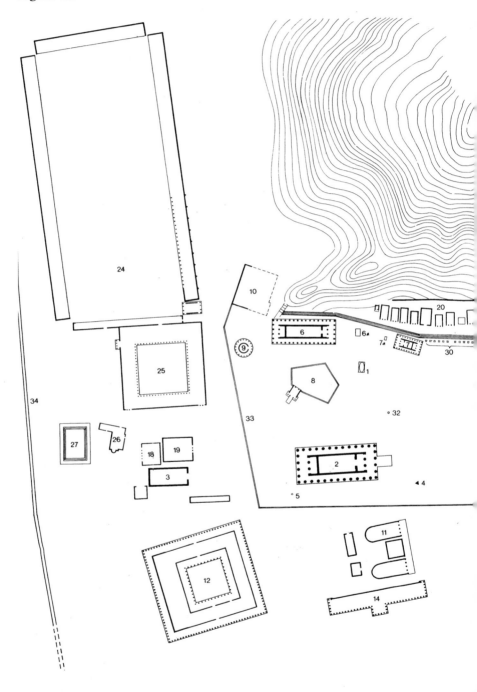

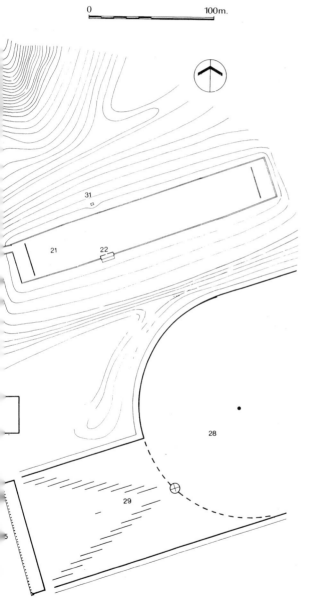

Plan of Olympia
c.100 BC

Key

1   Great Altar of Zeus
2   Temple of Zeus
3   Pheidias' workshop
4   Statue of Victory by Paionios
5   Sacred olive-tree
6   Temple of Hera
6a Altar of Hera
7   Temple of Meter
7a Altar of Meter
8   Pelopion
9   Philippeion
10 Prytaneion
11 Bouleuterion
12 Leonidaion
13 Echo Colonnade
14 Southern Colonnade
15 Colonnade of Agnaptos
16 South Eastern Colonnade
17 'Greek building'
18 Heroon
19 'Theokoleon'
20 Treasuries
21 Stadium
22 Judges' stand
23 Entrance tunnel to stadium
24 Gymnasium
25 Palaistra
26 Bathing facilities
27 Swimming pool
28 Hippodrome
29 Starting gate for horse-races
30 Zanes (statues of Zeus)
31 Altar of Demeter Chamyne
32 Pillar of Oinomaos
33 Altis wall
34 Retaining wall of river
    Kladeos
35 Hill of Kronos

mound in honour of the god, who was believed to take sustenance from the smoke.

If the sanctuary at Olympia at first had a rustic air, from the fifth century BC onwards it became heavily developed, with the erection apace of both religious and secular buildings. Figure 1.1 shows a plan of Olympia around 100 BC and illustrates the extent of the development. The most impressive of the new buildings was the Temple of Zeus, which took a decade to build and was completed in 450 BC. This housed the massive statue of Zeus, one of the 'seven wonders of the world'. Forty feet high and wrought of gold and ivory, it was designed and its construction supervised by the noted Athenian sculptor Pheidias from his workshop nearby.

In the early centuries of the Olympic Games the athletes used an open, level stretch of ground with a line scratched in the sand to mark the start (hence the expression 'starting from scratch'). In keeping with the religious nature of the festival the finishing line was close to the altar of Zeus. Spectators stood on the lower slopes of the Hill of Kronos. In time, a rudimentary rectangular stadium was constructed, but it was not until 350 BC that an impressive new stadium with a capacity of around 40,000 was specifically built (Crowther, 2001). By then the Games were established in their own right. 'Originally Zeus had been glorified for granting powers of strength and physical endurance to the athletes; now the athletes were becoming increasingly professional and beginning to gain recognition as cult figures themselves' (Swaddling, 1982: 24). Reflecting this change, the new stadium was located *outside* the sacred precinct.

The stadium track measured 600 Olympic feet, or 192.28 metres, and was of clay with a light covering of sand. There were stone sills towards each end to mark the start and finish of the races. Circumscribing the racing arena was a channel conducting water round the stadium; this was discharged at intervals into basins for the refreshment of spectators wilting in the sun. A natural rise of ground to the east and artificial embankments to the north, west and south made for the accommodation of 40,000–45,000 spectators.

It seems that neither the stadium nor the other buildings constituting the sports complex at Olympia were much used during the period between the games. Preparations for competition were therefore intense and protracted. The main officials of the games, the *Hellanodikai*, began their work ten months beforehand. Ten in number for most of the history of the games and chosen by lot, they were housed in Ellis. One acted as supervisor-in-chief while the others formed three groups to preside over, first, the equestrian events, second, the pentathlon and third, the remainder of the competitions.

The athletes were also required to train in their home towns for ten months before the games. For the final month they had to travel to Ellis for compulsory training under the strict supervision of the *Hellanodikai*.

During this month the judges were fully occupied with various tasks: they disqualified those who were not fit, checked on parentage and Greek descent, and resolved any disputes concerning the classification of men and boys, horses and colts. The training was renowned for its harshness: the athletes had to observe a strict diet, carry out a gruelling regime of exercise and obey every word of the *Hellanodikai*. (Swaddling, 1982: 35–6)

Significantly, for many centuries only reasonably affluent citizens became involved because they alone were able to devote the necessary time to such preparations (McIntosh, 1993). Women, slaves and foreigners were specifically excluded from participation. Women were also banned as spectators, although slaves and foreigners were allowed to attend. Women did have their own festival at Olympia however, the *Heraia*, or games held in honour of Hera. These were held every four years and consisted of a single foot-race, the track being shortened by one-sixth to around 160 metres. Winners were awarded crowns of olive like male Olympic victors.

Two days prior to the start of the Olympic Games the assembly of *Hellanodikai* and other officials, athletes and their trainers, horses and chariots, together with their owners, jockeys and charioteers, travelled the 58 kilometres from Ellis to Olympia. Meanwhile the spectators were arriving, their safety while travelling guaranteed by the Olympic 'truce'. The terms of this truce were engraved on a bronze discus maintained in the Temple of Hera in the Altius: it forbade all states participating in the games to take up arms, to pursue legal disputes or to exercise death penalties. Initially lasting one month, it was extended to two, then three months, to cover spectators coming from further afield. While it afforded real protection to those travelling to the games, the truce did not, of course, cause all wars, even local ones, to cease, as has sometimes been suggested. Moreover, travel itself was arduous and not without risk, especially for those braving pirates at sea (Crowther, 2001).

Swaddling (1982: 36) paints the following graphic picture:

Princes and tyrants from Sicily and southern Italy sailed up the river in splendid barges; ambassadors came from various towns, vying with each other in dress and paraphernalia. The rich came on horseback, and in chariots; the poor came on donkeys, in carts and even on foot. Food-sellers came loaded with supplies for there was no town near Olympia. Merchants flocked in with their wares. Artisans came to make figurines that pigrims could buy to offer to their god. Booths and stalls were set up; tents and huts were erected, for only official delegates were given accommodation in the magnificent guest-house known as the *Leonidaion*. Most visitors looked for a suitable spot to put down their belongings and slept each night under the summer skies.

The fact that the Olympic Games constituted a religious as well as a sporting or athletic festival does not mean that spectators were unduly inhibited. Finley and Pleket (1976: 57) describe the crowds as every bit 'as partisan, as volatile, and as excitable as at any other period of time'. As Guttman (1986) has pointed out, the names of the assistants appointed by the *Hellanodikai* to police both athletes and spectators (*mastigophoroi* or 'whip-bearers', and *rabdouchoi* or 'truncheon-bearers') imply a measure of disorderly conduct and a need for organized restraint.

Not surprisingly, the programme of Olympic rituals and competitions underwent a number of changes over the centuries. The programme outlined in Figure 1.2 is a hypothetical reconstruction reflecting events around AD 100, although, for interest, it incorporates some contests that had been abandoned by that time. Figure 1.3 lists the dates when the various sporting events were first introduced to the games. We shall

Figure 1.2 The Programme

Day One	**Morning** Swearing-in ceremony for competitors and judges in the Bouleuterion (Council-House) before the altar and statue of *Zeus Horkios* (Zeus of the Oaths). Contests for heralds and trumpeters held near the stadium entrance. Boys' running, wrestling and boxing contests. Public and private prayers and sacrifices in the Altis; consultation of oracles. **Afternoon** Orations by well-known philosophers and recitals by poets and historians. Sightseeing tours of the Altis. Reunions with old friends.
Day Two	**Morning** Procession into the hippodrome of all those competing there. Chariot- and horse-races. **Afternoon** The pentathlon: discus, javelin, jumping, running and wrestling. **Evening** Funeral rites in honour of the hero Pelops. Parade of victors round the Altis. Communal singing of victory hymns. Feasting and revelry.
Day Three	**Morning** Procession of the Hellanodikai (Judges), ambassadors from the Greek states, competitors in all events and sacrificial animals round the Altis to the Great Altar in front of the Temple of Zeus, followed by the official sacrifice of one hundred oxen given by the people of Elis. **Afternoon** Foot-races. **Evening** Public banquet in the Prytaneion.
Day Four	**Morning** Wrestling. **Midday** Boxing and the *pankration*. **Afternoon** Race-in-armour.
Day Five	Procession of victors to the Temple of Zeus where they are crowned with wreaths of wild olive by the Hellanodikai, followed by the *phyllobolia* (when the victors are showered with leaves and flowers). Feasting and celebrations.

Swaddling, 1982

Figure 1.3 This programme is hypothetical since it contains not only all the events held around 100 BC (the period represented by the model), but also, for interest, various contests which had been discontinued by that time. The dates when the various events were introduced are listed below. The order of contests at the festival is based as accurately as possible on the surviving literary evidence.

Dates for introduction of events

Olympiad	Year, BC	Event
1	776	Stade-race (short foot-race)
14	724	*Diaulos* (double-length foot-race)
15	720	*Dolichos* (long-distance foot-race)
18	708	*Pentathlon* and wrestling
23	688	Boxing
25	680	*Tethrippon* (four-horse chariot-race)
33	648	*Pankration* (type of all-in wrestling) and horse-race
37	632	Foot-race and wrestling for boys
38	628	*Pentathlon* for boys (immediately discontinued)
41	616	Boxing for boys
65	520	Race-in-armour
70	500	*Apene* (mule-cart race)
71	496	*Calpe* or *anabates* (race for mares)
84	444	*Apene* and *calpe* discontinued
93	408	*Synoris* (two-horse chariot-race)
96	396	Competitions for heralds and trumpeters
99	384	Chariot-racing for teams of four colts
128	268	Chariot-racing for teams of two colts
131	256	Races for colts
145	200	*Pankration* for boys

Swaddling, 1982

concentrate here on events associated in the modern world with the sport of track-and-field, principally the running races and the pentathlon.

The short foot-race of approximately 200 metres was the most ancient event, and indeed the *only* event at the first thirteen Olympiads. The winner was held in the highest esteem: not only was the Olympiad named after him but the list of victors came to be used as the linchpin of Greek chronology, 'the only common denominator in a country where every city counted years by a different series of magistrates' (Robertson, 1988: 12). Over time additional foot-races were included: the *diaulos*, named after the musical double-pipes, consisted of two lengths of the stadium (about 400 metres), and the *dolichos*, the only 'long' race, consisted of 24 lengths (just under 5000 metres). In both these races athletes ran up and down the track and around turning posts at each end. Although rules prohibiting tripping and bumping existed, there is no doubt that they were limited in their effectiveness.

Often there would be many entrants for races and so lots were drawn beforehand to determine heats. After a few warming-up exercises the athletes would line up, not crouching as they do now, but standing with arms stretched forward, one foot a few inches in front of the other, and toes gripping the grooves of the starting sill. The races would be started by a herald's trumpet or the shout of *Apite* – Go! Perpetrators of false starts were penalized by flogging, although the numbers of these were reduced when starting gates were introduced in the fifth century BC. As in contemporary races, running styles varied according to the length of the race. Swaddling (1982: 48–9) adds:

> The postures of figures on the vases are not always entirely accurate since artists relied heavily on conventional poses, but nevertheless they are an informative guide. Sprinters display the most vigour, arms and legs darting furiously to and fro in a flat-out dash down the track. The *dolichos*-runner, on the other hand, reserved his energy by keeping his arms bent close to his sides, and swinging them in relatively relaxed fashion. Only on the final lap did he suddenly sprint towards the finishing post making violent arm movements like the sprinter. Presumably the technique of the *diaulos*-runner was somewhere midway between the two.

It seems that in the earliest Olympiads athletes wore a type of shorts, but this practice was soon discarded and athletes competed nude. There are various accounts of why this change occurred. One dates it from the time a runner in Athens was leading a race when his shorts came adrift and, impeded, he fell. A law that all athletes should perform naked was subsequently passed to prevent further accidents of this kind. Another links the change to the victory of Orrhippos (or Orsippos) of Megara in the short foot-race at Olympia in 720 BC: he lost his shorts while winning and, in doing so, pioneered a new trend. A simpler and more likely explanation may lie in the intense pride Greek men had in their muscular physiques (Swaddling, 1982; see Scanlon, 2002). To the Greeks 'the youthful male figure, quite undraped, seemed ... a thing supremely beautiful' (Lawton, 1903: 38).

The remaining athletic events with which we are familiar today were contained in the *pentathlon*, as in modern games a test for the all-round athlete. It seems that if any competitor was first in three events that automatically ended the contest; otherwise there was a reduced field for the final event, the wrestling. The five events, in the order in which they were held, were: discus, jumping, javelin, running and wrestling. The first three of these were found only in the *pentathlon*, while running and wrestling also existed as events in their own right. It is the events exclusive to the *pentathlon* on which I shall briefly concentrate here.

Since there is enormous variation in both the size (17–35 centimetres in diameter, with a thickness of 1.5 centimetres) and weight (1.5–6.5 kilograms) of the 20 or so ancient – usually bronze – discuses that have survived, we cannot be clear about the dimensions of competitive discuses at Olympia. It is known, however, that three 'official' discuses were kept in the Treasury of the Sikyonians, presumably to ensure fairness in competition. Nor is there any certainty about the method of throwing, although depictions in painting and sculpture suggest that athletes made no more that a three-quarter turn before releasing the discus. Robertson (1988) makes the point that the narrowness of the stadium and proximity of the spectators would not permit the risk of loss of control which necessarily attends modern discus throwing, in which athletes turn a full circle, or even two, before release. There are no convincing records of distances achieved: one documented throw of 30 metres by Phaullos, who won two victories in the *pentathlon* and one in the short foot-race in Delphi at the end of the fifth century BC, seems too slight to impress. Each competitor at Olympia was allowed three or five throws (sources vary), only the best counting and being marked by a peg.

The long-jump was the only type of jumping competition in Greek athletics but is surrounded by more doubt and controversy than almost any other event. It is not even known whether athletes always utilized a running start. What does seem clear is that they invariably used weights or *halteres*, although those that have survived, like the discuses, vary considerably in their dimensions.

> The jump was accompanied by flute music, which must have helped to time the rather complex movements of running, swinging the weights, and finally jumping. The jumper would run up to the take-off point, swinging the weights back and forth at arms length. We often see athletes practising arm movements alone, and sometimes the coach pointing out a flaw. When the jumper took off, he swung his arms (still holding the weights) and his legs forward. As he was about to land, he swung his arms backward, just like a modern jumper. (Robertson, 1988: 17)

Once again there are few recordings of distances jumped. The Greeks rarely maintained records of either times or distances achieved in athletic competition, their interest being confined to victory/failure. But one long-jump success was documented: the same Phaullos who managed a meagre 30 metres, or 95 feet, with the discus is said to have jumped a staggering 55 feet in the long-jump! In the mid-nineteenth century some English athletes experimented with weights and claimed to have jumped 30 feet, but there are strong doubts about the reliability of these claims.

There are three possible interpretations of Phaullos' leap. The first is that the Greek long-jump corresponded to the modern triple jump (that is, it involved a hop, skip and jump). Indeed, it was this understanding of the ancient long-jump that led to the introduction of the triple jump into the modern Olympic programme. There is, however, no evidence – via ancient depictions or illustrations – to warrant this interpretation. A second possibility is that the Greeks used a different and smaller foot to measure jumps, but once again supportive evidence is lacking. The third interpretation is that the distance ascribed in an epigram to Phaullos in *both* the discus and the long-jump are simply unreliable, 'respectively a comic exaggeration and a comic underestimate: he could jump nearly as far as he could throw the discus' (Robertson, 1988: 18).

The final *pentathlon* event to be highlighted here is the javelin. As with the discus, competitors had three to five throws, only their best counting. The javelin was made out of elderwood, roughly the height of the thrower, blunted at the end, and thrown with the aid of a leather thong or *ankyle*.

> A cord, 30–45 cm in length, was wound tightly round the shaft near the centre of gravity, leaving a loop of 7–10 cm which was grasped by one finger. The effect was both to give the arm additional leverage and to impart a spin to the javelin in flight, thereby helping it to retain its direction and to carry much further. (Finley and Pleket, 1976: 32)

It has been mooted that distances of around 300 feet were possible, although no records of actual throws have survived.

These, then, were the principal athletic events in the five-day Olympic programme. But what of the athletes themselves? We have noted in passing that they were male and tended to be recruited from a narrow social band; that they were compelled to train vigorously, at least for a prescribed period before the games began; and that those who were victorious, above all in the short foot-race, were fêted and became social celebrities. It is to a fuller consideration of these issues, and especially of the changes that occurred over the 1000 years of the ancient games, that we now turn.

Athletes: Specialization and Commercialization

Scholars are agreed that only in the earliest games at Olympia were contests treated as leisure activities appropriate to nobles and warriors, although even then victors in local games were substantially rewarded, often with tripods or silver bowls. As the Olympic programme became diversified and began to draw competitors from southern Italy, Sicily and Asia Minor, athletics increasingly became 'a profession marked by specialization, and it remained that until the end of antiquity' (Finley and Pleket, 1976: 69). To specialization many historians would add enhanced commercialization. McIntosh (1963: 17) writes:

> Popular heroes became pot-hunters like Theagenes, winner of more that one thousand four hundred prizes in different festivals. By the end of the fifth century BC the appellation 'athlete' was no longer a badge of honour but was a label of a special class who dieted and trained for their careers in such a way as to set them apart from ordinary citizens.

Euripides, one of the harshest critics of this change, blamed spectators for what he saw as the decline of athletics: it was their fanaticism, adulation and money which led inexorably to increasingly valuable prizes for victors and to full-time athletic careers.

How did this change, which many modern commentators after the manner of Euripides interpret as a 'decline', come about? It has been noted that early Greek sport was tied to religion. It was also seen as preparation for war. This is reflected in the very nature of the Olympic events (see Figure 1.2 above). And no body of citizens was more warlike than the Spartans. After Sparta's early conquest of Messenia, its male citizens, numbering only 10,000 or so, were on a permanent war-footing (Finley and Pleket (1976: 70) refer to them as constituting 'a full-time, inflexible military machine'). A system of rigorous physical and mental training for war, initiated at the age of 7, made Spartans highly competitive in athletics: they contributed about half the Olympic victors down to 600 BC, mostly in the running and *pentathlon* events. But by the close of the next century Spartan dominance had ended: 'sergeant-majors could not compete with the professional trainers who emerged elsewhere in Greece by 600, nor could their pupils match the increasingly specialized athletes' (Finley and Pleket, 1976: 70).

Finley and Pleket tell how Aristotle once compared a combat between armed and unarmed men with a contest between professional and non-professional athletes. For Greeks the concept of 'professional' was applied to men who were properly trained and dedicated more or less full-time to a particular activity. The modern distinction between professionals and non-professionals in terms of *payment* did not arise. As we have seen, even the earliest 'non-professional' aristocratic runners were frequently awarded prizes for their successes.

It is likely that the Greek aristocracy provided the first professional athletes in European – and perhaps world – history. Only aristocratic families would have possessed the wealth to promote a career in athletics, to hire the best trainers and coaches, to guarantee diets, and to provide general and continuing financial support. Athletes intent upon Olympic honours would have needed additional funding to cover their travel costs, the ten months' full-time preparation leading up to the games, and the final compulsory month in Ellis. Gradually, however, gymnasia, centres of training 'for the body and the soul', introduced in the sixth century BC and soon spreading to all Greek cities, brought training opportunities to youths from non-aristocratic families. And in addition, alternative sources of funding emerged. If a young man without wealth showed unusual talent his native city would often sponsor him from public monies; occasionally private patrons would come forward; and after the Roman conquest associations or guilds of professional athletes would sometimes help. The return from this investment was political and commercial.

There has been a good deal of speculation about the value of the prizes available to athletes. It is possible that prizes of value were given at Olympia prior to 752 BC, when the olive wreath was first introduced; after this date, although no prizes of material worth were awarded to victors at the games, there is no doubt that an Olympic victory guaranteed future financial well-being. Nor did the Greeks have any objection to material rewards. This is shown by the fact that in about 594 BC Solon passed a law in Athens which led to the awarding of 100 drachmas to victors at the Isthmian Games and 500 drachmas to winners at Olympia. The high value of these awards is revealed by the fact that a single drachma was then sufficient to buy a bushel of grain. Five hundred drachmas would have elevated a man into the 'top financial category of Solon's division of citizens' (Glader, 1978: 47). Young (1988) has offered a tongue-in-cheek calculation that 500 drachmas in Solon's Athens was equivalent to something like US $338,000 in 1980. Solon's ambition was to increase the number of Athenian victors because this would contribute directly to the prestige and commercial prosperity of the city. Moreover it appears to have worked:

> One of the immediate results of Solon's law must have been that competition in the national festivals became less exclusively the privilege of the wealthy few. With such inducement a person could afford to leave gainful employment long enough for the journey to Olympia and the month of training there. The Isthmus, being nearer, entailed less expense. The investment by the city of such sums, possibly provided by the state-owned silver mines at Laurium, must have paid dividends far exceeding Solon's expectations, for Athens from that time began her rise to first place in Greece on all matters athletic. (Robinson, 1955: 59)

Over the centuries the sums accruing to athletes grew with the continuing commercialization of their sport. Gardiner (1930) reports evidence that in the third century AD some athletes automatically gained pensions for life, plus exemption from taxes, following successes even at local games. He gives the example of one 'ordinary' athlete who gained two victories at games over a four-year period and received a double pension worth two talents and 3,900 drachmas, adding:

> Of the value of these pensions we can judge from the fact that workmen engaged in building a public stoa, presumably therefore skilled men, received only four drachmas a day, and the average wage for a day's labour must have been about one drachma. When an ordinary athlete could earn such a pension, what must have been the pension of an Asclepiades or Demostratus? (Gardiner, 1930: 113)

The Demise of the Ancient Olympic Games

The conventional historical view is that the Olympic Games were progressively undermined by specialization, commercialization and, above all, the influence of Rome. This adds up to a partial truth. We have seen that specialization and growing commercialization were real phenomena, and when Olympia became a part of the Roman province of Greece in 146 BC this undoubtedly had very significant implications for the games. But, as Scanlon (1988: 38) writes:

> The interpretation of Olympian development as a gradual decline or distancing from high classical ideals to profit-minded professionalism is essentially erroneous ... The professional Greek athletes of Roman times were carrying on fundamentally the same, if somewhat better organized, traditions of competing for money or for valuable prizes.

In the Roman era the games underwent a gradual but permanent metamorphosis. While the Romans mostly preserved the outward trappings of the religious and athletic traditions of the Greek festival, they incorporated the cult of the emperor into the sanctuary and encouraged a much more cosmopolitan pool of competitors. Scanlon (1988: 38) maintains that the 'farce of Roman indignities' – which many analysts have emphasized – was 'occasional and short-lived'. The Olympic Games, for example, remained largely unscathed by the Roman propensity for brutal spectacle and 'entertainment', as opposed to athletic competition. And only rarely did emperors or leaders intervene destructively – as Sulla did in 86 BC when he plundered Olympia's statues and treasures to fund his military campaigns, and again in 80 BC when he transferred the Olympic Festival to Rome to celebrate his elevation to dictator; or as Caligula did a century later when he ordered Pheidias's statue of Zeus to be transported to Rome, where he intended to replace its head with his own.

The Emperor Augustus breathed new life into the games. His victory (as Octavian) over Anthony at Actium in 31 BC secured his position in Rome. In 28/27 BC he established the Aktian Games as a quadrennial celebration of his success, and these games were incorporated into the sacred circuit of traditional Greek festivals. Indeed, the Romans even started to count years in Aktiads from 28/27 BC, that is, four-year periods analogous to Olympiads. Olympic 'spinoffs' or 'isolympian games' proliferated in this era. Augustus may not have especially favoured the Greeks, former allies of Anthony, but his admiration of 'classical' Greece and, perhaps more decisively, his policy to revive religiosity and cults throughout the empire were part and parcel of a larger plan 'to conquer by assimilation of cultures, or by what may be called *syncretism*' (Scanlon, 1988: 43). Augustus was quick to establish the presence of the cult of the emperor next to that of Zeus at Olympia. Scanlon (1988: 60) again: 'Rome never truly dominated Olympia, but rather joined it to control political allegiance, just as Olympia welcomed Roman rulers in order to finance the Games.'

The fortunes of the Olympic Games fluctuated depending on which Roman emperor held power. A low point was reached with Nero, who arranged for the Olympic Games due in AD 65 to be postponed and for all the circuit games to be held in one year, AD 67, so that he could compete and win in each and thus become a *periodonikes*. This he duly accomplished, even winning the Olympic ten-horse chariot race despite falling from his chariot and withdrawing. 'Not only did he fail to foster the new spirit of the ecumenical Games revived under Augustus, but he even brought upon himself the enmity of the Olympic officials who declared these games invalid, an "Anolympiad"' (Scanlon, 1988: 46).

After Nero's farcical intrusion the games languished for over half a century until Hadrian and his successors revived them once more. Hadrian, who was to accept the title 'Olympian' and was worshipped in the East as 'Zeus Panhellinios', accorded the Greeks full citizenship rights under Rome and assiduously propagated Greek ideals and values. As part of this programme the athletic facilities at Olympia were improved and extended. There was also a proliferation of *new* games in his honour, hosted by, among others, Alexandria, Anazarbos, Ankyra, Antiochia, Athens, Ephesos, Gaza, Hadrianeua, Herakleia, Kyzikos, Smyrna and Tarsos. Politically, Hadrian proved as skilful as Augustus in his calculated pursuit of syncretism.

By Hadrian's time, however, *popular* interest in athletics, and especially in the traditional track-and-field events, was beginning to diminish in Greece and the East. Whereas traditionally the foot-races and *pentathlon* had attracted the most prize money, increasingly the more brutal and 'entertaining' boxing, wrestling and all-out *pankration* contests were taking over. After the third century AD there are relatively few records of events and happenings at Olympia. It seems that the games, 'like the Roman Empire itself, underwent a slow process of disintegration and ultimately death' (Scanlon, 1988: 56). Scanlon highlights a number of external threats to the games in this late period, all of which probably contributed to their demise: adverse ideologies, natural disasters, barbarian invasions, a failing economy on the Greek mainland, and the eclipse of the stabilizing central authority of secular Rome. The date of the final games is not known, although references survive to those of AD 261. It is unlikely that they continued beyond the banning of all pagan cults by Theodosius I in AD 393; but there are scholars who argue that they may conceivably have lasted until an edict of Theodosius II in AD 426 to destroy all pagan temples in the Eastern Mediterranean (Swaddling, 1982).

Continuity and Discontinuity

At the start of this chapter it was emphasized that ancient, modern and postmodern concepts of sport are different, that there is both continuity and discontinuity between past and present. In selectively reconstructing the activities and social environments of the ancient games at Olympia I have necessarily applied what Grandy (1973) calls the 'principle of humanity'. This states that if we are to understand participants in a culture that is radically divergent from our own, like that of ancient Greece, we *must* assume that the imputed pattern of relations among beliefs, desires and the world be as similar to our own as possible. In Lukes's (1982: 264) words, the principle of humanity 'prescribes the minimizing of unintelligibility – that is, of unintelligible agreement and disagreement'. Meaningful discussion of continuity and discontinuity between past and present presupposes the acceptance of this principle, or something very like it. The need for great caution in comparing past and present is obvious.

The account offered here debunks several potent myths surrounding the ancient games at Olympia. It has been shown, for example, that it is erroneous to regard Greek athletics as an 'amateur' pursuit, either in the sense that it went materially unrewarded or in the sense that it was for long a part-time or leisure activity. In this final section Guttman's (1978) seven defining characteristics of *modern* sport are utilized to make explicit some of the most salient continuities and discontinuities between the Greek past and the Western present. Themes are introduced that in some respects afford a framework for subsequent discussion.

Guttman's first characteristic of modern sport is *secularism*. He observes that in primitive cultures the activities we associate with sport were almost always bound up with religious rituals and ceremonies. For all that it may appropriately be seen as the ancestor of much modern sport, Greek athletics as practised at Olympia, Delphi, Corinth, Nemea and elsewhere was closer to the contests found in primitive cultures than to the nineteenth-century reconstruction of the Olympics. 'The relative familiarity of Greek culture and the revival of specific track and field sports in our own time act to obscure fundamental similarities between the sports of the Athenians and those of the Apaches and Aztecs' (Guttman, 1978: 20). The ancient games at Olympia were sacred festivals, integral to the religious life of the Hellenes; they had their roots in religion.

It is also reasonable to suggest, however, that sport emerged as 'a more or less secular phenomenon' under the Greeks, especially during the Roman period. Guttman (1978: 23) quotes the German writer Kamphausen here:

> When one speaks in this context of 'secularization', one does not mean that an originally religious phenomenon becomes worldly but rather that an athletic games (*sportliches Spiel*), originally laden with religious significance, concentrated itself upon its own essential elements – play, exercise, competition.

Sport, in other words, became an increasingly routine aspect of the life of the Greek *polis*, as well as a means of worship. Thus it seems plausible to identify precursors to the secularism of sport in Greek culture while acknowledging that only in modern sport has the bond between the sacred and secular been truly broken.

The second characteristic is *equality* – of opportunity to compete and in conditions of competition. Guttman's point here is that modern sports *assume* equality, even though in practice, as we shall observe later, numerous inequalities persist. In primitive cultures the relationship between the principles of equality and achievement has to be interpreted differently. Equality of opportunity to compete and in conditions of competition were largely irrelevant because the outcome of competition 'was more likely than not determined by the gods rather than by the relative skill of the participants' (Guttman, 1978: 27).

More emphasis was placed on achievement in Greek culture than in many primitive cultures. Indeed, it has been written of Greek athletic contests that: 'Every competitor had the same formal rights, under the same rules, and could claim the prize if he won; only his skill and strength mattered. In a world of built-in inequalities, that was a significant rarity' (Finley and Pleket, 1976: 58). It has been seen that even seemingly minor infractions of the rules were vigorously punished at Olympia. However, this equality in the conditions of competition has to be assessed against the background of 'built-in inequalities' of class, race and gender. Slaves and 'barbarians' (or non-Greeks) were automatically excluded from athletic competition, and women were banned from Olympia and almost all other games.

Guttman's third defining property is *specialization*. Specialization in modern sport and athletics has reached astounding levels and continues to grow apace. The difference between Greek and contemporary worlds is remarkable; but, crucially, it remains one of degree. We have noted in some detail how, after an early and relatively short-lived era of non-professional aristocratic dominance, athletic professionalization in ancient Greece became ubiquitous, extending beyond the class of aristocrats to less prosperous but talented male citizens, for whom civic funds bought the time, facilities and expertise to construct and execute careers as athletes. In many ways Euripides' disgust at this new breed of manufactured sportsmen – 'of all the countless evils through Hellas none is worse than the race of athletes' – anticipates protests against the *scientific* screening, recruitment and training programmes directed at child sporting prodigies in the contemporary world.

Rationalization is the fourth characteristic, referring to the fact that the rules in modern sports are perceived as means to an end, as cultural artefacts rather than divine instructions. In sociological terms, sports are rationalized in Weber's sense of *Zweckrationalitat*. Greek sports lay somewhere between the perception of rules as sacred found in many primitive cultures and their perception as useful conventions in the modern world. Guttman (1978: 43) illustrates the difference between ancient and modern by focusing on the discus. He points out that although participants in a Greek games almost certainly used the same set of discuses when competing with each other, 'the standardization of equipment stopped at precisely that point'. As we have documented, the dimensions and weight of discuses varied considerably between games. One might add that the Greek stade also varied from festival to festival: at Olympia it was 192.28 metres, at Delphi 177.5 metres, at Epidaurus 181.13 metres, and at Pergamon 210 metres. The

Greeks, and more so the Romans, were technologically sophisticated enough to have standardized these distances, but they elected not to. The issue was not salient for them.

The fifth defining characteristic of modern sport is *bureaucracy*. In the modern world the rules of sport and their administration are in the hands of a bureaucratic organization, a form of organization all but unknown in primitive societies. Once again Guttman argues that we can look to the Greeks for intimations of the modern: they may be said to have developed a nascent form of sports bureaucracy.

> The Athenians and others with democratic tendencies elected officials or selected them by lot. Each Greek city had its *gymnasiarch* or ruler of the gymnasium. Athletic competitors were usually administered by an *agonathete*. How much of the administration remained in priestly as opposed to secular hands is hard to say. What is certain is that the germs of sports bureaucracy flowed in Roman times. The most famous administrator was Herodes Atticus, whom the emperor Hadrian appointed as *athlothete*, who endowed the great stadium at Athens. (Guttman, 1978: 45)

Another example of bureaucratic organization in the Roman period was the creation of associations or guilds of athletes, an imperial enterprise by AD 150, with elected leaders, elaborate rules and regulations, entrance requirements, membership certificates, codes of appropriate conduct, and so on (Finley and Pleket, 1976). But these are essentially Roman rather than Greek accomplishments.

Guttman's (1978: 47) penultimate characteristic is *quantification*. Whereas in primitive cultures there was minimal quantification in sport, modern sports 'are characterized by the almost inevitable tendency to transform *every* athletic feat into one that can be quantified and measured'. Track-and-field athletics is a prime example of the accumulation of statistics of performance based on an increasingly precise technology of measurement. For all their mathematical subtlety the Greeks were never interested in quantification beyond that required to distinguish victory from defeat. As Robertson (1988: 18) remarks, 'what excited them most was the momentary competition, not the long-term record'. Guttman (1978: 49) puts it more philosophically: 'For them, man was still the measure of all things, not the object of endless measurements.' Given this approach to athletic contests, it is of course not surprising that standardization of equipment across games was neither sought nor achieved.

Finally, and relatedly, Guttman lists *records* among his characteristics. He defines this in terms of a combination of the impulse to quantification with the desire to win, to 'be the best'. A record is 'a marvellous abstraction that permits competition not only among those gathered together on the field of sport but also among them and others distant in time and space' (Guttman, 1978: 52–3). There is evidence that primitive peoples occasionally maintained records but lacked our 'mania' for quantification. The

Greeks appear not to have possessed the concept of 'record' at all. It seems they simply had no way of referring to the setting or breaking of a record. It has been suggested, in fact, that the concept only dates from the 1880s, a key period in the historical evolution of sport which is a focus of the next chapter.

Guttman closes his discussion of modern sport by indicating whether or not the seven characteristics might be said to apply to sport in other ages. In his comparisons with ancient Greece he cautiously concludes as follows: secularism (yes and no), equality (yes and no), specialization (yes), rationalization (yes), bureaucracy (yes and no), quantification (no) and records (no). Guttman's definition of 'modern sport' has served this discussion well, but the issue of the genesis and definition of modern sport is of course far from unproblematic; and it is to this issue that Chapter 2 turns.

2

The Genesis of Modern Sport

The formal characterization of modern sport encountered at the close of Chapter 1 commands considerable sympathy among historians and sociologists. But the transition from ancient to modern sport occurred irregularly and over centuries and was neither exclusive to the West nor linear. Rather, it was characterized by interminable hiccups of time and place. Coakley (2001) has usefully adapted Guttman's model to spell out some of the more significant changes that took place between the ancient games at Olympia and the emergence of modern sport in England, emphasizing in particular shifts during the medieval period (500–1300) and from the Renaissance to the Enlightenment (1300–1800). His revisions are summarized in Table 2.1.

Table 2.1 Historical comparison of organized games, contests, and sport activities

Characteristic	Greek Games and Contests (1000 B.C. to 100 B.C.)	Roman Sports Events (100 B.C. to A.D. 500)	Medieval Games and Tournaments (500 to 1300)	Renaissance and Enlightenment Games and Sport Activities (1300 to 1800)	Modern Sports
Secularism	Yes and no★★	Yes and no	Yes and no	Yes and no	Yes
Equality	Yes and no	Yes and no	No	Yes and no	Yes
Specialization	Yes	Yes	No	Yes and no	Yes
Rationalization	Yes	Yes	No	No	Yes
Bureaucratization	Yes and no	Yes	No	No	Yes
Quantification	No	Yes	No	Yes and no	Yes
Records	No	No	No	Yes and no	Yes

★Modified version table 2 in Guttmann (1978).
★★This characteristic existed in some sports during this time, but not in others.

Coakley (2001)

Unsurprisingly, there is less than unanimity among historians about the nuts and bolts of the genesis of modern sport in the West. Drawing on Elias's (1978) classic account of the 'civilizing process', some have stressed the importance for its growth of the displacement of 'force by finesse' during the shift from medieval to Renaissance times (Mehl, 1993). Elias and Dunning (1986) have made the case for a two-fold process of *sportization* of English pastimes. The first phase, they contend, took place in the seventeenth and eighteenth centuries and saw the radical transformation of pastimes such as cricket, fox-hunting, horse-racing and boxing; while the second phase occurred during the early and mid-nineteenth century and witnessed soccer, rugby, tennis and track-and-field athletics adopting modern formats. Maguire (1999) assimilates these two phases into a five-phase model, which is reproduced in full in Figure 2.1. His third phase of sportization is also pertinent to aspects of this chapter: it covers the period from the late nineteenth to the early twentieth centuries and represents the 'take-off' and differential diffusion of 'English sports' to continental Europe and to what Maguire and colleagues (2002: 10) refer to as 'both the formal and informal British Empire'.

Figure 2.1 Phases of Sportization

Phase One	Early transmission of English pastimes like cricket, fox hunting, horse racing and boxing into sports in seventeenth and eighteenth centuries.
Phase Two	Further sportization of English pastimes like football, rugby and track-and-field in the early and mid-nineteenth century.
Phase Three	The 'take-off' and differential diffusion of English sports throughout continental Europe and to the formal and informal British empire during the late nineteenth and early twentieth centuries.
Phase Four	Western (Anglo/Euro-American) hegemony over sport, including sports organizations, the surplus and ideology associated with sporting festivals, from the 1920s to the 1960s.
Phase Five	Changing balance of power over rapidly globalizing sport, with African, Asian and South American nations increasingly challenging Western control since the 1960s.

(Maguire, 1999)

This chapter focuses on the varied – sometimes mundane and predictable, sometimes dramatic – emergence of modern sports in England, and often very shortly after in countries within its reach, through Maguire's first, second and, to a more limited extent, third phases. In the interests of space and to further and deepen comparisons with events held at the ancient games at Olympia, special attention will be paid to pedestrianism and track-and-field athletics.

Sport in Pre-Victorian England

Localized sporting activity in rural England doubtless predates the earliest surviving historical evidence. Frequently cited as an early source is the Venerable Bede's praise of the seventh-century saint, Cuthbert, for his jumping, running and wrestling skills. Sufficient scattered references to sporting pastimes as ingredients of seasonal 'folk games' from Cuthbert's time exist to suggest that they were commonly and competitively practised, although there is a paucity of empirical detail (Harris, 1975). During the reign of Henry II in the twelfth century, open spaces near the city were made available so that Londoners could practise 'leaping, wrestling, casting of the stone, and playing with the ball' (Watman, 1968: 15). Indeed, there is some indication that activities such as 'casting the stone', the precursor of shot-putting, became so popular as to threaten people's commitment to archery practice; and for this reason Edward III felt obliged to issue an edict in 1365 prohibiting weight-putting. The Scottish Highland Games, still held today, date back to the fourteenth century or earlier.

It seems probable that games organized around local or national festivals ebbed and flowed through the Middle Ages and beyond, often in accordance with wider social changes. The variable history of the annual Cotswold Games is illustrative of this. Whitsuntide games on the boundaries of the parishes of Weston and Campden had had a long and colourful history through the Middle Ages, but had all but died out – not least because of local Puritan activity – prior to the arrival of Robert Dover in the Cotswolds around 1608. Dover was a committed Royalist and traditionalist and as keenly anti-Puritan as he was an advocate of sport. In reviving the Cotswold Games around 1612 his intent was not only to promote sport as intrinsically pleasurable, but to re-establish medieval folk games by associating them with the Renaissance and with Crown and Church. In Brailsford's (1969: 13) words: 'This was to be the coming together of the two cultures of sporting activity, the courtly and the popular, and deliberately contrived to that end.'

Bidding to attract the gentry, Dover incorporated hunting, gaming and chess-playing in his programmes; he even had a blind Homeric harpist in simulation of the spirit of the ancient games at Olympia. Predominant, however, were the more popular rural recreations. Brailsford (1969: 113) again: 'Apart from "leaping", "dancing", "leap-frog", and a strange contest of "shin-kicking" . . . the games for the commoners included wrestling, pitching the bar, throwing the hammer, and foot races.' Throwing contests of one sort or another were doubtless widespread, and a contribution to *Annalia Dubrensia* indicates that sometimes a round rock or boulder was used as a missile, although an actual shot was probably used on occasions. Foot-races were also popular. At the same time as they were coming under Puritan attack, and consequently disappearing in some places, they were also elsewhere becoming more regulated, using set courses and ceasing to be point-to-point scrambles. Races for women and girls attracted much attention from the few early commentators, as they doubtless did also from the spectators. The usual prize was a smock (hence, 'smock races'), which at the Cotswold Games as at many others was displayed on a tall pole before the event. It should be added here that part of the attraction of smock races was the flimsy and revealing garments of the participants. Mandell (1984: 145) reports that in London in 1725 substantial crowds were drawn by the prospect of witnessing a four-mile race by two young women running nude, although in the event they were obliged to wear loose blouses and bloomers. 'Military' events in the Cotswold Games included single-stick contests and handling the pike; but archery, prescribed by statute throughout the Middle Ages but in relative decline by the early seventeenth century, was not included.

Dover's success with the Cotswold Games, in many ways reflecting the sympathies of the Stuart sovereigns, James I and his son Charles I, was achieved in the face of growing Puritan pressure for sporting constraint. In his analysis of Puritanism, Weber notes that its asceticism

> turned with all its force against one thing: the spontaneous enjoyment of life and all it had to offer. This is perhaps most characteristically brought out in the struggle over the Book of Sports which James I and Charles I made into law expressly as a means of counteracting Puritanism, and which the latter ordered to be read from all the pulpits. (See Turner, 1992: 166–7)

What Weber refers to as the 'anti-authoritarian ascetic tendency of Puritanism' was interpreted as a clear threat to the state. When the Parliamentarians eventually took over government in the 1640s and 1650s a radical and repressive sporting policy was implemented. According to Brailsford (1991: 36), the thoroughness of this policy 'has never been rivaled in Britain, and seldom anywhere in the world. It was no less than an attempt to rewrite the whole sporting calender.' He refers to a rapid series of statutory prohibitions on Sunday activities, each finding a fresh target:

> In 1644 it was wrestling, archery, bell-ringing, feasting, dancing, and the catch-all of 'Games, Sports or Pastime whatsoever'. In the next year the proscribed Sunday activities were extended to specify dicing, card-playing, football, stoolball, hawking, hunting, fishing and fowling. By 1657 there was little that the imagination could add – 'leaping' was thrown in, presumably to make it clear that children's sports were also included, and finally 'all persons vainly or profanely walking on that day' were to be prosecuted. The ambition of government to control its citizens' bodily movements could hardly be pushed further. (Brailsford, 1991: 36)

And as if this was not enough, the 'papist festivals' of Christmas, Easter and Whitsuntide, traditional occasions of popular play, were struck from the calendar.

The effect of these edicts was of course limited due to difficulties of enforcement. Sport was certainly not eradicated under the Common-wealth, especially for the upper classes, but popular recreation was 'constrained' and 'forced into unfamiliar moulds' (Brailsford, 1991: 38). With the Restoration of the Stuart monarchy in the form of Charles II in 1660, however, sporting festivals and meetings that had been temporarily dormant, clandestine or necessarily distorted were quickly re-established. It has been suggested that one permanent lesson of the Puritan interlude is that laws banning sporting pastimes and recreation are likely to be only partially effective or lasting if they lack popular assent; indeed, the methods required for their enactment may prove even more unacceptable than the laws themselves.

If the chronicle of early sporting activities in England was largely one of (periodically disrupted) association with traditional festivals, this link had been all but severed by the beginning of Victoria's reign. The circumstances of the emergence of England as a major imperial and industrial power are too well known to need rehearsing again in any detail here. The expansion occurring during the period from the 'long sixteenth' to the mid-eighteenth century had been characterized by the establishment of small but prosperous trading posts and settlements close to the sea, backed up by naval strength. After 1750 imperial rule progressed steadily inland. With the weakening between 1790 and 1830 of all the other European empires (that is, the Spanish, Portuguese, French and Dutch), by the time of the enthronement of Victoria in 1837 'the British empire was not only the largest empire the world had even seen, it was the only flourishing and functioning empire in existence' (Lloyd, 2001: ix). The English empire dwarfed that of Hellas. England had of course also become by this time an industrial as well as an imperial force. Of some significance in the severance of sport from festival was the marked curtailment of leisure in the name of labour discipline at the hands of a new style of entrepreneur.

> Those who invested large sums in capital equipment for the textile industry, for example, were anxious to get the most out of their machinery and this in turn meant instilling regular habits of work into their employees. The well-documented and strenuous efforts that were made in the creation of a new work discipline by certain employers have been seen as a major cause of the decline of traditional forms of recreation . . . The clock and the factory hooter were after all no respecters of ancient amusements. (Holt, 1989: 37)

Such entrepreneurial initiatives were by the second quarter of the nine-teenth century complemented both by evangelical agitation against traditional sporting festivals, especially those which involved fighting, and by changes in popular taste pioneered by the skilled 'labour aristocracy' (Holt, 1989).

Pedestrianism

Sporting endeavours outlived the festivals, fairs and wakes that spawned them. One way of encapsulating this transition is through a consideration of the phenomenon known as *pedestrianism*, which may be defined here as running, or walking, for wagers. Pedestrianism, or 'professional racing', was promoted and patronized initially by the gentry, although it was their footmen – faster and more reliable for carrying messages than horse-drawn coaches until roads were improved towards the end of the eighteenth century – who usually did the competing. Pedestrianism certainly occasioned much interest and business long before the demise of popular sporting festivals. Some £6000 was said to have been wagered in 1618 on a race before James I between an Irish and an English footman (Mandell, 1984: 144). On 30 July 1663 Samuel Pepys wrote: 'The town talk this day is of nothing but the great footrace run this day on Banstead Downs between Lee, the Duke of Richmond's footman, and a tyler, a famous runner. And Lee hath beat him; though the King and Duke of York and all men almost, did bet three to four to one upon the tyler's head' (quoted in Watman, 1968: 16).

Pedestrianism was at its most fashionable at the end of the eighteenth century and the beginning of the nineteenth: Mason (1988) dates its peak between 1790 and 1810. Spectators were attracted in considerable numbers. In the early 1800s, for example, a young Scottish landowner, Robert Barclay Allardice, known later by his military rank as Captain Barclay, drew huge crowds for his feats of walking and running: he remained unbeaten as a runner through a series of contests over distances ranging from 440 yards to 2 miles. In 1809, 10,000 came to Newmarket to see him walk 1000 miles at the rate of one mile in each of 1000 hours. For this he collected no less than £16,000, equivalent to approximately £180,000 in 1980, 'probably the largest amount ever earned by an athlete for a single race' (Lovesey, 1979: 15).

By the time Victoria came to the throne pedestrianism had played a major part in taking competitive spectator sport to the growing towns and cities and still had a substantial following. When *Bell's Life* published its first annual 'Chronology of Pedestrianism' in 1838 a large number of enclosed grounds serving primarily as venues for pedestrianism were identified. In fact, this period was to see the first purpose-built tracks of modern times. The public was as familiar with Borough Gardens in Salford, the Hyde Park Ground in Sheffield, and Hackney Wick and Old Brompton in London as it was with cricket venues like Lord's and Trent Bridge. Moreover, 49 of the 60 events listed by *Bell's Life* were located in the expanding industrial areas of the Midlands and the North.

By this time, however, and notwithstanding the participation of gentlemen in the fashion of Barclay, pedestrianism was long outside the control of the aristocracy. Those gentlemen who did compete for staked bets called themselves 'amateurs' in order not to be classified with the 'peds'. One such, John Astley, recalled in his memoirs: 'In those days . . . an amateur meant a gentleman, whether he ran for money or honour, or both – and I used to combine the two' (quoted in Lovesey, 1979: 16). Brailsford (1991: 64–5) summarizes pedestrianism's transformation into a working-class sport:

> Pedestrianism lacked any central organization and was entirely in the hands of individual small-scale entrepreneurs for whom there were no hindrances to the attractions of quick profit, at whatever cost to fair and open competition. It became more and more a purely working-class sport, surviving largely in the absence of any sporting alternatives elsewhere. It became associated with the near-criminal edges of urban life through its crooked gambling, fixed matches, and general dishonesty. To become part of the later Victorian sporting pantheon, the athletic sports of running, jumping, and throwing had to take on a new mantle of amateurism, socially acceptable but economically of little account until well into the twentieth century. Meanwhile, it played its considerable part in asserting the demands for sporting time being made by a considerable part of the population.

We now turn to the gradual supercession of the professional 'ped' by the amateur athlete.

Amateurism and Respectability

With control of pedestrianism transferred to the taprooms of public houses in Birmingham, Manchester, Newcastle, Sheffield and London, increasing numbers of those with talent in or on the margins of poverty took to running as a source of income, even if the winnings were small by pre-Victorian standards. 'The stake was usually £5 a side, rising to £100 for a race of championship quality' (Lovesey, 1979: 15). And malpractice was common, including *roping*, or holding back to lose a race, *running to the book*, or disguising form to conserve a good handicap, and *ringing in*, or the fixing of handicaps by conspiring promoters.

If it had unquestionably grown shabby, pedestrianism had also paved the way for modern track-and-field athletics. Not only were there at least a dozen specially designed tracks by 1850, generally faced with gravel, but more precise time-keeping allowed the publication of reliable records. Lovesey (1979: 15–16) writes:

> The standard events of the modern track and field programme began to emerge, as championship cups and belts were offered for competition over popular distances: 110 yd, 440 yd, 880 yd, 1 mile, 2 miles, 4 miles, 6 miles, 10 miles and jumping. There was a strong enthusiasm, too, for hurdling in the forties. And in dress the 'ped' of 1850 looked distinctly modern. He wore spikes and brief silk shorts. Only if ladies attended would he put on tights and a long-sleeved vest.

There were some impressive achievements too. An American who settled in Britain, George Seward, was credited with 9.25 seconds for the 100 yards in 1844, when timing was to the nearest quarter of a second. Henry Reed registered 48.5 seconds for the 400 yards in 1849, and 1 minute 58 seconds for the 880 yards in 1854. And William Jackson, known as the 'American Deer', ran 11 miles 40 yards in one hour in 1845 (Lovesey, 1979).

But by 1850 too the 'cult of athleticism', a by-product of the moral earnestness of Thomas Arnold, Headmaster of Rugby from 1828 to 1842, and epitomized by the concepts of 'manliness' and 'muscular Christianity' associated with authors such as Thomas Hughes and Charles Kingsley, had spread from the major public schools to a wider, if still privileged, public arena. It was a cult, of course, of transparent ideological import. Referring to the 'mania' especially for team games in the public schools, Hargreaves (1986: 43) writes:

> In organized sports the scions of the ruling classes absorbed a uniquely British 'bourgeois ideology' and rehearsed the practices that were necessary in order to integrate successfully into the social order. It was in games primarily that one learned how to be a gentleman and through them that the model of gentlemanly behaviour was exemplified and spread. Participation in school sport was a way of learning to be the kind of individual who would fit in with the class ally and learn how to rule over subordinates. Confidence and self-reliance, learning how to take the initiative and responsibility, how to control aggression and yet act decisively in a determined manner, the necessity of conforming to the established way of doing things, and above all, loyalty to one's group, were all being taught.

In 1850 a group of undergraduates at Exeter College, Oxford, deflated by their poor showing in the College steeplechase, staged a 'foot grind' across country, and an 'Exeter Autumn Meeting', organized on Jockey Club lines and encompassing the weighting of top runners and a 'Consolation Stakes' for beaten 'horses' (Lovesey, 1979: 16). Under the influence and rubric of athleticism, this bizarre initiative was succeeded by sporting moves at other Oxford and Cambridge colleges. In 1853 Cambridge extended an invitation to John Howard, a professional long-jumper, to perform before faculty and students; using weights, he cleared 28 feet, or 8.53 metres. Four years later Cambridge held its first University Sports, Oxford following suit in 1860.

During this period a Cambridge solicitor, Jack Macdonald, acted as adviser to University athletes, even coaxing them into shorts and spikes. Like Astley, he had made 'amateur matches' on the running tracks and therefore knew some of the pedestrian performers. In 1861 he brought the most famous pedestrian of the time, the American Native Indian 'Deerfoot' (Hagasadoni, better known as Louis Bennett) to Cambridge.

A crowd of 6000, including the Prince of Wales, watched the visitor win a 6 mile race. That the future King should have patronized a pedestrian match and afterwards received the runner and dined with him in Trinity College caused a minor scandal, but manifestly strengthened the athletic movement, at Cambridge and more widely ... Athletics became respectable again. It was the turn of the middle classes. (Lovesey, 1979: 16)

Athletic activity soon spread beyond the closed communities of the public schools, universities and army regiments. Professionals, civil servants and businessmen sought exercise on newly available Saturday afternoons, a habit for which many had been prepared by public school curricula. Traditionally, pedestrianism and numerous other sports and entertainments had peaked on 'Saint Monday' (spectators' pay having been distributed late the preceding Saturday). In 1856 pedestrianism was still predominantly a Monday sport, with *Bell's Life* reporting 200 of the 260 matches over one three-month period taking place then. But by 1867 half the contests were occurring at the weekend, with less than a third on a Monday.

By then, the movement towards a free Saturday afternoon was being carried along by the widespread preference for shorter hours over higher wages that characterized the whole period (and affected all classes) between 1840 and 1870. It was encouraged, too, by the general prosperity which pushed up real wages by an average of some 20 per cent in the 1860s and 1870s. (Brailsford, 1991: 105)

Gentlemen in pursuit of sporting activity on a Saturday afternoon could row or play cricket, but there were no athletic clubs prior to the 1860s. In 1861, however, the West London Rowing Club hired the Brompton ground, which had long been used by 'peds' for running matches, and held some track races for its members. These were sufficiently popular to prompt regular meetings, which were subsequently opened up to non-members. In 1862 William Price, manager of the running ground at Hackney Wick, offered a silver cup for a handicap open to 'gentlemen amateurs'. The following year a group of City businessmen founded the first athletic club in London, the Mincing Lane Athletic Club. The respectable 'club model', as Crump (1989) calls it, was important in distancing the sport from freelance pedestrianism. Moreover, 'athletics stressed individual achievement to an extent which could undermine the team spirit fostered by other games favoured by the Victorian middle class. The club provided an element of collective endeavour' (Crump, 1989: 44).

A year before this, in 1862, two ardent disciples of 'muscular Christianity', Charles Melly and John Hughes, had founded the Liverpool Athletic Club, which developed in co-operation with the local Volunteer Brigade. On 14 June 1882, an 'Olympic Festival' was arranged by the Liverpool AC. Events untried in London were included in the programme: in addition to running and walking races, there were high- and long-jumps, pole-leaping, throwing the cricket ball and disc, together with boxing, wrestling, fencing and gymnastics. Nearly 10,000 spectators 'of a highly respectable class' attended. In 1863 the festival was repeated with equal success, drawing competitors and spectators from all over the country; Melly and Hughes were encouraged to rename the organizing committee the Athletic Society of Great Britain. Further festivals followed in 1864 and 1865. Late in 1865 Melly and Hughes took another initiative, the latter chairing a meeting of delegates from the North, Midlands and South that resolved to form a National Olympian Society 'for the encouragement and reward of skill and strength by the award of medals and other prizes, money excepted' (quoted in Lovesey, 1979: 18). This move reverberated around the running-grounds of London. Paraphrasing Lovesey, it was as if the French had landed. The London contingent had been mobilized.

The Birth of the English Amateur Athletic Association

The following announcement was made on 23 December 1865, in the *Sporting Gazette*:

> The Amateur Athletic Club will hold their first annual champion games on the day immediately preceding the University Boat Race, on some ground in London. The programme will consist of the following events:
>
> Flat races: 100 yd, 440 yd, 880 yd, 1 mile, 4 miles, 7 miles walk. 120 yd hurdle race over 10 flights of hurdles 3 ft 6 in high. High running jump, long running jump and high pole jump. Putting the weight (16 lb) and throwing the hammer (16 lb).
>
> The entrance fee for each of these competitions will be one guinea. The competitions will be open to any gentlemen amateur, and the club lays down the following rule, which will be strictly enforced: that no gentleman who has ever run in any open race or handicap can enter for the club races.
>
> C. Guy Pym. Secretary pro tem.

The Amateur Athletic Club (AAC) was managed by an elite committee, the most influential member of which was probably John Chambers. A former all-round athlete of distinction, Chambers had played a key role in drawing up the programme of the first meeting between Oxford and Cambridge Universities in 1864. He was instrumental, too, in devising the AAC Championship programme for 1866. Lovesey (1979: 19) claims this programme 'has formed the basis of track-and-field meetings ever since'. Nine of the eleven events in the AAC Championships of 1866 − or their metric equivalents − are still contested in the Olympic Games. Moreover, the hammer and shot still weigh 16 lb and the hurdles are still 3 ft 6 in high.

The AAC Championships of 1866 held at Beaufort House on 23 March were the first English – and more pertinently the first *national* – championships ever held (Quercetani, 1990). Significantly, they went more smoothly and generated more public enthusiasm than the rival National Olympian Society meeting held at Crystal Palace, London, the following August (during which W. G. Grace won the hurdles while officially fielding in a cricket match at the Oval). Subscriptions to the AAC came in thick and fast. Lovesey (1979: 22) again:

> A Club gymnasium was opened off the Strand. The committee took over management of the Beaufort House Ground, put Chambers in charge, and replaced the old gravel track with a new circuit of cinders. They staged a range of other sports: football, cricket, swimming, billiards and boxing. The Marquess of Queensbury donated a set of challenge cups for the first national amateur boxing championship (1867), so Chambers sat down and wrote the famous Queensbury Rules.

Intriguingly, the AAC also organized regular meetings for pedestrians, the first one taking place at Crystal Palace on 8 October 1866. This attempt by the amateur elite to resuscitate professional athletics may be interpreted as an exercise in Victorian philanthropy. But there was to be less charity in the years ahead.

The amateur/professional dichotomy requires further comment here. In Chapter 1 we saw that it had very different connotations for the Greeks than it came to have for the gentlemen of Victorian England. It is in fact a dichotomy with a complex history (Glader, 1978). In British athletics the first 'amateurs' were spectators, equivalent to late twentieth-century 'fans'. Its usage in relation to sportsmen derived from rowing. Lovesey (1979: 22) writes: 'In 1835 *Bell's Life* defined an amateur as anyone who rowed and was not a waterman or otherwise engaged in rowing for a living.' However, by mid-century there was a marked narrowing of emphasis:

> the term was used to dignify people of the middle and upper classes who indulged in sports also practised by the low class. An amateur was a gentleman. *The Rowing Almanac* (1861) defined amateurs by listing the universities, schools and institutions that nurtured these superior beings, ending with an absolute exclusion of 'tradesmen, labourers, artisans or working mechanics'.

Initially, the AAC was less exclusionary, employing a definition that left involvement open to all parties: 'An amateur is any person who has never competed in any open competition, or for public money, or for admission money, and who has never at any period of his life taught or assisted in the pursuit of athletic exercises as a means of livelihood' (quoted in Lovesey, 1979: 22). By 1867, however, the AAC's more illiberal members had added: '. . . or is a mechanic, artisan or labourer'. And the following year the opening words of the definition were amended to: 'An amateur is any gentleman . . .' The AAC, with private rooms at 6 Pall Mall, had rapidly become the exclusive body it had always threatened to be. But if it had turned exclusive as a club, working-class participants were in practice never banned from its championships. Alfred Wheeler, for example, a London cart-driver, was runner-up in the four-mile race for three consecutive years, 1871–3.

For all the merits of the track at Beaufort House, the fact that the ground was shared with a farmer did present occasional problems. In the 1868 Championships, Edward Colbeck contrived to collide with a sheep, breaking the animal's leg in the process, although he still defeated the world 440 yards record, setting a time of 50.4 seconds which was to stand for 11 years (Lovesey, 1979). In 1869 the AAC negotiated a new home for amateur athletics at the Lillie Bridge Ground, adjacent to West Brompton Station. John Chambers took over its general management with his customary verve.

The AAC had it rivals. Gradually, under the influence of James and William Waddell, London Athletic Club became prominent among these. Adopting an anti-elitist membership policy to outmanoeuvre the AAC, the Waddells had recruited nearly 900 members, substantially increasing London AC's profits, by 1874. Meanwhile the less flexible AAC was in relative decline. Direct confrontation between the two clubs became inevitable when London AC invested in a new track at Stamford Bridge in 1877. 'Its proximity to Lillie Bridge was more than provocation; it was a challenge to the death' (Lovesey, 1979: 27). In the same year the AAC championships attracted a mere 26 athletes for 12 events. The challenge came to a head in 1879, when the AAC held its championships in the spring as usual while London AC held its championships in the summer. 'The result was a stalemate. The Lillie Bridge meeting was practically an Oxford and Cambridge affair, boycotted by London AC members. The Stamford Bridge meeting drew only four entries from outside London. Athletics was close to anarchy' (Lovesey, 1979: 28–9). There were rumbles of dissatisfaction and threats of new anti-elitist and anti-London initiatives too from the North and the Midlands.

It was the sporting Oxford alliance of Clement Jackson, Bernhard Wise and Montague Shearman that rescued British track-and-field from near dissolution. Jackson and Wise were the originators of a scheme subsequently put to Shearman. This involved the formation of an Amateur Athletic Association (AAA), which would be composed of all the principal clubs in the country and would both legislate for the sport and assume responsibility for the championships. It was a scheme, it was hoped, that would conclude the 'state of war' between the AAC and the London AC and prevent an irredeemable rift with the North and Midlands. The response of the AAC and London AC was less than encouraging. But Jackson, Wise and Shearman were more anxious to enlist the support of the North and the Midlands, the price of this being an end to the injustice and exclusivity implicit in the category of the 'gentleman amateur'. It was a price the Oxford trio were willing to pay.

Skilful and sustained diplomatic work by the three men eventually paid off. On 24 April 1880, 28 delegates from the North, the Midlands and the major athletic and cross-country clubs in the South came together at the Randolph Hotel in Oxford. The AAA was formally established, the Objects of Association being:

1) to improve the management of athletic meetings, and to promote uniformity of rules for the guidance of local communities;
2) to deal repressively with any abuses of athletic sports;
3) to hold an annual championship meeting.

Plans were made for 'a Championship Meeting open to all amateurs, and a definition that made no social discrimination' (Lovesey, 1979: 31). The original Rules of Competition are reproduced in Figure 2.2. The Waddells had consolation in an agreement that the championships would occur in the summer and incorporate two events, the 10-mile and 2-mile steeple-chase, hitherto featured in the London AC programme; and Chambers was pacified by a promise that the first championships would be held at Lillie Bridge, thereafter to rotate between the South, North and Midlands. Even Walter Rye of the Thames Hare and Hounds, long a vehement and obdurate spokesman for the 'gentleman amateur', ceased his campaigning.

On 16 April 1887, after nearly 18 months of research, the AAA pro-duced a list of British records. This list, the first to be ratified by an official governing body anywhere, was all but a world record list. Only in the 880 yards was a superior record known, the 1 min 55.6 sec of the American athlete Lawrence Myers. Figure 2.3 gives the inaugural list of records for events still contested – if over metric distances – in the AAA Championships.

The English Initiative in Perspective

It seems evident that the somewhat tortuous emergence of the AAA in England marked the transition to *modern* track-and-field athletics, at least if Guttman's (1978) defining characteristics of modern sport are accepted. And it was of course 'quantification' and 'records' that Guttman noted were entirely absent from ancient Greek competition. While commenting on the importance of sport in the socialization of both bourgeois and proletariat, he argues that it was 'inevitable' that England, 'the home of industrial capitalism, was also the birthplace of modern sports'. He goes on to offer a graphic elaboration of this claim:

The astonishing readiness of the English to wager money on horse races, foot races, and boxing was commented on by many observers. In the words of an eighteenth-century French commentator on English customs, 'The probability of life, and the return of ships, are the objects of their arithmetic. The same habit of calculating they

Figure 2.2 The Original Rules

For its inaugural Championship Meeting in 1880, the AAA published its first Rules for Competition, reproduced below. It is notable that the essentials of the modern internationally recognized rules, including sizes and shapes of weights and throwing areas, were here established. A century later, there are 114 AAA Rules for Competition.

1.–No attendant to accompany a competitor on the scratch, or in the race.

2.–Any competitor starting before the signal to be put back at the discretion of the starter, who shall have power to disqualify him on a repetition of the offence; all questions as to starts to be at the discretion of the starter.

3.–In Hurdle races each competitor to keep his own hurdles throughout the race. The hurdles to stand 3 ft 6 in out of the ground.

4.–In Sprint racing each runner to keep his own side of the course.

5.–Wilfully jostling, or running across, or obstructing another, so as to impede his progress, to disqualify the offender.

6.–In Pole Leaping and High Jumping, three tries at each height allowed. Each height to be determined by the Judges; displacing the bar only to count as a try.

7.–In Broad Jumping, Putting the Weight, or Throwing the Hammer, three tries only to be allowed. The best three competitors of the first trial to be allowed three more tries each for the final. The farthest Throw, Put, or Jump of the six attempts to win.

8.–The Hammer to be thrown from a circle of 7 ft diameter; the throw to be measured from the nearest point of the edge of the circle to the edge of pitch of the ball of the Hammer.

9.–In Broad Jumping, Weight Putting, and Hammer Throwing, crossing the Scratch in the attempt, to count as 'A Try'; all Broad Jumps to be measured from the scratch to the nearest place where any part of the body touches the ground.

10.–The weight of the Hammer (head and handle) and Weight to be 16 lbs respectively.

11.–The Weight and Hammer head to be of iron and spherical, and the Hammer handle to be of wood.

12.–The length from the end of the handle of the Hammer to bottom of the ball not to exceed 4ft over all.

13.–The Weight to be delivered from the shoulder with either hand, from a seven feet circle; no Put to count if delivered or followed with any part of the body touching the ground over the mark; all puts to be measured from the nearest point of the circle, to the edge of the pitch of the Weight.

14.–In Walking Races cautions and disqualifications to be left to the discretion of the Judges.

15.–The decision of the Judges in each competition to be final.

16.–All cases of dispute and any questions that may arise, not provided for in these rules, or the interpretation of any of these rules, to be referred to the Committee of Management at the time, whose decision shall be final.

Lovesey (1979)

extend to games, wagers, and everything in which there is any hazard.' This readiness to wager on horses, cocks, bears, ships, and pugilistic butchers paralleled the increased willingness to risk venture capital in the development of England's expanding industry. From the eagerness to risk and wager came the need to measure time and space. The capitalist's ledgers are close kin to the scorecard. We suddenly enter the world of the bookkeeper and the bookie. (Guttman, 1978: 60)

Figure 2.3 British Records, 1887

On 16 April 1887, the AAA ratified a list of British records. It was the result of 16 months' investigation by a special sub-committee. The records were the first to be ratified by an official governing body anywhere in the world. Below are listed the inaugural records for events still contested (although over metric equivalent distances) in the Championships.

	min	sec			
100 yd		10.0	Arthur Wharton	Stamford Bridge	3 July 1886
220 yd		22.0	William Phillips	Stamford Bridge	25 May 1878
440 yd		48.8	Lawrence Myers (USA)	Lillie Bridge	6 June 1885
880 yd	1	56.0	Lawrence Myers (USA)	Stamford Bridge	2 July 1881
mile	4	18.4	Walter George	Birmingham	21 June 1884
3 miles	14	39.0	Walter George	Stamford Bridge	17 May 1884
6 miles	30	21.5	Walter George	Stamford Bridge	28 July 1884
120 yd hurdles		16.0	Clement Jackson	Oxford	14 Nov 1865
		16.0	Samuel Palmer	Lillie Bridge	15 Apr 1878
		16.0	Charles Daft	Stamford Bridge	3 July 1886
2 mile walk	14	21.4	Henry Meek (USA)	Stamford Bridge	12 July 1884
6 mile walk	45	04.0	Harry Webster	Lillie Bridge	7 Apr 1879
high jump	6 ft $2\frac{3}{4}$ in/1.90 m		Pat Davin	Carrick-on-Suir	5 July 1880
pole jump	11 ft $5\frac{1}{4}$ in/3.48 m		Tom Ray	Whitehaven	13 Aug 1886
long jump	23 ft 2 in/7.06 m		Pat Davin	Monasterevan	30 Aug 1883
	23 ft 2 in/7.06 m		Pat Davin	Portarlington	27 Sept 1883
shot	43 ft 9 in/13.33 m		James O/Brien	Dublin	3 July 1886
hammer	119 ft 5 in/36.40 m		James Mitchell	Limerick	16 June 1886

This was practically, in effect, a world record list. Only in the 880 yd was a superior record known, and that was by Myers, with 1 min 55.6 sec in America. The same runner's 48.6 sec for 440 yd in the 1881 Championships was disallowed as a record because of the gradient in the Aston track.

Lovesey (1979)

Unquestionably, the English 'model' for sport and its rapid export overseas were a function of England's pioneering experience of and role in industrial capitalism. Moreover, well into its 'second phase' of industrialization by 1880, England seemed at the peak of its power, the seeds of immanent (if relative) decline largely unrecognized. The extent of its empire and economic dominance were without historical rival. Interestingly, Guttman tentatively suggests that the export of the English model for sport closely followed the chronology of industrial development. Quoting Rostow's (1960) assertion that the first five nation-states to 'take off' into a stage of sustained economic growth were Britain, France, the USA, Germany and Sweden, he highlights the fact that these five nation-states were also the first to establish truly national organizations for modern sport. Taking into account football, swimming, cycling, rowing and lawn tennis as well as athletics, he ventures:

If we calculate Kendall's coefficient of concordance, which will be 1.0 if the sequence is always England-France-America-Germany-Sweden and 0 if the sequence is always reversed, the coefficient of

concordance is quite high, .637, which strongly suggests *some* relationship between the pace of industrialism and the spread of modern
sports. (Guttman, 1978: 61–2)

As far as track-and-field is concerned, the order precisely follows Rostow's:
the founding of the AAA in 1880 was followed by equivalent initiatives in
France in 1887, the USA in 1888, Germany in 1891 and Sweden in 1895.
Table 2.2 gives the foundation years for both British and international
federations across a range of modern sports.

Table 2.2 Foundation years of international amateur sports federations

Sport	British Federation	Year	International Federation	Year
Athletics	AAA	1880	IAAF	1912
Boxing	ABA	1880	IBU (professionals)	1911
			FIBA (amateurs)	1920
Fencing	AFA	1902	FIE	1913
Football	FA	1863	FIFA	1904
Gymnastics	AGA	1890	FIG	1897
Ice skating	NSAGB	1879	ISU	1892
Lawn tennis	LTA	1888	ILTF	1913
Rowing	ARA	1882	FISA	1892
Swimming	ASA	1886	FINA	1908

Kruger (1999)

For all the signal significance of the English model, it would be quite
wrong to assume that other nations lacked their own distinctive and formative traditions. Consider, for example, the USA. There is no space to
provide an outline of American premodern athletic activity to parallel that
of the English provided earlier, although the richness of, for example,
American Native Indian sporting history needs to be noted (Nabokov,
1981). Instead we shall focus on selected antecedents of the Amateur
Athletic Union of the USA, which was formed in 1888.

Track-and-Field in the USA

Professional pedestrianism in the USA had gained a considerable following
by the 1840s and 1850s. The famous Caledonian Games too were held
annually from at least as early as 1853, organized by various Scottish
immigrant associations. They reached their peak in the immediate after-
math of the American Civil War, although by this time traditional activities
like tossing the caber and playing the bagpipes were little in evidence. If
they belonged in many ways to the same tradition as pedestrianism –
crucially, they were professional – 'in terms of athletic events, the Caledonian Games were the forerunners of their amateur successors' (Redmond, 1971: 101). Rader (1990: 56) writes:

From the 1850s to the mid-1870s, the Caledonians were the single most important promoters of track and field in the country. Even old-stock Americans exhibited an enthusiasm for the annual games. Huge crowds, as many as 20,000 in New York City, turned out in the 1870s to view competition in footracing, tug o'war, hurdling, jumping, pole vaulting, throwing the hammer, and putting the shot. In 1886 the New York Caledonian Club even added a 200-yard dash for women, which resulted in the crowd breaking through the ropes in order to get a better view.

The Caledonians recognized the potential financial return on athletic meetings, opening competition to all ethnic groups, charging for admission and giving cash prizes to winners. By the final quarter of the nineteenth century, however, Scottish immigration had slowed down and Scots had assimilated and had less need for the symbolism of ethnic community. The Caledonian clubs also had new rivals for participation and patronage in the growing numbers of 'amateur' American athletic clubs. Their demise was quite rapid.

As early as the 1860s the New York Caledonian Club was not New York's only athletic club. Inspired by the formation of the London AC in 1863, as well as by the activities of the New York Caledonian Club, three young athletes founded the New York Athletic Club (NYAC) in 1866. 'Apparently the founders simply wanted an opportunity to engage in track and field with men of similar social standing and congenial interests' (Rader, 1990: 86). In line with the English experience, all three were at the time members of local boating clubs. In 1868 the NYAC sponsored the first open amateur track-and-field meeting. A special invitation having been afforded to the New York Caledonian Club, this meeting was advertised as 'an international match – America against Scotland'.

As clubs sprang up in other American cities from the 1870s, the NYAC assumed a leadership role. It built the first cinder track in the country at Mott Haven, introducing the use of spiked shoes, and in 1876 it sponsored the first National Amateur Championships in track-and-field. Then, on 22 April 1879, seven clubs became charter members of the National Association of the Amateur Athletes of America (NAAAA); these clubs were the NYAC, Scottish-American AC, Manhattan AC, Staten Island AC, American AC, Plainfield AC and the Union AC of Boston. The NAAAA immediately assumed control of the National Amateur Championships, and Article IV of the Constitution prescribed the events to be included (Redmond, 1971: 103):

Running – 100 yards, 220 yards, quarter mile, half mile, 1 mile, 3 miles.

Hurdle races – 120 yards, 10 hurdles, 3 ft 6 in high.

Walking – 1 mile, 3 miles and 7 miles.

Running high jump, running broad jump, pole leaping.

Putting the Shot, 16 lbs, throwing the hammer, 16 lbs, throwing the 56 lb weight.

Bicycle race – 2 miles.

Individual tug o'war, tug o'war, teams of 5 men.

Axiomatically, it is a programme that bears the stamp of the Caledonian legacy.

In 1885 the NAAAA sought to extend its jurisdiction to cover virtually all athletic activities, which caused some dissent. For all that 'the American amateur code, unlike its British counterpart, rested neither upon a body of established customs or the sponsorship of an inherited aristocracy' (Rader, 1990: 90), squabbles were plentiful about the amateur standing of individual athletes, including the great Lawrence Myers from the Manhattan AC who at one time held every American record from 50 yards to 1 mile. The upshot was the withdrawal of the NYAC from the NAAAA in 1886. The following year the NYAC led the initiative to form a rival association, the result, in 1888, being the successful launching of the Amateur Athletic Union (AAU). Article XV of the AAU's Constitution claimed jurisdiction over a range of 'amateur athletic exercises' well beyond those acknowledged within track-and-field competition, including boating, boxing, cycling, bowling, football, lawn tennis, racquets, skating, fencing, wrestling, gymnastics, quoits and lacrosse (Redmond, 1971: 104). The AAU's indebtedness to British sporting precedent was, and is, recognized:

> The house of the AAU was literally built upon the bricks of the early pioneers who came from Europe, particularly England, and carried with them their love for sports and games . . . and the athletic-loving Scotsmen who pursued their native games at the Caledonian outings and provided entertainment for more spectators at any single track meet than any other organization had been able to do until well into the twentieth century. (Korsgaard, 1952: 68)

This brief survey of events leading to the founding of the AAU in 1888 would be incomplete without some reference to college and university athletics in the USA, the more so since the collegiate scene has remained significant through to the present, and not just for American-born athletes. In response perhaps to the Oxford–Cambridge meeting first scheduled in 1864 in England, as well as to the Scottish-American Caledonian tradition, the foundations of American student track-and-field were laid in 1869 with the formation of the Columbia College Athletic Association, which that same year initiated meetings with several other student bodies. In 1869 too a pre-eminent Caledonian athlete, George Goldie, was appointed gymnasium director at Princeton University. 'By 1876 eleven institutions engaged in track and field athletics, and in addition in that year the Intercollegiate Association of Amateur Athletes of America (ICAAAA) was established – the oldest continuing collegiate athletic organization in the United States' (Spears and Swanson, 1988: 140).

Special impetus was given to student competition in 1873 when James Gordon Bennett Jr, publisher of the *New York Herald*, donated a cup to the winner of a 2-mile race held as part of the intercollegiate rowing regatta of that year. In 1874, five athletic events were included alongside the rowing contests: 100 yards, 1 mile, 3 miles, 120 yards hurdles and a 7 mile walking race. A number of colleges participated, including Columbia, Princeton, Cornell, Harvard and Yale. Over the next few years intercollegiate track-and-field gradually built up its own independent following, with the ICAAAA assuming responsibility both for hosting an annual championship meeting and for regulating the sport at college level. But the ICAAAA was not immune from changes elsewhere. 'Caught in the controversy between the NAAAA and the newly formed AAU, the ICAAAA chose to affiliate with the AAU. By 1885 track-and-field took its place with football, baseball, and rowing as a main feature of the college athletic scene' (Spears and Swanson, 1988: 140).

If intercollegiate athletic competition had been pioneered – and initially regulated – by students, college and university faculty soon moved to exert a degree of control. Some complained of absenteeism from classes, others of an unacceptable rate of student injuries. In 1882 Harvard appointed a small faculty committee to investigate complaints arising out of student commitments to baseball. One indirect product of this Harvard initiative was the Intercollegiate Athletic Conference, held in New York City in 1883. Spears and Swanson (1988: 141) summarize:

> In this first attempt by college faculty to exercise some control over intercollegiate athletics, eight resolutions were passed dealing with subjects such as the prohibition of college teams playing against professional teams; the prohibition of receiving coaching from professional athletes; limiting competition to four years for each student; requiring all games to be played on the home field of one of the competing institutions; and having a standing faculty committee supervise all contests.

Only Harvard, Princeton and Cornell ratified these resolutions, so much was left in the air; but the intention on the part of college and university faculty and bureaucrats to wrest control of student athletics from the students themselves had been signalled.

Track-and-field athletics was selected to afford a degree of continuity through this opening historical section of the book, from the ancient games at Olympia (Chapter 1) through the modernization of sport in industrial England (Chapter 2) to the 'reinvention' of the Olympics by de Coubertin at the tail end of the nineteenth century (Chapter 3). The account of the rebirth in 1896 and unfolding of the Olympic movement beyond 2000 in the next chapter sees track-and-field athletics buffeted by the vagaries of social change from liberal through organized to disorganized capitalism.

3

The Modern Olympiads

There were several attempts to breathe new life into the Olympic Games between the demise of the ancient games and, approximately 1500 years later in 1896, the first of the new series of modern games in Athens. According to Redmond (1988), the earliest documented instance of what he calls 'pseudo-Olympics', that is, meetings utilizing an Olympic label, was Dover's Cotswold Games in early seventeenth-century England (see Chapter 2). While it is evident that Dover had no true aspiration to revive the Olympic Games, the allusions to the ancient pan-Hellenic festivals that his Cotswold Games engendered undoubtedly helped keep alive the memory of the ancient games at Olympia (Ruhl, 1985). Moreover, Redmond (1988: 74) suggests,

> they are the most prominent example of the fact that long before 1896 or even the beginning of the nineteenth century, the adjective 'Olympic' (whether deliberate or deserved or not) was becoming the most prized description for an athletic festival, embarking on its way to represent the modern epitome of athletic excellence as well as of ancient deeds.

References or allusions to the ancient Greek games were not uncommon in seventeenth-century Europe, but, with hindsight, it was from the early 1800s that the inexorable movement towards an international Olympic revival really began. Only a few of the more significant initiatives will be mentioned here. In 1834 what MacAloon (1981: 147) has termed 'the first true prototype of the modern Games', a pan-Scandinavian festival defined by the contemporary press as 'Olympic Games', was organized in Sweden by Gustav Schartau. Wrestling, jumping, climbing and running events were included, and the festival was held for a second – but final – time in 1836. In 1844 the 'Olympic Club' of Montreal organized a two-day gathering dubbed the 'Montreal Olympic Games', incorporating no fewer than 29 events. This festival has encouraged some Canadian commentators to describe Montreal as one of the birthplaces of modern organized sport. But the festival was never to be repeated.

By contrast, Dr W. P. Brooks' annual 'Olympic Games' held in a valley outside the village of Much Wenlock in Shropshire, England, were repeated for more than 40 years. The Olympic pageantry and symbolism of Brooks' festivals were conspicuous. A silver urn was donated by the Greek King in Athens for the victor of the pentathlon. 'Other events included cricket (which was incorporated in the programme for the 1896 Olympic Games in Athens but then cancelled because no one entered), jumping, running, tilting at a ring from horseback, and "prizes for literary competitions and other artistic works" ' (Redmond, 1988: 77). Coubertin himself was invited by the industrious Brooks to attend the Much Wenlock festival, and did so in 1890, apparently being 'entranced' by the spectacle. Young (1984: 59) has suggested, in fact, that so enthused was Coubertin by his trip that it might reasonably be contended that 'even the name of his Olympic Games, like their philosophy, came more from England than from Greece'.

Greece too had its 'Olympic Games' in the nineteenth century. Under the auspices of a wealthy grain dealer, Evangelios Zappas, festivals were held in Athens in 1859, 1870, 1875 and 1889. The 1859 games took place in a flat city square, Place Louis, because no stadium was available.

> Among the events included were sprint and distance races appropriately called *diaulos* and *dolichos*, jumps, discus and javelin throws, rope climbing and wrestling. Competitors took an oath that they would not cheat or foul their opponents. Olive wreaths, money and other prizes were distributed by the King before an enthusiastic but disorderly crowd that had to be vigorously controlled by police and soldiers. (Redmond, 1988: 78)

To some it is these games that truly comprise 'the first Olympic Games of the modern era' (Messinesi, 1973). In Young's (1984) opinion the next games in Athens in 1870 were the most modern and sophisticated that had been held up to that time. Although Zappas had died in 1865, a site had been acquired using the Olympic Trust Fund that he had established and to which he had left the greater part of his considerable fortune (Hill, 1996). A fusion of ancient and modern events, these games were celebrated on the site of the centuries-old Panathenaic stadium in front of 30,000 spectators and were widely praised. While the later games in the 'series', in 1875 and 1889, attracted fewer spectators and plaudits, there is no doubting the historical significance of these pre-Coubertin Olympic Games in Athens. Only recently, however, has their impact on Coubertin himself been stressed.

Coubertin and the International Olympic Movement

Coubertin was born into an aristocratic family in Paris in 1863. Reared in a household convinced that the French defeat in the Franco-Prussian War was due to general decadence, he drew on a somewhat stereotypical conception of English youths – formed out of early acquaintance with Hughes's *Tom Brown's Schooldays* and a dozen or so excursions to England in the 1880s – to elaborate a programme of pedagogical reform. Arguably, Thomas Arnold, headmaster of Rugby School from 1828 to 1842, was 'the single most important influence on the life and thought of Pierre de Coubertin' (Lucas, 1988: 90). Certainly Arnold's brand of moralism found an echo in Coubertin's prescriptions for change in French education. Coubertin became convinced that the English public school system, premised in part on the formative potential of athletic proficiency, had provided the foundation for the consolidation of the vast British empire.

> The genius of Arnold had sown the seed. The genius of Coubertin responded. The latter's life-long devotion to the Hellenic trinity of body, mind and spirit, coupled with a compelling faith in the character-building qualities of English sport education, formed the rationale for his dream of universal amateur athletics. (Lucas, 1988: 91)

The efforts of Coubertin and his allies were not without their rewards in France, with many schools taking a new interest in physical education and sport and rowing and athletic clubs springing into existence in Paris and provincial towns. By the early 1890s, however, Coubertin's ambitions were international rather than merely national. With hindsight, it is apparent that his political footwork was remarkably sure during the critical period between 1892 and 1896, but his own confidence in realizing his newly defined project of re-establishing the ancient Olympic Games on an international basis rose and fell through a multiplicity of alliances and meetings. He first publicly floated his idea of reviving the games of Olympia in his conclusion to a speech at the Sorbonne on 25 November 1892. The idea was keenly received, but more as a vivid rhetorical device, a piece of symbolism, than as a practical proposition. Disappointed, Coubertin reconciled himself to a more thorough preparation of the soil in which his idea might eventually take root. He set off on visits to a number of other countries, making speeches and securing support.

After meticulous international diplomacy and planning, crucially involving Charles Herbert from the Amateur Athletic Association in England and the influential William Milligan Sloane from the USA, Coubertin arranged a second gathering at the Sorbonne from 16 to 23 June 1894, where 79 delegates from 12 countries attended, primarily to discuss the still thorny issue of amateurism. The idea of reviving the Olympic Games was clearly on the agenda, but it is debatable how many delegates had appreciated the salience of this item prior to their arrival in Paris (Hill,

1996). In the event, the delegates divided into two 'commissions', one on amateurism and one on the games proposal. A well-rehearsed spell was ultimately cast over those present: 'There were poems, music and songs. And after every delegate had heard the hymn to Apollo, discovered at Delphi in 1893 and set to music by Gabriel Fauré and sung by Jeanne Remacle from the Paris Opera, the assembly, unanimously and by acclaim, decided to restore the Olympic Games' (Eyquem, 1976: 139).

The commission's deliberations on the re-establishment of the Olympic Games did not depart significantly from Coubertin's own blueprint.

> The Games were to be held at four-yearly intervals; they were not to imitate the ancient Games, but to be exclusively modern in character – what mattered was the spirit of Olympism rather than the specific nature of the events; the Games for boys between the ages of twelve and eighteen were not to be reproduced: in the absence of birth certificates they had given great trouble to the judges. Coubertin was also to have full responsibility for the designation of an international committee whose members would represent Olympism in their countries. (Hill, 1996: 21)

The plan for the initial games to be held in Athens had not been Coubertin's – who had envisaged Paris as host city in the early 1900s – but he did not dissent. It was agreed that the presidency of the new International Olympic Committee (IOC) should revolve, resting with the country selected to host the next games. Accordingly, Demetrius Bikelas was elected first president, with Coubertin serving as secretary-general. Coubertin succeeded as president after the first games in Athens in 1896, since the games of 1900 were to be held in Paris. He was then invited to continue as president, which he did until 1925. The pattern of long tenure had been established (see Figure 3.1).

Figure 3.1 Presidents of the International Olympic Committee

1894–1896	Demetrius Bikelas (Greece)
1896–1925	Baron Pierre de Coubertin (France)
1925–1942	Count Henri de Baillet-Latour (Belgium)
1946–1952	J. Sigfrid Edstrom (Sweden)
1952–1972	Avery Brundage (USA)
1972–1980	Lord Killanin (Ireland)
1980–2001	Juan Antonio Samaranch (Spain)
2001–	Jacques Rogge (Belgium)

The basic concept of the IOC from the outset was that of independence for each member. Thus the original 15 members in 1894 were neither elected by, nor representative of, their countries on the IOC; rather, they were representatives of Olympism to all nations. 'The very fact that this Committee is self-recruiting makes it immune to all political interference, and it is not swayed by intense nationalism' (Coubertin, 1951: 15). This independence, if increasingly controversial, remains jealously guarded over a century later.

Apart from Charles Herbert and William Milligan Sloane, Coubertin's original, hand-picked and overwhelmingly European IOC included a number of active participants, notably Viktor Balck (Sweden), Alexander Butkowski (Russia), Jiri Guth-Jarkovsky (Bohemia) and Ferenc Kemeny (Hungary), as well as an assortment of inactive noblemen whom Coubertin was later to dismiss disdainfully as *une façade* (Guttman, 2002). It was to be an influential body.

Krotee (1988) has argued that Coubertin's IOC *appeared* to conform to Weber's idea type of a formal, rationally organized bureaucracy: essentially, there were clearly defined goals and patterns of activity, with acceptable regulations and controls functionally related to the attainment of the goals. But it is *in reality* Michel's 'iron law of oligarchy' which is the more pertinent. At the core of Michel's theory is the contention that oligarchy, or rule by the few, arises even in the most idealistic of organizations, the ideals over time serving as mere rationalizations to preserve power in the hands of the few. Moreover, little has changed since Coubertin's era: 'Like the initial Committee membership selected by Coubertin, today's IOC, as well as its past presidents, seems to be dominated by the elite upper class and, for the most part, European patrimony' (Krotee, 1988: 117). This is an issue to which I shall return.

The IOC needed all its influence between 1894 and 1896 to pave the way to Athens. Greek politicians were unenthusiastic and fickle; the Prime Minister, Charilaos Tricoupis, came out against holding the games in Athens. By late 1894 Stephanos Dragoumis, Bikelas's choice to mastermind the preparations, was recommending the postponement of the games for four years when Paris might host them. Coubertin, with a reserve location (Budapest) up his sleeve, travelled to Greece to negotiate (whilst simultaneously working to reduce tensions further afield – many of his fellow French citizens, for example, had not forgiven Germany its victory in 1870 and were violently opposed to German participation in the games). Gradually the momentum for the Athenian games began to grow. The Crown Prince Constantine, who played an instrumental role in rekindling enthusiasm, appointed Timoleon Philemon, a former Mayor of Athens, to lead a reconstituted organizing committee. The ancient stadium was reconstructed in white marble, thanks to the sponsorship of a wealthy Greek, George Averoff. And as the commencement of the games drew closer, Athens warmed: 'Every house was decorated with flowers and flags. A triumphal arch was erected on the theatre square, myriads of lanterns lined and spanned the streets, bearing the letters "OA" ' (*Olympiakoi Agones* – Olympic Games) (Lucas, 1988: 95). So enthusiastic were the Greeks by the time of the opening ceremony on Easter Sunday, 5 April 1896, that many assumed they would also host the games of 1900; indeed, some reached the conclusion that the modern Olympic Games, like their ancient predecessors, rightfully belonged to Greece. In his subsequent speeches and writings, the 33-year-old Coubertin's resentment at what he saw as a calculated Greek attempt to diminish his own vision, diligence and achievement, and to present the games as a native accomplishment, is manifest. Scholars, however, vary in the distribution of their sympathies between Coubertin and the Greeks.

As in the ancient games, track-and-field athletics contributed most events (12) to the 1896 festival. The other sports contributing events were gymnastics (8), cycling (6), shooting (5), swimming (4), fencing (3), weight-lifting (2), tennis (2) and wrestling (1). There were no female athletes in any sport, a policy over which Coubertin himself was entirely adamant (although it is said that one woman, Melpomene, having been denied entry to the marathon, nevertheless completed the race alongside the male athletes). The conditions for the track-and-field events were far from ideal. Because of Greek inexperience, Charles Perry, caretaker of the Stamford Bridge track in London, was commissioned to lay the track-and-field facilities at the Averoff Stadium. Perry found himself short of time, materials and water, and the result was an uncongenial, dry and loose-surfaced cinder track. Moreover, the track was built to the same specifications as at ancient Olympia: there was a lone straight in excess of 200 metres and extremely sharp bends; and races were run clockwise rather than, as today, anti-clockwise.

Approximately 40,000 spectators watched the events, the winners receiving a wreath of wild olive from Olympia, a diploma drawn by a Greek artist, and a silver medal prepared by the celebrated French engraver, Chaplain. The first three in each event were received on a podium, where the symbols of victory were distributed by the president of the IOC or his representative, and the flag of the winner's country raised while the national anthem played. There were in fact relatively few competitors, and these arrived individually rather than in national teams. The Americans, mostly members of the Boston Athletic Association or students from Princeton University, were conspicuously successful, although standards tended to be moderate. Figure 3.2 lists the track-and-field events held, and the winners, winning performances and numbers of competitors for each event.

The event that warrants its own account was the only one specially designed for the occasion, the marathon. 'In contrast to the ancient Games, which did not include a marathon race, Coubertin included a race to honour the Greek who ran almost twenty-five miles from Marathon to Athens in 490 BC to tell the Athenians that they had won the Battle of Marathon' (Spears and Swanson, 1988: 364). No Greek had won any event in any sport in the 1896 games: it is part of modern Olympic folklore that the unexpected victor was a Greek shepherd, Spiridon Loues. A traveller who witnessed Loues's entrance to the Averoff Stadium is worth quoting at some length:

Figure 3.2 Winners of the track-and-field events at the 1896 Olympic Games

100 metres
Thomas Burke (USA)   12.0

400 metres
Thomas Burke (USA)   54.2

800 metres
Edwin Flack (USA)   2:11.0

1500 metres
Edwin Flack (USA)   4:33.2

Marathon (40,000 metres)
Spiridon Loues (Greece)   2h 58.50

110 metres hurdles
Thomas Curtis (USA)   17.6

High jump
Ellery Clark (USA)   1.81m

Pole vault
William Hoyt (USA)   3.30m

Long jump
Ellery Clark (USA)   6.35m

Triple jump
James Connolly (USA)   13.71m

Shot put
Robert Garrett (USA)   11.22m

Discus
Robert Garrett (USA)   29.15m

It is impossible to describe the enthusiasm within the Stadium – nay, in the whole of the city of Athens – over the result of this the most important contest in the games during these ten days. The Stadium packed with over 50,000 people; the walls around it, the hills about, covered with a human crowd that from the distance looked like bees clustering over a comb; and this mass of humanity rising in one great shout of joy with the advent – the one runner who was first to cross the line within the Stadium, caught in the arms of the Crown Prince, who led him before the King, embraced and kissed by those who could get near him; all this and much more sent a thrill through every heart which few could have experienced before with the same intensity. It might almost have been Philippides of old bringing to the anxious inhabitants of Athens the news of their glorious victory, the salvation of their country and home.

Consolidation and Development

It is neither possible nor necessary here to detail a century of modern Olympiads. Instead a largely chronological outline will be provided, addressing the themes of *consolidation* and *development*, punctuated by fuller accounts of selected games, namely, those in Berlin in 1936 and Los Angeles in 1984.

An Olympic congress held at Le Havre in 1897 put an effective end to any Greek ambitions to usurp the modern games. But the frenetic haggling so characteristic of the period before the 1896 games was to continue. Coubertin actually withdrew from the organizing body for the Paris games of 1900 in despair. For him, neither the Paris games nor those in St Louis in 1904, tacked on to a world's fair to celebrate the centennial of the Louisiana Purchase, were successes, not least because they were haphazardly organized, involved athletes from relatively few countries – 432 of the 554 participants in St Louis were American, with Americans winning 22 of the 23 track-and-field events – and were held over several months; he did not even attend in 1904. While Coubertin had expressly excluded women in 1896, however, some did take part in subsequent games, initially, in 1900, in tennis and golf.

The 1906 'interim' games were held in Athens, partly because so few Europeans had been able to compete in St Louis, but also because Coubertin was anxious to reassert his concept of the Olympic ideal. These 'unofficial' games, while modest in impact, seemed to have appeased Coubertin. After Rome's late withdrawal, London hosted the 1908 games. Perhaps remembered most for local arrangements for the marathon – which started at Windsor Palace as a favour to the royal family and finished at Shepherd's Bush, exactly 26 miles, 385 yards away, a distance which has stuck – 1908 was characterized by strong nationalist sentiments, disputes and accusations of bias, the IOC deciding that thenceforth officials should be as international as the athletes. At a ball at Grafton Gardens, Coubertin quoted approvingly the words first uttered by an American prelate: 'The importance of the Olympiads lies not so much in winning as in taking part' (cited in Guttman, 2002: 31).

It was Stockholm's turn in 1912. Symbolic of the Swedes' mastery of all organizational aspects of the games, remarked upon favourably by a young Avery Brundage (later IOC president from 1952 to 1972), was their pioneering use of electronic timing for the foot-races. Coubertin, Guttman (2002: 32) writes, 'was ecstatic about the splendidly constructed stadium, "a model of its type", and about the way the Swedish organizing committee orchestrated events'. The number of women was growing slowly, up from 36 in 1908 to 57 in 1912 (the figures for men being 1,998 and 2,447 respectively), although there was continued opposition to their inclusion, most notably from Sullivan, representing the USA.

The sixth Olympiad, scheduled for Berlin in 1916, 'was drowned out by the roar of canon and the moans of dying men' and cancelled (Guttman,

2002: 37), Antwerp being the diplomatically – if hurriedly – chosen successor for 1920. But should the Germans be invited to participate? The organizing committee for the 1920 games was not instructed by the IOC to exclude them, simply encouraged not to issue an invitation (an expedient also adopted by the Parisians in 1924). Antwerp could not in the time available match the cool efficiency of Stockholm. It also marked the end of American domination of track-and-field. Ominously, the 'flying Finn', Paavi Nurmi, won three gold medals in distance races.

In 1921 Coubertin announced his intention to retire as president of the IOC and asked, as a favour, if the 1924 games might be held in Paris; this was granted, although furious Italian advocates of the city of Rome walked out. At the same meeting the IOC decided to establish an executive board, and the French cleric Père Henri Didon ventured what became a lasting motto for the Olympics: *Citius, Altius, Fortius* (Faster, Higher, Stronger). The Paris games, preceded by a few months by the first ever winter games, witnessed new forms of chauvinism (accompanied by unofficial 'points tables'). The Finns again impressed, in medals per capita of population by far outshining Britain and the USA; the astounding Nurmi set Olympic records for the 1500 and 5000 metres, won the 10,000 cross-country race, and was a member of Finland's victorious teams in the 3000 metres relay and 10,000 metres cross-country relay. The games also featured Harold Abrahams' victory in the 100 metres and Eric Liddell's win in the 400 metres, performances re-created in 1981 in the 'somewhat fictionalized, beautifully sentimentalized feature film *Chariots of Fire*' (Guttman, 2002: 43; see also Magnusson, 1982).

Between the games in Paris and those in Amsterdam in 1928 there was some acceleration of the 'bureaucratic tendency to regularize and standardize' (Guttman, 2002: 44). The longstanding issue of amateurism versus professionalism continued to exercise the IOC and its executive board. At an important Olympic congress in Prague in 1925 the case for compensation was put and defeated, although athletes were to be allowed expenses for up to 15 days. At the same congress government-funded training was roundly condemned and Belgium's Comte Henri de Baillet-Latour was elected as Coubertin's successor for an eight-year term. This was the year too of the First Workers' Olympics at Frankfurt, a four-day 'extravaganza' involving 'one hundred thousand workers as athletes, as participants in parades, pageants, and massed demonstrations, and as spectators' (Guttman, 2002: 45). So successful were these games that they were repeated in 1929, 1933 and 1937 (see Scambler, forthcoming).

The otherwise largely uneventful 1928 Amsterdam games were the first to see women competing in the core track-and-field programme. The International Amateur Athletic Federation (IAAF), formed in 1912, had voted in 1926 to sanction women's track-and-field events but not at that juncture to push for their inclusion in the Olympics Games. A mere two years later, however, not only had the IAAF been pressurized into a more militant advocacy but the IOC had accepted its recommendation that women be permitted to participate in 'a restricted number of athletic events' – in fact, five – on an experimental basis. The British women were so incensed at this grudging concession that they boycotted the games. Nurmi, it should be noted, won the 10,000 metres and was runner-up in the 5000 metres and the 3000 metres steeplechase.

In defiance of growing pressure to be more accommodating to female athletes, Baillet-Latour moved for their exclusion from the Olympic Games destined for Los Angeles in 1932; but his will did not prevail. Nor was Los Angeles, despite some trepidation on the part of non-Americans, the shambles that St Louis had been in 1904; moreover it took on a Hollywood aspect. An Olympic village was constructed for the male participants, and a further innovation was a 'victory platform upon which the medal winners were to stand while their national flags were raised and their national anthems played' (Guttman, 2002: 50). Nurmi, to wrap up an extraordinary Olympic biography, was judged to have turned professional and therefore to be ineligible to compete. The IOC decision to hold the Olympic Games for 1936 in Berlin was announced on 15 May 1931. It had been a difficult, and was to prove a controversial and fateful, judgement.

'The Nazi Olympics'

If there had been doubts about the choice of Los Angeles, mainly around the distances non-American athletes would have to travel to compete and the enthusiasm for and organization of the games, there had been many more about Berlin. As Guttman's (1984) study elucidates, in some respects Nazi ideology appeared inimical to sport (gymnastics, through the traditional *Turner*, excepted), let alone to Olympism. Later he writes:

> most *Turner* remained devoted to gymnastics as their nation's sole authentic form of physical exercise. These believers in German gymnastics condemned competition, which is an inherent aspect of sports, and they were appalled by the specialization, rationalization and quantification that are characteristic of modern sports. (Guttman, 2002: 54)

It is not of course necessary to reject the philosophy of the *Turner* to recognize likely quandaries for the IOC. And then there was the contradiction between the Olympic Charter and the open racism of the Nazi regime: 'American, British, and French leaders of the International Olympic Committee well knew of Nazi discrimination against non-Aryans, and certainly of their policies against Jewish athletes' (Baker, 1982: 251–2). As early as 1933, for example, Jewish teams were formally forbidden to play Aryan teams in any sport. Baillet-Latour, recently re-elected for a second eight-year term, sought reassurances. Discussions quickly centred on the rights *not* of foreign Jews to compete, but of German Jews to try out for *their* national team. An 'unambiguous' written guarantee was obtained from German members of the IOC that no such restraints would be permitted. Doubts were not fully assuaged, however, and an American withdrawal was threatened. Brundage, by now president of the American Olympic Committee, journeyed to make an on-the-spot inspection and was quickly and easily satisfied by his hosts. He gave short shrift to continuing American opposition to the Berlin venue, crassly demanding that Jews and Communists 'keep their hands off American sport' (Guttman, 2002: 61). Predictably, the Nazis were to renege on their undertaking.

Baker (1982: 251) offers a perspicacious observation of the Berlin games:

> Born of a nationalistic age, from their beginnings in 1896 the modern Olympic Games had been played amid a martial display of flags, military marches, patriotic anthems, and nationalistic rivalries. The Nazis did not create this atmosphere; they merely carried it to its absurd limits. They cloaked the Olympics of 1936 in political and military garb, using them as a showpiece of German engineering skill, cultural taste, and athletic prowess.

The games were certainly 'spectacular' (and I shall have more to say about both sport *as spectacle* and modernity's Olympic Games as *mega-events* in later chapters (see Roche, 2000)). Twelve days before the opening of the games on 1 August a torch was lit from the sacred alter at Olympia (see Chapter 1), to be transported by 3075 runners – each covering about one kilometre – to arrive at the magnificent *Deutsches Stadion* in Berlin at precisely the right moment. More than 110,000 people heard 30 trumpets announce Hitler's arrival. An ageing Richard Strauss led the orchestra in a rendering of *Deutschland über alles* and *Horst Wessellied*, followed by his own 'Olympic Hymn'. Sixty-year-old Spiridon Loues, winner of the marathon in 1896, headed the Greek team's march-past, after which a further 51 national teams paraded by, some giving the Nazi salute, some not. A recorded message from a terminally ill Coubertin was played: 'The important thing at the Olympic Games is not to win, but to take part, just as the important thing about life is not to conquer, but to struggle well' (quoted in Baker, 1982: 254). Hitler departed at 6 p.m., again to a fanfare of trumpets, and the evening was then given over to a no less grand Festival of Olympic Youth. Outside the stadium the Jewish population enjoyed a temporary respite from anti-Semitic slogans and, to a point, active persecution.

As for the sporting activity, overall the Germans won more gold, silver and bronze medals than any other team, with the Americans placed second and the Italians third. The Americans came out on top, however, in the track-and-field events, winning 12 of the 24 gold medals. Moreover, most of the American track-and-field victors were black, with Jesse Owens outshining all others: he won gold medals and set new Olympic records in the broad (or long) jump, the 200 metres, and the 400 metres relay, and tied the record while taking the gold medal in the 100 metres. Hitler is alleged to have snubbed Owens, declining to meet him after having personally and publicly congratulated earlier German victors. But the truth is more prosaic: he had just been informed by Baillet-Latour that he should congratulate *all* or *none* of the winners, and thenceforth refrained from meeting German as well as foreign athletes. As has often been remarked, rarely without irony:

> Owens' subsequent treatment exposed a dark side of American life more tellingly than it reflected Nazi racism. 'I wasn't invited to shake hands with Hitler', he later noted, 'but I wasn't invited to the White House to shake hands with the President either' ... For all their ruthlessness, the Nazis had no corner on prejudice. (Baker, 1982: 256)

Although the number of lynchings in the USA fell from 18 in 1935 to 8 in 1936, on 15 August 1936, the penultimate day of the games, a crowd of more than 10,000 held all-night parties at Owensboro, Kentucky, jostling for a good view of the execution of Rainey Bethea, a black who had abducted and killed a 70-year-old white woman (Hart-Davis, 1986: 229). Not so long after the Berlin games Owens was reduced to racing against dogs, horses and cars to make ends meet (see McRae's (2002) account of the post-games deprivations of both Owens and his friend Joe Louis, who had been world heavyweight boxing champion for 12 years).

If the feats of Jesse Owens represent one ready folk image of the 1936 Berlin games, so too does *Olympia*, the classic film of the games made by the German film-maker and Fascist fellow-traveller, Leni Reifenstahl, and released in 1938 (Roche, 2000: 115). Reifenstahl's production is frequently interpreted as one ingredient of an effective Nazi propaganda coup. But were the Berlin games the legitimating device Hitler and his political allies may have hoped for at that juncture, even required? The verdict is mixed. Roche (2000: 117) rightly insists that the lead-up years of 1933–36 were as important as the games themselves:

> In these crucial early years of the Nazi revolution, as with any revolution, the legitimacy and authority of the new state was vulnerable and conceivably it could have been short-lived. However, the coming of the Olympic event, when the eyes of the world would be on the new Germany, together with the production of the facilities, and preparation and rehearsal of its organization, were significant factors in legitimizing and popularizing the regime internally and in legitimizing and sanitizing it internationally.

All this was no less evident to political opponents of the Nazi regime and of the Berlin games. But as Roche (2000: 121) shows, the IOC proved a willing 'collaborator' with the 'supernationalistic politics of fascism'; moreover, the IOC went on in 1936 to award the 1940 games to Japan, a decision it was content to ratify as late as 1938 (only to be rebuffed by Japan prior to the cancellation of the war-time games of 1940 and 1944).

In his last public pronouncement, Coubertin described the Berlin games as 'grandiose' and organized with 'Hitlerian strength and discipline'; they had, he judged, 'magnificently served the Olympic ideal' (quoted in Guttman, 2002: 70). Undoubtedly the watching world was impressed with the organization and staging of the games. Brundage, predictably, echoed Coubertin's enthusiastic celebration of the games for their contribution to 'international peace and harmony'. He strongly denied that they constituted a propaganda victory for the Nazis, sanguinely proclaiming that while it was true that 'the Hitler regime made every effort to use for its own purposes this great festival of the youth of the world ... it was arranged and controlled entirely and exclusively by non-Nazis for the benefit of non-Nazis' (quoted in Guttman, 1988: 214). Certainly, as Brundage remarked, a popular Jesse Owens was fêted by German athletes and spectators alike, a point emphasized by Guttman (1988: 216) in what is probably a fair judgement: 'To the degree that Owens made a mockery of the Nazi myth of "Nordic" superiority, the games were not a propaganda coup, *but the overall impression of the games must have added to Hitler's prestige*' (emphasis added). Furthermore, as Hart-Davis (1986) sensibly insists, it is no more possible to determine whether an Olympic boycott would have constrained or provoked Hitler than it is prudent to guess. That the games were a personal propaganda coup for the ambitious Brundage, however, is less equivocal.

Postwar Renewal

Brundage characteristically resisted the cancellation of the 1940 games, even in the face of threatened boycotts on the part of the Empire Games Federation and the British AAA in 1938 ('Why do the athletes meddle with politics – have they no foreign office?' (Brundage, quoted in Guttman, 2002: 73)). When later that year Japan withdrew on the grounds that the games would be a costly distraction, the IOC unanimously and revealingly sanctioned a return to Berlin. Even when Hitler invaded Poland on 1 September 1939, Brundage, for one, persisted in the illusion that the games could go ahead. Only when the Germans called off the winter games and the Soviet Union invaded Finland on 30 November did they give up. Baillet-Latour died of a stroke in 1942, to be replaced by his vice-president, the Swede Sigfrid Edstrom. Edstrom was at the time over 70 years old and Brundage was soon after appointed by a majority vote his second vice-president (moving up to first vice-president and likely successor in 1946). A mail ballot led to London's hosting of the first postwar games in 1948.

The London games took place in a Europe that had been devastated by the war. Visiting athletes appeased a querulous local citizenry by bringing their own food and distributing any surplus to British hospitals. They were lodged in army barracks and other makeshift accommodation. Guttman (2002) makes the point that the track-and-field competition was unsurprisingly dominated by non-Europeans: the Americans carried off ten gold medals in the men's events, and the Swedes, neutral in the war, six. However the athletic star was a woman, Holland's Francina Blankers-Koen. She had competed as an 18-year-old in 1936 (tying for sixth in the high jump); now, having in the interim married and had two children, she took gold medals in the 100 metres and 200 metres, the 80 metres hurdles and the 400 metres relay (because of Olympic restrictions on the numbers of events one could enter, she was unable to tackle the long and high jumps, for both of which she was world record-holder). Brundage, not known for his support for women athletes, was bowled over, referring to 'a new type of woman . . . lithe, supple, physically disciplined, strong, slender and efficient, like the Goddesses of ancient Greece' (quoted in Guttman, 2002: 82).

Edstrom's term of office expired in 1952, the year of the subsequent games in Helsinki. Brundage was the hier apparent, although he was vigorously opposed in the early rounds of voting by the Marquess of Exeter. The 20 years of the 'Brundage era' were to be characterized by resistance to *politics*, that is, government 'interference', on the one hand, and *professionalism*, that is, payments to athletes, on the other. The games of 1952 took on a new political dimension and gave rise to novel tensions with the first participation of the Soviet Union (see Shneidman, 1979). It marked the return too of teams from (West) Germany and Japan. American track-and-field athletes were again dominant, the men's team taking 14 of the 24 gold medals. The Soviet men missed out on men's golds, although there was compensation in the performances of Czechoslovakia's Emil Zatopek, who set Olympic records in winning the 5000 and 10,000 metres and the marathon (famously asking of the English runner Jim Peters 15 miles into the marathon: 'Excuse me, I haven't run a marathon before, but don't you think we ought to go a bit faster?').

The Melbourne games of 1956 were jeopardized by two wars, precipitated by Egypt's seizure of the Suez Canal and the entry of Russian tanks into Budapest. Brundage was prompted to ask why modern nation-states might not sign up to an 'Olympic truce', erroneously assuming that wars had been halted to accommodate the ancient games, whereas the truce had in fact merely guaranteed safe travel to and from the Olympia site (see Chapter 1). A number of countries boycotted the Melbourne gathering. US athletes again dominated track-and-field, taking 15 of the 24 gold medals. Among the outstanding individual performances, Al Oerter's victory in the discus (the first of four consecutive gold medals for the American) and the Russian Vladimir Kuts's Olympic records in the 5000 and 10,000 metres stood out. Guttman (2002: 101) writes:

Considering the unresolved political crises that wracked the world, one can conclude that the games were – despite flashes of anger – remarkably ironic. The IOC's desire to create an oasis of amity in a desert of hostility was not entirely quixotic. At the closing ceremony, the athletes took matters into their own hands. Rather than march as members of their national teams, they broke ranks, joined hands, embraced, sang and danced. Together, spontaneously, they created one of the more humane traditions in modern sports.

In 1955 the Soviet Union released East Germany from its status as the Soviet zone of Germany and recognized it as an independent state. The IOC provisionally recognized the East German National Olympic Committee (NOC), but only on condition that it co-operated in forming a single German team. This provisional recognition of East Germany continued and the Germans managed, with difficulty, to compete as a joint team at Rome in 1960 (and in Tokyo in 1964) (Hill, 1996). For Brundage this was a vindication of his notion of sport: 'in sport we do such things'. The Rome games were transmitted 'live' throughout Western Europe and CBS-TV paid $660,000 for the right to fly film from Rome to New York for prime-time telecasts. The sale of television rights netted the Italian NOC approximately $1.2 million, and despite his distaste for commercialization Brundage accepted 10 per cent of the profits on behalf of the executive board of the IOC. Wilma Rudolf won the 100 and 200 metres and anchored the US team to victory in the 4 × 100 metres relay; Ludmilla Shevtsova won the women's 800 metres, restored for the first time since the experiment in 1928; Al Oerter captured his second discus title; and Abebe Bikila of Ethiopia became the first black African to win a gold medal, in the marathon (a feat he was to repeat at Tokyo). Significantly too, in Rome for the first time – the initial international games for 'disabled athletes' were held in Stoke Mandeville in 1952 – the Paralympics took place at the same venue as the Olympic Games.

By the time the games had reached Tokyo in 1964 the South African NOC had been suspended as a result of its apartheid policies. As South African involvement in international sport faded, other independent African nations came within the orbit of Olympism. Symptomatic of future Olympiads, however, was NBC-TV's decision to delay the West Coast broadcast of the Tokyo opening ceremony until 1 a.m. to avoid a clash with Johnny Carson's *Tonight Show*, a decision condemned by the US State Department as well as the IOC. Track-and-field stars included the 'metronome on legs', Abebe Bikila, who won his second marathon, the New Zealander Peter Snell, who won the 800 metres, and of course Al Oerter.

In advance of the games of 1968 in Mexico City the American TV rights were sold for $4.5 million. By this time the NOCs were flexing their muscles, with some representatives, notably the Italian Onesti, pushing for a Permanent General Assembly (PGA) of NOCs, effectively to reign in the – increasingly wealthy – executive board of the IOC. An embattled Brundage had his work cut out to secure his second term of office. Intransigence on the part of the South African NOC led to its continued exclusion from the 1968 games. The games themselves were preceded not only by the Warsaw Pact's intervention in Prague but by social unrest in

Mexico during which more than 250 students were killed. In the event the games were sheltered from local disturbances. Wyomia Tyus excelled on the track, dominating the 100 metres. Dick Fosbury pioneered the *Fosbury flop* in the high-jump, and Bob Beamon floated through the thin air to shatter the world long-jump record with a distance of 8.90 metres, 63 centimetres beyond the old mark and at the time of writing the longest surviving Olympic track-and-field record. Al Oerter recorded his fourth discus win. Most memorable, however, was the protest by the male sprinters Tommy Smith and John Carlos, who raised their black-gloved fists in a black-power salute on the podium during the playing of the 'Star-Spangled Banner'. Then, on the day these two athletes were suspended by the US NOC, Lee Evans set a world record for the 400 metres and, accompanied by Larry James (second) and Ron Freeman (third), wore a black beret on to the podium; all three removed their berets during the playing of the national anthem but waved them with obvious intent when it finished. Brundage was incensed: 'warped mentalities and cracked personalities seem to be everywhere and impossible to eliminate' (cited in Guttman, 2002: 132).

The games of 1972 took place in a Munich still triggering memories of Hitler's rise and Chamberlain's folly. Black nations lobbied and threatened a boycott to secure the expulsion of the Rhodesian team shortly after Ian Smith had declared independence from Britain on behalf of his white minority government. The athletes from East Germany competed for the first time with their own uniforms, flag and anthem. Borzov took the 100 and 200 metres gold medals for the Soviet Union, while Lasse Viren of Finland won both the 5000 and 10,000 metres. Munich is remembered most, however, for the siege in which a group of Palestinians, demanding the release of 234 fellow countrymen held in Israel as well as of Andreas Baader and Ulrike Meinhof who were being held in West Germany, took a number of Israeli hostages in the Olympic village on 5 September. Several captors and captives died when the German police eventually made a bid to rescue the hostages at Furstenfeldbruck airport as they made their way to board a plane destined for an Arab airfield. A memorial service was held on 6 September, after which Brundage, an autocrat throughout the tragedy, insisted, rightly according to most IOC members, that 'the games must go on'.

Montreal won the battle to host the 1976 games against opposition including both Moscow and Los Angeles. By the time they were held, the 58-year-old Irishman Lord Killanin had been elected to replace Brundage. But the Montreal games were in trouble long before 1976. The games were to cost $2 billion rather than the estimate of $125 million advanced by local mayor Jean Drapeau. Not only were the building and other preparations held up but the games were again overtaken by political trouble. Killanin's passivity in the face of the representations of *both* Taiwan *and* the Republic of China to attend – compounded by what Espy (1981) describes as his political naivety and lack of political acumen – precipitated a crisis when Pierre Trudeau, the Canadian Prime Minister, unexpectedly withdrew recognition from Taiwan. In addition, 28 African teams withdrew as the IOC declined to ban New Zealand for permitting rugby tests against South Africa. The most conspicuous performances in track-and-field came from Cuba's Alberto Juantorena, who won the 400 and 800 metres, and from Lasse Viren, who repeated his twin successes of 1972 (although amidst rumours of 'blood doping'). To American consternation, and some international suspicion, 'communist' athletes won all but one event in women's track-and-field. Drugs were beginning to replace 'professionalism' as the principal nightmare haunting the IOC.

Montreal had witnessed a quantum leap in the bidding for television rights, ABC winning with an offer of $25 million. In advance of the 1980 games in Moscow, the Soviets struck a deal with NBC for $85 million. The choice of Moscow was not, in Killanin's (1983) words, 'universally welcomed'. Unsurprisingly, politics once more intruded, this time with the Soviet invasion of Afghanistan at the tail end of 1979. On 4 January 1980 Jimmy Carter mooted the possibility of an Olympic boycott; on 21 January the US House of Representatives endorsed a firm proposal in favour of a boycott by 386 votes to 12; and on 29 January the proposal was approved by the Senate by 88 to 4. The US NOC was not obliged to acquiesce but did so. NBC-TV cancelled its deal. The boycott was rapidly endorsed by Thatcher's government in Britain, but the British NOC did *not* acquiesce. Other leading nation-states divided, some supporting the boycott, some not. The competition was severely depleted with the absence of teams from America, Canada, West Germany, Japan and Kenya. For Britain, Alan Wells won the gold medal in the 100 metres, while Steve Ovett defeated Seb Coe in the 800 metres, with Coe getting his revenge in the 1500 metres. Daley Thompson took the decathlon title. Overall, however, it was the Soviet and East German athletes who dominated.

The Capitalist Games in Los Angeles

The Nazi Olympics of 1936 were pinpointed earlier as an exemplar of the political use of a mega-event: the games projected the false but expedient image of 'a powerful but peace-loving Germany' (Byrne, 1987: 113). Having characterized *all* the postwar Olympics, socialist as well as capitalist, as in general reflective of vested interests, Gruneau (1984: 2) writes in similar vein of the Los Angeles Olympics, claiming that 'they are best understood as a more fully developed expression of the incorporation of sporting practice into the ever-expanding marketplace of international capitalism'. It was after the Los Angeles games, Burbank and his colleagues (2001: 7) add, that the Olympics became '*the* urban mega-event'.

Certainly the omens were not good and Los Angeles, the only candidate city, had to surmount its share of obstacles, most notably the financial challenge that Montreal had failed to rise to, leaving the city and Quebec with long-term debt, and the Soviet-inspired retaliatory boycott (the Soviet Union and 16 of its allies stayed away). Furthermore Jimmy Carter and Thomas Bradley, Mayor of Los Angeles, both declined to underwrite financially the games of 1984, prompting amendments in the Olympic Charter and the city's charter. But these precautionary amendments proved unnecessary.

> Led by the dynamic Ueberroth, the LAOOC sold television rights to ABC for $225 million; the European networks Eurovision and Intervision together paid another $22 million, and the Japanese added some $11 million to the coffers. The LAOOC raised another $130 million from thirty corporate sponsors, including American Express, Anheusser-Busch, Canon, Coca-Cola, Levi's, IBM, Snickers, and Sanyo ... In addition, the Southlands Corporation built a velodrome for the cyclists, the Atlantic-Richfield Company refurbished the Los Angeles Coliseum, General Motors donated Buick automobiles, and Xerox gave copiers. (Guttman, 2002: 160)

In addition, no fewer than 43 companies were licensed to sell 'official' Olympic products (for example, McDonalds marketed the official Olympic hamburger and the Mars Bar was the official Olympic snack food). There was to be no shortage of funding.

The opening ceremony was pure show-biz. Ronald Reagan appeared relaxed and at home as 84 grand pianos gave vent to Gershwin. A procession of covered wagons recalled the early pioneering days. Guttman (2002) notes the British sociologist Tomlinson's scathing reaction to this 'world of Disney'. But while Tomlinson bluntly condemned what he perceived as the 'heights, depths, and breadths of shallowness, over-simplification and superficiality', Guttman (2002: 161) records that the American spectators – for the most part – seemed to display an 'uncritical acceptance of patriotic kitsch'. Frank about the ubiquitous charge of American jingoism, Guttman is almost plaintive when he adds that there was none of the spectator violence often associated with soccer in Europe and Latin America.

As far as the competition was concerned, the home athletes were dominant in track-and-field and elsewhere, capturing in all 174 medals, including 83 golds. Carl Lewis, winner of four gold medals (in the 100 and 200 metres, the long-jump and the 4 × 100 metres relay) and Ed Moses, winner of the 400 metres hurdles, were outstanding. For Britain, Seb Coe and Daley Thompson established Olympic records in the 1500 metres and decathlon respectively. Mary Decker Slaney was notoriously brought down during the 5000 metres by her controversial rival Zola Budd, a South African who had hastily been granted British citizenship to permit her to compete for her 'new country'.

American athletes, it has been estimated, received 45 per cent of ABC's total television coverage. As had been the case since the founding modern games of 1896, coverage of track-and-field, which Americans dominated, featured prominently (with the men's events occupying two-thirds and the women's one-third). But what most characterized the Los Angeles games, of course, was the entrepreneurial acumen of Peter Ueberroth's network and the resultant profit. The figures, collated by Guttman (2002), are revealing. Aided by the US successes, ABC was able to hold its audiences: on the opening day of the games it drew in 55 per cent of the viewers while CBS and NBC managed a mere 18 per cent. Despite its huge investment of $225 million for the American rights, plus the extra sum committed to the costs of production, ABC 'earned' a profit of $435 million. One means to this profitable end was the scale of its advertising revenue: it charged up to $250,000 for a 30-second prime-time advertisement. McDonalds paid $30 million for its series of commercials. The Los Angeles Olympic Organizing Committee raised so much money from TV and sponsorship deals that it found itself with a surplus of $200 million. Ueberroth promptly awarded himself a bonus of $475,000. For all that the Los Angeles games have been portrayed as a tribute to American capitalism, however, as Guttman (2002: 163) succinctly and wistfully puts it, 'for any television viewer who preferred sports to hamburger commercials, the critics had a point'.

From Seoul to Sydney, then Athens Again

The decision to award the 1988 games to an Asian country was made in 1981, a year after Juan Antonio Samaranch succeeded Killanin as President of the IOC. Seoul in South Korea was a controversial choice because its government was authoritarian and it was the capital of a divided nation. After some haggling North Korea withdrew, as did Cuba; but the Soviet Union, with Gorbachov now in the Kremlin, rejoined the Olympic movement. By now TV was less a spectator than a key organizer of the games (Hill, 1996); but there was a 14-hour difference between Korean and American east coast time, making it difficult to schedule events for prime-time US TV (8 pm to midnight): the result was a 'disappointing' sale of TV rights to NBC for $300 million (to recoup this sum NBC had to charge $285,000 for a 30-second commercial). Technically, Seoul ended up with a profit of $497 million, thus exceeding Los Angeles; however this figure did not represent a surplus on operations but rather included donations and premiums on the sale of apartments amounting to $347 million (Hill, 1996: 178). The extent to which the games contributed positively to political relations in the area remains a matter of dispute.

Track-and-field once more attracted the most coverage, with American Florence Griffith-Joyner emerging as the most flamboyant athlete, winning the 100 and 200 metres and anchoring the 4 × 100 metres relay; meanwhile her sister-in-law Jackie Joyner-Kersee took the gold medal in the long jump and the heptathlon. Athletes from the Soviet Union featured in the field events and the Kenyans in the longer distance races. An abiding memory for many, however, was Ben Johnson's dramatic victory over Carl Lewis in the 100 metres in a world record time of 9.79 seconds and his subsequent disqualification after a positive test for anabolic steroids. Lewis also won the long-jump and took the silver medal in the 200 metres. Lewis was not alone in his barely veiled suspicion that a physically transformed Griffith-Joyner, like Johnson, may have benefited from the use of anabolic steroids. Perhaps he should have kept his own counsel (see Chapter 4).

The Spaniard Samaranch was comfortably re-elected in 1989, the year in which the Cold War came to an end and three years before the Barcelona games. The games of 1992 opened with the most elaborate pageantry and symbolism yet: 'To the music of the Japanese composer Sakamoto Ryuichi, a gigantic metal figure representing Hercules moved its arms to symbolize the formation of the Straits of Gibraltar, through which the waters of the Atlantic flowed to create the Mediterranean Sea. Across this sea, represented by hundreds of blue-clad dancers, the good ship *Barca Nona* made its perilous way to the shores of Spain, where its crew founded the city of Barcelona' (Guttman, 2002: 183). It was a symbolism too complex for most spectators and many TV commentators, but both opening and closing ceremonies impressed. Barcelona emerged from the staging of the games with a modest financial surplus of $3.27 million (Hill, 1996); and by common consent with an enhanced international reputation and quality of life for its citizenry (Brunet, 1993).

With the Cold War at its end, 498 athletes from the former Soviet Union, representing 12 newly independent nation-states, competed in Barcelona as a 'Unified Team'. The success of these athletes in track-and-field was limited. Britain's Linford Christie won the gold medal in the 100 metres, while Carl Lewis won further golds in the long jump and 4 × 100 metres relay. Gail Devers and Gwen Torrence from America took golds in the women's 100 and 200 metres; France's Marie-Jose Perec ruled supreme in the 400 metres. Algeria's Hassiba Boulmerka, the first Islamic woman to become a world-class runner, was victorious in the 1500 metres despite having received death threats from Islamic fundamentalists for refusing to wear a tracksuit that covered her arms and legs, a putative violation of Islamic religious doctrine.

The awarding of the Centennial games of 1996 to the American city of Atlanta, capital of the New South, caused some anxiety. Relations between the Atlanta organizers – that is, enthusiastic entrepreneur Billy Payne backed by a rather weak city administration – and both the IOC and the US NOC remained strained through the early stages of preparation (Hill, 1996); but the election of Bill Campbell as Mayor, and a (belated) commercial 'call to arms' by Coca-Cola chairman Robert Goizueta, led to a city bond referendum and subsequent issue that allowed the Olympic building programme to get properly underway. The largest single source of income, predictably, was the sale of broadcasting rights (for £568 million). Burbank and his colleagues (2001: 113–14) offer a summary assessment of Atlanta's efforts. On the positive side of their balance sheet, 2.5 billion

viewers worldwide came to associate Atlanta with an inspiring and spectacular event, 'a rare achievement among cities'. On the negative side,
Atlanta attracted a lot of criticism, if mostly from overseas. The international press complained of bungled accommodation and transportation
(hence the ubiquitous 'bad press'); and many deemed 'Atlanta's commercial zest and undistinguished venues . . . tacky in comparison to Barcelona's
cultural and architectural heritage'. Home evaluations were less scathing.

As far as the track-and-field competition was concerned, the outstanding
figure was Michael Johnson, who won the 200 and 400 metres, the former
in an astonishing world record time of 19.32 seconds. Johnson's gold
medals were among 10 captured by American athletes (out of a total of 24).
Canada's Donovan Bailey also beat the world record to win the 100 metres
in 9.84 seconds, Linford Christie having been disqualified for two false
starts. Perec matched Johnson by taking the women's 200 and 400 metres.
Carl Lewis won his ninth Olympic gold in the long-jump; and Merlene
Ottey from Jamaica added two silver medals to her Olympic total of ten
finals with two silver and five bronze medals.

Samaranch had been re-elected for a third term in 1993. In 1997 he
expressed a wish to remain for a fourth term, for which the IOC would
have to extend the mandatory age of retirement from 75 to 80. By this
time, however, opposition to him had grown, not least as a result of the
publication in 1992 of *The Lords of the Rings* by two British journalists,
Simson and Jennings (see also Jennings, 1996). They criticized Samaranch
for his overly enthusiastic identification with Franco's Fascist regime, his
drive to maximize the commercial potential of the Olympics, his apparent
indifference to the growing use of performance-enhancing drugs, and for
what they defined as his personal lust for power. Guttman (2002) treads a
middle path, tempering these criticisms with a record also of Samaranch's
achievements. In any event, Samaranch was eventually succeeded in office
by Jacques Rogge of Belgium in 2001.

The Millennium games in Sydney were preceded by Aboriginal protests
highlighting historical and outstanding injustices. A decision was taken late
not to disrupt the games themselves, partly influenced it seems by the
selection of Cathy Freeman to light the Olympic flame. The temperature
dropped further when Cathy Freeman went on to win the 400 metres and
to carry the Aboriginal flag as well as the Australian national banner on her
victory lap. In fact for once the media seemed more focused on the
women's track-and-field performances than the men's, perhaps principally
because Sydney's relatively trouble-free 17-day extravaganza also incorporated the American Marion Jones's assault on an unprecedented five gold
medals: she was to accomplish three – in the 100 and 200 metres and the 4
× 100 metres relay – winning bronzes in the long-jump and 4 × 400
metres ('probably the most successful "failure" in Olympic history'
(Guttman, 2002: 191)). For the men, the Americans Maurice Green and
Michael Johnson captured the 100 and 400 metres respectively, while
Konstantinos Kenteris sprang a surprise by winning the 200 metres, the first

Greek victor since Spiridon Loues in 1896. The East Africans dominated the longer races, Kenyans coming in first and third in the 1500 metres, first and second in the 3000 metres steeplechase, and second in both the 10,000 metres and the marathon, while Ethiopians came first in the 5000 metres and first and third in the 10,000 metres and the marathon.

In Sydney, competitors from 52 nation-states shared a total of 298 gold medals. Of the protagonists, the Americans won 39, the Russians 32, the Chinese 28 and the Australians 16; Germany (14), France (13) and Italy (13) accounted for nearly a third of Europe's 132 victories; 22 Asian nation-states won 40 golds (of which 28 went to China); Cubans took 11 of the 14 going to participants from Latin America and the Caribbean; and African competitors had to be satisfied with a total of 9. Citing these figures, Guttman (2002: 194) broaches the issue of 'cultural imperialism':

> Another way to think about this is to consider that the Europeans and North Americans who invented the modern games continue to claim over three-fourths of all the gold, silver, and bronze medals. In short, while the disparities among nations are certainly much reduced from what they were twenty years earlier, the men and women – especially the women – of Asia, Latin America, and Africa continue to play ancillary roles on the Olympic stage.

For details of the top ten medal-winning nation-states during the period of the modern Olympiad, see Table 3.1; and, no less revealingly, for equivalent data for the Paralympics, see Table 3.2.

Guttman concludes that 'the root difficulty is that modern sports, like the universalistic political ideals institutionalized in the Olympic Games, are themselves a product of Western civilization. Paradoxically, the success of the baron's dream is one of the things that prevents the dream's full and complete realization' (see also Eichberg, 1984, and Guttman, 1994). This charge of cultural imperialism, as well as the sharper ones of class, ethnic and gender stratification it subsumes, even masks, will be examined in more detail in subsequent chapters, and not only in relation to track-and-field athletics and the modern Olympic movement. But the data collated in Tables 3.1 and 3.2, and the summary overview of the degree of expansion of the modern games since 1896 represented in Table 3.3, bear comprehensive testimony to the emergence of one of occidental modernity's core urban mega-events.

To pull the threads together, this opening section of the book has taken a selective socio-historical look at three significant 'long moments', concentrating for convenience on track-and-field athletics, pertinent to the wavering, stop-start accommodation and institutionalization of sporting activity in ancient, premodern and modern (and for some, postmodern) worlds, albeit with a focus on Western domains. For all their apparent theoretical innocence, however, even straightforward edited historical narratives such as these are reflective of, or anticipate, theoretical stances. In

Table 3.1 Top 10 all-time medal-winning countries

Country	Gold	Silver	Bronze	Total
1 USA	872	658	586	2116
2 Russia★	498	409	371	1278
3 Germany#	214	242	280	736
4 United Kingdom	180	233	225	638
5 France	188	193	217	598
6 Italy	179	143	157	479
7 Sweden	136	156	177	469
8 East Germany	159	150	136	445
9 Hungary	150	135	158	443
10 Australia	102	110	138	350

★ Including USSR (1952–88) and United Team (1992)
Including West Germany (1968–88)

Ash and Morrison (2002)

Table 3.2 Top 10 medal-winning countries at the Summer Paralympics★

Country	Gold	Silver	Bronze	Total
1 USA	576	523	522	1621
2 UK	389	401	387	1177
3 Germany/West Germany	404	385	361	1150
4 Canada	311	250	262	823
5 France	279	264	241	784
6 Australia	240	248	228	716
7 Netherlands	219	179	153	551
8 Poland	194	184	148	526
9 Sweden	197	190	135	522
10 Spain	156	137	152	445

★ Excluding medals won at the 1960 Rome and 1968 Tel Aviv Games – the International Paralympic Committee has not maintained records of medals won at these Games

The first international Games for the disabled were held in Stoke Mandeville, England, in 1952, when 130 athletes from just two countries competed. The first Paralympics to take place at the same venue as the Olympic Games was in Rome in 1960. Since then, the Paralympics have been held every four years, and, since Seoul in 1988, at the same venue as the Summer Olympics. Four hundred athletes from 23 countries took part in 1960. In Sydney in 2000, a total of 3,843 athletes from 127 nations competed. The most medals won at one Games is 388 by the United States in the 'dual' Paralympics of 1984. Their total of 131 gold medals is also a record for one Games.

Ash and Morrison (2002)

Table 3.3 Participation in the Summer Olympic Games

Olympiad	Year	Venue	Male Athletes	Female Athletes
1	1896	Athens	295	0
2	1900	Paris	1066	11
3	1904	St Louis	548	6
4	1908	London	1998	36
5	1912	Stockholm	2447	57
6	1916	Games not held		
7	1920	Antwerp	2527	64
8	1924	Paris	2939	136
9	1928	Amsterdam	2681	290
10	1932	Los Angeles	1204	127
11	1936	Berlin	3652	328
12	1940	Games not held		
13	1944	Games not held		
14	1948	London	3677	385
15	1952	Helsinki	5349	518
16	1956	Melbourne	2958	384
17	1960	Rome	4785	610
18	1964	Tokyo	4903	683
19	1968	Mexico City	5845	781
20	1972	Munich	6595	1299
21	1976	Montreal	4938	1251
22	1980	Moscow	4835	1088
23	1984	Los Angeles	5429	1626
24	1988	Seoul	6941	2476
25	1992	Barcelona	6648	2715
26	1996	Atlanta	6582	3779
27	2000	Sydney	6582	4069
28	2004	Athens	–	–
29	2008	Beijing	–	–

Adapted from Guttman (2002)

Part Two of the book the salience and purchase of theory become more apparent through wide-ranging discussions of exercise, sport and health, incorporating a brief discussion of drug use in sport (Chapter 4), the suggestion of a 'de-civilizing spurt' in contemporary sport (Chapter 5), and the colonization and mediation of sporting activities, most conspicuous in Europe in professional football (Chapter 6).

PART TWO

Features of Contemporary Sport

4

Exercise, Sport and Health

With the displacement of the premodern world by the modern, or modernity, traditional institutions of *social* integration, such as kinship systems and ritual exchange, no longer sufficed to co-ordinate power and exchange relations, with the result that certain mechanisms of *systemic* organization were 'uncoupled' from the mundane but immediate sphere of everyday social intercourse. In short, areas of life were transferred from the lifeworld to the system. Habermas's (1984, 1987) distinction between system and lifeworld is in some respects a reconceptualization of Marx's distinction between base and superstructure. Hanks (2002: 83–4) puts it neatly:

> One theoretical and practical result of Marx's distinction was the ability to analyze aspects of society not immediately available to consciousness ... Habermas describes the uncoupling and rationalization of system and lifeworld as aspects of modernity. The lifeworld reproduces itself through the symbolic interactions of people in their everyday lives. The subsystems of the economy and state reproduce themselves through the media of money and power. The social distortion that Marx sought to explain is explained by Habermas as the process whereby the reproduction of everyday life becomes directed by considerations of money and power and not through the communicative interactions of people. This is the colonization of the lifeworld. The effective pursuit of goals that we never debated becomes the point of our lives.

The principal focus of this chapter is on the colonization of exercise and sport via the steering media of money and power, especially in the era of global or disorganized capitalism dating from the mid-1970s. It was apparent through Part One that athletic activity has always been associated historically with varying forms of material assets and rewards and power. What is different about the modern period, and never more so than during the disorganized capitalism of high or late modernity, is the nature and extent of the systemic and colonizing intrusion of money and power into athletic activity.

The first section of this chapter expounds on the basic distinction between exercise and sport. Attention is drawn in particular to linkages between exercise, sport and health. In the second section rates and patterns of participation in exercise and sport are further explored in the figuration of the British nation-state in terms of the logics of the regime of capital accumulation of the economy (and its relations of class) and the mode of regulation of the state (and its relations of command) (Scambler, 2002). Attention is paid also to the heightened topical concern with what some deplore as an epidemic of obesity, associated not only with ubiquitous fast-food chains but also with diminishing exercise in the early phases of the lifecourse. Finally, the lively and worrying issue of drug usage in sport is addressed. The sociological utility of the system/lifeworld distinction and of the notions of system rationalization and lifeworld colonization, not least in respect of sport, becomes apparent through these analyses.

Exercise, Sport and Health

The notion that sport is 'good for you' has a long and varied pedigree but has been especially prominent since its modernization, courtesy of the ('ruling-class', masculine, white) public school ethos of Victorian England (Mangan, 1981) (see Chapter 2). As the era of liberal capitalism gave way to that of organized capitalism, the emphasis on sport's potential both to build character appropriate to elite standing and governance and to offer a means of discipline for working-class youths yielded increasingly to an emphasis on its general capacity to enhance individual health. Each emphasis, or rhetoric, owed much to system imperatives. But is sport good for you? Is it conducive to positive health and longevity? Setting aside the ideological baggage such a proposition almost always conceals, we need to remember that sport conjures up activities with no discernible core properties in common but rather with 'family resemblances' (Wittgenstein, 1958). Some sporting activities may be conducive to health and longevity, others not; and it is likely often to be a matter of degree (Scambler et al., 2004).

In assessing the evidence it is helpful to distinguish between sport and exercise since it is the latter that features in most neo-positivist studies (see Waddington, 2000, 2000a; McKenna and Riddoch, 2003). The general conclusion of these studies is that 'moderate, rhythmic and regular exercise has a significant and beneficial impact on health' (Waddington, 2000: 411). Regular aerobic exercise like walking, jogging, dancing or swimming seems to bear positively on both physical and psychological health (Royal College of Physicians, 1991). The Health Education Authority (1996: 1) has summarized the health return on this form of exercise as follows: lower levels of all-cause mortality; reduced risk of developing coronary heart disease, stroke, hypertension and non-insulin dependent diabetes mellitus; better control of obesity; possible protection against some cancers; decreased levels of moderate depression and anxiety; maintenance of healthy bones and possible prevention of osteoporosis; and benefits for those with existing diseases, particularly for those with controlled hypertension, hyperlipidaemia, mild depression and chronic anxiety. It is important to stress that moderate, rhythmic and regular exercise is defined here as ranging from 'brisk walking, running or swimming for 20–30 minutes about three times each week' (Smith and Jacobson, 1988: 126), to 'energetic getting about' or the regular climbing of stairs for older people (Morris et al., 1980).

Evidence-based guidelines from the English health authorities suggest that whether an individual is exercising on his or her own or in a group, it is a focus on self-development, effort and mastery of tasks that most impacts on mood and psychological well-being (Grant, 2000). This 'task orientation' is compared favourably to 'ego orientation', where exercisers strive to be better than others and where a competitive ethos prevails. Many sports are of course inherently competitive. Waddington (2000: 413) affirms that non-competitive exercise and competitive sport tend to involve different sets of social relations, and that the former is more likely than the latter to involve rhythmic movements and to be under the control of the individual participant. Sport is the more complex activity (see Elias and Dunning, 1986). Given the 'game pattern' of most sports, the individual participant has no choice but to cede control over his or her own movements and the pace and intensity at which he or she is able to play. Movement easily becomes the antithesis of rhythmic and bursts of anaerobic activity become paradigmatic (Waddington, 2000).

The degree to which sport has been competitive has varied historically, but it seems likely that sport's trajectory in disorganized capitalism has augmented a postwar trend. Now, as Donohoe and Johnson (1986: 93) maintain, 'athletes are forced to train longer, harder, and earlier in life. They may be rewarded by faster times, better performances and increased fitness, but there is a price to pay for such intense training.' One such price is a threat to health, and unsurprisingly this threat is most apparent at the elite level. Former England soccer captain Gary Lineker resented the routine use of pain-killing injections, commenting on his retirement (occasioned by a chronic foot injury): 'it is as if a huge weight has been lifted from me. I no longer have to worry whether I'll be fit enough to get through a match and I will no longer have to suffer the dizzy spells and stomach complaints that come with a dependency on anti-inflammatory drugs' (quoted in Waddington, 2000: 416).

Overuse injury is commonplace in elite sport:

Overt and covert pressures are brought to bear on injured athletes to coerce then to return to action. These may include certain 'degradation ceremonies' ... such as meal areas, constant questioning from coaches, being ostracized at team functions, or other special treatment that clearly identifies the injured athlete as separate. (Young et al., 1994: 190)

One study of Danish soccer players found that 37 per cent of injuries were overuse injuries (Lynch and Carcasona, 1994). But such injuries are not, or are no longer, confined to professional or elite competitors. A survey conducted in England and Wales for the Sports Council discovered that one-third of all injuries resulting from participation in sport/exercise were recurrent injuries. Extrapolating from these data, the Sports Council estimated that there are 10.4 million incidents per annum leading to recurrent injuries (that is, in addition to 19.3 million resulting in new injuries) (Sports Council, 1991: 25).

The Sports Council also distinguished different sports by risk of injury. Top of the list was rugby, with an injury rate of 59 per 100 participants per four weeks. Second in dangerousness was soccer (39), followed by martial arts (26), hockey (25) and cricket (20). Rugby also headed the list of high-risk sports in a New Zealand study (Hume and Marshall, 1994). A number of distinctions are relevant to the differential risk of injury. That between exercise and sport remains basic, but to this might be added others, for example between (professional) elite and (amateur) mass sport, and between contact and non-contact sports. Table 4.1 presents a provisional typology of exercise/sports ranked in terms of their injuriousness to health. Only type 1 might be described as typically health bestowing, although types 2 to 6 intermittently accommodate elements of type 1, not least in aspects of training. There is of course nothing sacrosanct about the labels chosen to represent each of these pursuits. In fact many individuals would lay claim to proprietorship of more than one label, and many activities might be assigned to more than one category (swimming, for example, can be a form of exercise, a non-competitive sport and a non-contact competitive sport). The examples should be interpreted as paradigmatic, serving merely to anchor the categories. The typology's value is heuristic (Scambler et al., 2004).

Table 4.1 A typology of types of exercise/sport by risk of injury

1. Exercise	(*the exerciser*: e.g. jogging)
2. Non-competitive sport	(*the enthusiast*: e.g. orienteering)
3. Non-contact competitive sport	(*the competitor*: e.g. tennis)
4. Contact competitive sport	(*the contester*: e.g. rugby)
5. Combat competitive sport	(*the gladiator*: e.g. boxing)
6. Dangerous sport	(*the gambler*: e.g. mountaineering)

Scambler et al. (2004)

Of elite contact sports in the USA Young (1993: 373) bluntly asserts that,

> by any measure, professional sport is a violent and hazardous workplace, replete with its own unique forms of 'industrial disease'. No other milieu, including the risky and labour-intensive settings of miners, oil drillers, or construction site workers, can compare with the routine injuries of team sports such as football, ice-hockey, soccer, rugby and the like.

We have seen that modern rugby players, 'contesters' in the typology, are the most likely sportsmen to incur injury. In fact since Rugby Union went open in 1995 the risks to professionals seem to have grown. British journalist Paul Rees (2003) refers to an Australian study of elite players showing that while in the year before the game went open there were 47 injuries per 1000 player-hours, that figure increased by nearly 50 per cent to 69 injuries per 1000 player-hours, with 143 injuries recorded from 91 matches, in the following year. The fly-half was the most injured back and the lock the most injured forward. There may perhaps be discrete health-bestowing aspects to rugby training, but the sport itself is hazardous.

This enhanced rate of injury can be attributed largely to the fact that elite rugby players – like professional footballers and many other elite athletes – are now put under pressure to sustain a high level of performance week-in, week-out. Rees (2003) quotes Bristol coach Peter Thorburn:

> There is a conflict in the sport between the commercial and the playing sides. Clubs want to generate more money to balance the books but the risk is that too much is asked of the players. It is not just about matches, though I think there are too many: we have contact training twice a week, and even though players wear protective suits there is the risk of injury . . . The trouble with the British season is that there is little let-up in it. Once you start in September, you are involved in a non-stop process of build-up and playing. There is little room for recovery. Staleness and boredom creep in and injuries pile up. The busiest members of a club's management are the physio and the masseur . . . Players may be well paid but that does not mean we have bought their hearts and bodies. There is a danger we will turn them into a scrapheap . . .

Not only are players expected to train and play with unremitting commitment, many follow strict dietary regimes and take 'legal' performance-enhancing supplements such as protein and weight-gaining powders; and it would be disingenuous to deny that some also take 'illegal' performance-enhancing anabolic steroids. It has become routine also to undergo arduous psychological preparation (Scambler et al., 2004).

Howe (2001) has shown how the expectation and accommodation of injury has become one of a complex of factors constituting the *habitus* of a professional rugby club. Howe (2001: 292) adopts Bourdieu's (1977) notion to refer to the 'habitual, embodied practices that collectively comprise and define a culture', in this instance that of Pontypridd RFC. At the heart of the habitus of Pontypridd RFC is a determination to succeed on behalf of the club. No longer a 'community co-operative', the club has been transformed by processes of commercialization, or commodification, into a potentially lucrative business enterprise, with economic gain taking priority over 'championing community identity' (Howe, 1999). This commodification has been paralleled by the players' professionalization. Howe found that if a player, say, broke his arm, the pain was obvious but then 'disappeared', in the sense that no subsequent reference was made to it; if, however, an injury was *playable* then the player would let it be known that he was in pain. This latter strategy both gave the player the option of blaming a weak performance on the injury and afforded him elevated kudos within the club for his readiness to play through pain. However, how vocal a player was about his pain was contingent also on his hold on his position: there was a greater onus to 'deal with pain' when a player's position was under threat. It was an issue of costs and benefits.

Patterns of Participation in Exercise and Sport

There is concern in Britain that its citizens in general, and children in particular, are participating in less health-bestowing exercise in disorganized than in organized capitalism (and possibly in less than in later phases of liberal capitalism characterized by robust school sports for the upper and middle classes and military-style disciplinary 'drills' for working-class pupils). Hence, it is claimed, the rapidly increasing rates of obesity. In fact, obesity levels, defined in terms of Body Mass Index (BMI) – that is, weight in kilograms divided by the square of height in metres – seem to have risen steadily since the early 1980s. In England, for example, in 1980, 8 per cent of women and 6 per cent of men were obese; by 1998, these figures had almost trebled, standing at 21 per cent for women and 17 per cent for men. The rise in England was high relative to that in other European countries, more closely mirroring that in the USA, where by 2000, 30 per cent of the adult population was technically obese (Crossley, 2004). The dramatic rise in obesity in England has occurred in part, it is claimed, because physical activity in schools has fallen by 70 per cent over the last generation (Parkinson, 2003). Two-thirds of teachers in state schools believe their sports facilities have deteriorated over the last five years (Townsend, 2003). A Sport England study identified four groups of pupils: 'reluctant participants' (24 per cent), including *couch potatoes* who live a sedentary lifestyle and *tolerators* who have an average level of participation but do not enjoy it much (mostly primary-school girls and older boys); the 'unadventurous' (14 per cent) who participate little but more than the reluctant participants (mostly secondary pupils, especially girls aged 11–14, and including many children from ethnic minorities); those with 'untapped potential' (37 per cent) who are not averse to sport but spend relatively little time engaging (mainly younger people, especially girls); and 'sporty types' (25 per cent) who play sport regularly inside and outside school, and enjoy it (two-thirds of whom are boys) (Campbell et al., 2003). In the next few paragraphs I shall summarize present rates of participation in exercise/sport by age, gender and socio-economic group and offer a provisional comment on a state of affairs in disorganized capitalism about which medical experts and politicians alike have expressed anxiety.

The amount of time allocated to physical education (PE) in school curricula remains important, not least because for some young people this provides their only opportunity for sport. In 1994 the first national survey of sports participation for young people aged 6 to 16 in England was conducted, and this was repeated in 1999. Overall, the proportion of those between 6 and 16 spending an average of 30–59 minutes a week in PE lessons increased from 5 per cent in 1994 to 18 per cent in 1999. However the proportion spending two hours or more on PE decreased from 46 per cent to 33 per cent over the same period (ONS, 2001). Table 4.2 gives the most popular sports played in school lessons by gender, 1994 and 1999. Above all else, these data bear testimony to the longstanding division between 'masculine' (soccer, cricket) and 'feminine' (rounders, hockey) sports.

Table 4.2 Most popular sports played in school lessons[1]: by gender, 1994 and 1999

England	Percentages			
	Males		Females	
	1999	*1994*	*1999*	*1994*
Football	44	40	12	7
Gym/gymnastics/trampolining	30	36	36	41
Athletics	33	34	36	32
Cricket	24	20	8	7
Rounders	23	19	39	29
Hockey	12	16	23	24

1 Percentage of pupils aged 6 to 16 who participated ten or more times in the last year.
Source: National Survey for Young People and Sport, MORI for Sport England

ONS (2001)

Table 4.3 draws on the Health Survey for England to outline time spent in sports and exercise by age and gender for people aged 16 to 75+ in 1998 (ONS, 2001). While it is unsurprising that participation diminishes with age – with 23 per cent of males and 42 per cent of females aged 16–24, and 93 per cent of males and 96 per cent of females aged 75+, devoting 'no time' to exercise/sport – what is striking is the gender difference in early adulthood. Women are far less likely than men to participate in exercise/sport after school, at least until the age of 45 or so.

Another source of useful data is the *UK 2000 Time Use Survey* (ONS,

Table 4.3 Time spent participating in sports and exercise[1]: by gender and age, 1998

England								Percentages All aged
	16–24	*25–34*	*35–44*	*45–54*	*55–64*	*65–74*	*75 and over*	*16 and over*
Males								
No time	23	38	50	64	77	83	93	58
Less than 1 hour	14	20	17	14	9	8	3	13
1 hour but less than 3	22	20	20	14	7	5	2	14
3 hours but less than 5	13	10	7	4	3	2	–	6
5 hours but less than 7	9	5	3	2	2	–	–	3
7 or more hours	18	7	4	3	1	1	1	5
All	100	100	100	100	100	100	100	100
Females								
No time	42	50	57	64	74	84	96	64
Less than 1 hour	18	19	17	15	11	5	1	13
1 hour but less than 3	22	19	17	14	10	8	2	14
3 hours but less than 5	10	8	6	4	4	1	–	5
5 hours but less than 7	4	3	2	1	1	1	–	2
7 or more hours	5	2	2	1	1	1	–	2
All	100	100	100	100	100	100	100	100

1 Number of hours spent participating in sports or exercise each week.
Source: Health Survey for England, Department of Health

ONS (2001)

2003), which outlines time given daily to a range of activities. Under the category of 'sport and outdoor activities', those aged 8–15 were found to commit an average of 29 minutes per day; those aged 16–24, 20 minutes; those aged 25–44, 13 minutes; those aged 45–64, 15 minutes; and those aged over 65, 13 minutes. Among adults (that is, those aged 16 years or over), men spent an average of 18 minutes a day on sport and outdoor activities, and women an average of 11 minutes. When adult time spent on sport and outdoor activities was broken down according to socio-economic group, those in managerial and professional occupations committed an average of 16 minutes per day; those in intermediate or routine/manual occupations and those who had never worked, 13 minutes; and those 'not classifiable' (including students), 20 minutes.

Sticking with the figuration of the nation-state, two points are apposite on the contribution of social structures to explaining changing rates of participation in exercise/sport during disorganized capitalism. Each point picks up on a discrete set of logics/relations. The first highlights the logic of the regime of capital accumulation and relations of class. Self-evidently there is a great deal of money to be made from exercise/sport, and with less restraint in disorganized than in organized capitalism. The notion of identity, and especially that accomplished in and through the body, is particularly pertinent here. The issue of identity, linked as it is to globalizing tendencies, the reinvigoration of class relations, processes of individualization, the postmodernization of culture, and technologies of the self and governmentality, is increasingly salient to the recasting of both exercise and sport in disorganized capitalism. How is this?

The search for an abiding identity has become more urgent and more volatile, disinhibited and problematic in our postmodernized culture. Paraphrasing Lyotard (1984), identities are associated now with a multiplicity of promiscuous *petit* narratives rather than a handful of chaste *grand* narratives. Many analysts see identity as having a novel and pivotal salience to individuals (occasioning a crisis of identity) at an historical juncture – the advent of the postmodern culture of disorganized capitalism – when identity formation is theorized as an ever more elusive, fluid and impermanent project (leading to a crisis of 'identity') (Bendle, 2002). This is due in part to the culture-ideology of consumerism, itself the product of the resurgence of objective (if, paradoxically, *not* subjective) relations of class. Exercise, sport and health, and the bodily identities with which they have come to be intimately associated, have all become more malleable, primarily as a function of their hyper-commodification. People are 'seduced' by such forms of hyper-commodification. Their 'choices' of bodily identity, image and lifestyle owe much to the logic of the regime of capital accumulation and relations of class.

In terms of the health benefits of exercise/sport, this brings opportunities but also hazards. Positively, people have new rationales to opt for, forge and be rewarded for bodily identities through exercise and sports that are, fortuitously or otherwise, health bestowing. Aspects of the 'fitness industry', extending to club and leisure-centre membership and specially designed equipment and clothing, which resonate in the growing popularity of keep-fit/yoga sessions among largely middle-class women, afford examples. More negatively, and setting aside for the moment extreme cases of elite contact and combat sports, potentially health-bestowing activity can be subverted according the formula: *to look good is to feel good is to feel healthy* (Scambler et al., 2004).

Monaghan's (2001) study of bodybuilding is particularly instructive here. For those embroiled in the 'positive moment' of bodybuilding, he writes, this kind of activity is seen as beneficial to mental, physical and social health. In fact, the gym subculture to which such individuals belong consists largely of Foucauldian 'technologies of the self' that are affected by 'normalized subjects in pursuit of self-improvement, happiness and healthiness' (Monaghan, 2001a: 332). Why, he asks, are bodybuilders willing to engage in potentially health-damaging practices, even extending to steroid use, to secure 'strong, fit and healthy-looking bodies'? It is simplistic, he insists, to regard bodybuilding as indicative of either gender inadequacy or reverse anorexia or muscle dysmorphia; it cannot, in other words, be simply pathologized or medicalized. Healthy exercisers and bodybuilders share an attempt to 'embody and display a sense of empowerment and mastery' (Monaghan, 2001a: 334). However, for all that bodybuilding may be seen by its enthusiasts as health-enhancing, many are aware that lifting weights is primarily an anaerobic as opposed to an aerobic activity: bodybuilding requires relatively little of the cardiovascular fitness that health promoters consider so important for physical health. The overriding goal of bodybuilding is 'the look': to change one's body appearance so that it approximates to idealized images of health, youth, fitness and beauty (Featherstone, 1991), rather than to confer any direct benefit in internal physiological functioning (Monaghan, 2001a). It is the health of the 'outer body' that matters. For bodybuilders, then, the embodied pleasures and perceived psychosocial benefits of anaerobic exercise, combined with the 'postmodern imagery of muscle', are typically of high significance in sustaining the 'ongoing consumption of (risky) bodybuilding technologies' (Monaghan, 2001a: 335; Scambler et al., 2004). Sport, in summary, is not intrinsically healthy; and it is reasonable to argue that in disorganized capitalism the novel fluidity of identity-formation has permitted developments in sport that are objectively, if not subjectively, antithetical as well as favourable to health.

The second point concerns the logic of the mode of regulation and relations of command. The decline of PE in schools – in general exposing the command relations of the state as derivative of those of class (as epitomized in recent policy emphases, *for state schools*, on a national 'core curriculum', 'opting out' of local authority control, the re-introduction of partial selection, competitive league tables and vocational skills) – can be seen as piecemeal social engineering by the state in response to imperatives issuing from the economy. The selling off of school playing fields, which has fuelled the decline of sport in schools, was no less responsive to business interests. Associated with the Thatcher and Major years, during which period such sales were actively encouraged, it is a process that has continued under Blair, notwithstanding a change of rhetoric. According to government figures, 76 per cent of 38 applications for disposal or change of use of school playing fields 2000 square metres or larger (the Football Association's recommended area for games played by under-10s) were approved in 1999–2000, this proportion rising to 87 per cent of 31 for 2000–2001. Of applications relating to school playing fields smaller than 2000 square metres, 86 per cent of 50 were approved in 1999–2000, and 84 per cent of an admittedly reduced number of 19 in 2000–2001 (DCMS, 2003). It has been estimated that an astonishing 6000 school playing fields have been sold off since 1982 (Kelso, 2002).

That the New Labour government has largely failed to reverse the demise of school sport appears ironic given: (a) its public and financial commitment to do so (see, for example, 'Learning Through PE and Sport' (DFES/DCMS, 2003)); and (b) its no less public promotion of exercise as a means of improving population health, reducing health inequalities and, latterly, fighting escalating rates of obesity. At the level of policy, the government's apparent impotence is a function of the impact of its policy package *as a whole*; and at the level of social structure, its total policy package is a function of the re-invigoration of relations of class *at the expense of those of command*. Governments are required to balance the state's primary systemic task to deliver a mode of regulation appropriate to the regime of capital accumulation (in this case, of disorganized capitalism) with its continuing need for legitimation. Policy is therefore Janus-faced. It must secure the requisite mode of regulation while retaining the confidence of the electorate. Documents like 'Learning Through PE and Sport' should be seen, in Habermas' terms, as strategic not communicative. They exemplify either distorted communication (that is, manipulation on the part of policy makers) or, less typically, systematically distorted communication (that is, they 'take in' policy makers as well as the electorate), and are to be judged, systemically, not primarily in terms of their effectiveness but in terms of their perlocutionary effects (that is, in terms of their impact on the electorate).

New Labour's espousal of Clinton's 'third way', with its philosophy of personal responsibility, is functionally equivalent to Thatcherism: that is, it is no less friendly to Britain's capitalist-executive and no less unfriendly to the working class and its 'displaced segment', the so-called 'new poor' (Scambler and Higgs, 1999, 2001). Moreover, if children continue to *fail* to engage in health-bestowing exercise or sport, then the *blame* – to be experienced as *guilt* – will fall on parents and teachers, not on government or, of course, on the capitalist-executive. Responsible adults too must exercise on their own account. This has been discussed elsewhere as the reflexive and calculated honing of Foucauldian 'technologies of the self' by a (weakly globalized) state power-elite compelled in disorganized capitalism to respond positively to a (strongly globalized) capitalist-executive (Scambler, 2002).

Crossley (2004) asks why it is that in the era of disorganized capitalism, during which the salience of self and body image for identity formation has become paramount, obesity has yet emerged as a putative epidemic. The short answer is that there is serious money to be made from forms of exercise and dieting that can be linked with positive self and body image *and* from economical fast foods, soft drinks and passive high-tech modes of entertainment, including mediated sport (see Chapter 6), conducive to weight gain. Moreover, our more individualized postmodern culture allows for normative inconsistency. Against the background of altered relations of class and command, health policy sometimes seems an ineluctable or fateful product of political attempts to square circles.

Exercise, Sport and Drug Use

The use of recreational drugs has become commonplace since the 1960s, as have concerns about the use of 'doping' in professional elite sports. The most common arguments *against* performance-enhancing drugs in sport are that their usage is (1) unfair, (2) threatens the health of those athletes who take them, and (3) undermines the integrity of sport. That this is not all there is to it is demonstrated by the campaign against the use of recreational drugs by sports stars *qua* role models. Nobody has claimed that marijuana boosts performance, yet the 1990s signalled an end to the former tolerance of its enjoyment by elite athletes. The IOC in 1990 fell short of listing marijuana as a banned substance, but it did include it among those drugs 'subject to certain restrictions': it disparaged its usage as 'damaging to youth and a threat to world peace' (see Waddington, 2000: 110). In Britain athletes have been tested for marijuana since 1990 under a system of doping controls operated by the Sports Council; and the Sports Council has noted with concern growing usage of 'social drugs' throughout the 1990s.

Use of doping substances is not new. In light of the account of sport in archaic and classical Greece in Chapter 1 it should come as no surprise that the pioneering Greek physician Galenos mentioned the use of performance-enhancing substances. In the era of modernity the narrative is largely one of celebrated catastrophes, including the collapse of the American marathon runner Thomas Hicks in the 1904 St Louis Olympic Games, and the deaths of Danish cyclist Jensen in the 1960 Olympic Games in Rome and British cyclist Simpson during the 1967 Tour de France. In the 1950s a steroid component, Dianabol, was widely utilized by American and Soviet athletes. It has been argued that his helps explain 'irregular results' in the 1960 Olympic Games in Rome, after which knowledge of the benefits of steroid use rapidly became widely shared: 'the subsequent Olympic Games up to the late 1980s were probably as much influenced by illegal use of doping substances as any before and thereafter', not least because methods of detection were weak (Luschen, 2000: 463). In fact spectacular disqualifications of athletes only began to occur in the 1980s, with 19 athletes withdrawn from the PanAmerican Games in 1983, and the disqualifications of Canadian Ben Johnson at the Seoul Olympic Games of 1988 and of German Katrin Krabbe prior to the Barcelona Games of 1992.

Tables 4.4 and 4.5 are taken from a review of doping and sport by Houlihan (2003). Table 4.4 outlines the major drugs and banned practices based on the International Olympic Committee list, together with their medical uses and putative benefits in sport and their side-effects. Table 4.5 sets out the principal milestones in the development of anti-doping policy between the Rome Games of 1960 and those of Sydney in 2000.

The story can only be partial: not only is the future fairly unpredictable, but the past is constantly under reconstruction. It has emerged since Ben Johnson's dramatic exposure in 1988, for example, that the main and loudly pious beneficiary, second-placed American Carl Lewis, had himself been found positive for drug use, although this had been concealed; and later the athlete placed third, Britain's Linford Christie, was also banned for using illicit substances. At the time of writing, Christie's natural British successor, Dwain Chambers, has recently been banned for using designer steroid tetrahydrogestrinone (THG), and a series of American athletes also associated with THG and Victor Conte and his Balco Laboratory in California, including 100 metres world record holder Tim Montgomery,

Table 4.4 Major drugs and banned practices based on the IOC list: medical uses, benefits in sport and side-effects

Drugs and banned practices	Illustrative medical uses, if any	Claimed benefits for athletes	Selected side-effects
Stimulants: e.g. amphetamine	Relief of mild depression; eating disorders	Used to increase aggression in sports, e.g. American football; increase energy in endurance sport, e.g. cycling; suppress appetite in weight-related sports, e.g. judo	Addiction; may cause loss of judgement, psychotic behaviour, anorexia and insomnia
Narcotics: e.g. cocaine	Powerful painkiller	Painkillers	Addiction and loss of judgement regarding injury
Anabolic agents: anabolic androgenic steroids	The management of male development at puberty; anaemia; renal failure; treatment of burns	Increased strength and size; help athletes recover from training and train more intensively; increase aggression	In males: shrinkage of the testicles and the development of breast tissue. In females: masculinizing effects including deepening of the voice and growth of facial hair. For both males and females: increased aggressiveness and depression
Diuretics	Control the retention of fluids and high blood pressure	Used to flush out other drugs and to achieve weight in weight-related events	Dehydration and possible risks of muscle cramps and a reduction in muscle strength
Peptide and glycoprotein hormones and analogues: e.g. human growth hormone (hGH)	hGH is used to treat growth-deficient children	Aid growth and muscle development. Depress fat accumulation. Strengthen tendons (and thus overcome one of the problems of steroid use)	Over-growth of bones such as the jaw and forehead. Risk of infection from contaminated needles as drug has to be injected
EPO	Synthetic erythropoietin (EPO) is used to treat anaemia and renal disease	Increases the red blood cell count which in turn increases the oxygen-carrying capacity of the body	Increased blood pressure and risk of thrombosis and stroke
Prohibited methods: pharmacological, chemical and physical manipulation	This category covers a wide range of activities including the corruption of a urine sample with alcohol for example, the practice of catheterization whereby drug-free urine is introduced into the bladder so that a 'clean' sample can be provided, or the inhibition of renal excretion.		

Houlihan (2003)

Table 4.5 Milestones in the development of anti-doping policy

Year(s)	Event
1960	● Death of Knud Jensen at the Rome Olympics
1961	● IOC establishes a Medical Commission
1962	● IOC passes a resolution condemning doping
1963	● Convention of international federations led to the formulation of a definition of doping
mid-1960s	● Union Cycliste International introduce drug testing
1964	● IOC adopts a definition of doping
1965	● France and Belgium are among the first countries to introduce legislation concerning doping in sport
1966	● Five elite cyclists in the world road race championships refuse to provide a urine sample
	● FIFA conducts tests at the World Cup in England
1968	● IOC conducts tests at the summer and winter Olympic Games
1970	● Testing introduced at the Commonwealth Games
1971	● IOC produces the first list of banned substances and practices
1972	● IOC conducts over 2,000 tests at the Munich Olympic Games
	● Test for anabolic steroids piloted
	● IAAF establishes a Medical Committee
1974	● Testing conducted at the European Athletics Championships
1976	● First use of test for the detection of anabolic steroids at the Montreal Olympic Games
	● Accreditation of laboratories by the IOC introduced
1977	● First use of out-of-competition tests
1978	● Some harmonization on penalties between federations
	● Council of Europe formulates a recommendation to member states on doping
late 1970s and 1980s	● Series of international conferences to exchange information and discuss common problems
1981	● 11th Olympic Congress at Baden-Baden passed a resolution from athletes endorsing the IOC anti-doping policy
early 1980s	● Development of more sensitive testing methods based on gas chromatography/mass spectrometry (GC/MS)
1983	● A large number of athletes withdraw from the Pan-American Games when the use of GC/MS is announced
1988	● Canadian Ben Johnson, winner of the 100 m Olympic final, tests positive for steroids
1989	● IAAF establish 'flying squads' of doping control officers to conduct unannounced out-of-competition testing especially for steroids
	● Council of Europe publishes the Anti-Doping Convention
late 1980s	● Series of trials begin in Germany which expose the extent of state-organized doping in former East Germany
1998	● Near collapse of the Tour de France because of the seizure of drugs by customs officials and the subsequent police enquiries
1999	● Lausanne Anti-Doping Conference proposes a global anti-doping agency
	● World Anti-Doping Agency (WADA) formed
2000	● 2,500 tests conducted by WADA in the run-up to the Sydney Olympic Games

Houlihan (2003)

have been implicated; Montgomery's partner, triple Olympic champion Marion Jones, remains under suspicion. Moreover, a new twist to the ongoing dynamic between technologies of drug use and detection may be immanent. It is reported that undetectable gene doping may be the next form of high-tech cheating to hit athletic activity.

Gene therapy, soon to be entering human trials for muscle-wasting disorders, promises the restoration of muscle lost to age or disease. 'Unfortunately', Sweeney (2004: 37) opines,

> it is also a dream come true for an athlete bent on doping. The chemicals are indistinguishable from their natural counterparts and are only generated locally in the muscle tissue. Nothing enters the bloodstream, so officials will have nothing to detect in a blood or urine test. The World Anti-Doping Agency (WADA) has already asked scientists to help find ways to prevent gene therapy from becoming the newest means of doping. But as these treatments enter clinical trials and, eventually, widespread use, preventing athletes from gaining access to them could become impossible.

Sweeney asks whether we will one day be engineering superathletes, or 'simply' bettering the health of the entire population, with gene transfer. As Habermas (2003) has discussed, such matters, which threaten our taken-for-granted notions of human nature, have barely begun to be publicly considered, especially in the USA where the forces of the marketplace are least constrained.

If the deployment of performance-enhancing substances has always existed, why has it become in disorganized capitalism a topic of such intense concern and debate? Luschen (2000: 463–4) suggests six reasons. First, the potential to build and improve performance has become more widely known among athletes and their 'supporting cast'. Second, at a time of ever smaller differences in performance outcome, even a small enhancement through illicit means may deliver a win, thereby justifying the use of and rationalizing doping. Third, the money to be made out of modern sporting contests has increased exponentially for individual athletes, most significantly so after professionals were allowed to enter the Olympic Games and the Games were thoroughly commercialized. Fourth, pharmaceutical products are more easily accessed, and are becoming ever more, and more rapidly, refined. Fifth, the media have raised public consciousness of doping, hence exacerbating pressures to clamp down on illicit practices. Finally, methods of detection and control have become more sophisticated and effective, leading to more high-profile convictions. Luschen's analysis is adequate as far as it goes. It might usefully be complemented, however, by an examination of linkages between these six reasons and wider societal change. Once again, reference will be made to the logics of the regime of capital accumulation and its mode of regulation, and their respective relations of class and command, in the disorganized capitalism of the last generation.

It was suggested earlier that since the early to mid-1970s class relations have conquered territory occupied under organized capitalism by relations of command. It is the logic of capital accumulation and relations of class that have precipitated what Sklair (1998) terms the culture ideology of consumerism. The commodification of everything is the end-point of capitalism, whatever its phase. Too often the postmodernization of culture in disorganized capitalism is examined independently of the ideology of the capitalist-executive. While our postmodern culture is *not* wholly determined by the logic of capital accumulation and relations of class, it remains the case that only those cultural forms compatible with this logic and its relations were likely to emerge or to endure (Scambler, 2002). Phenomena mentioned earlier, such as the new salience of identity-formation, processes of individualization and technologies of the self, have their genesis in part in the shift from organized to disorganized capitalism. What I have elsewhere called 'self-turnover' also belongs in this category (Scambler, 2001). Self-turnover refers to the postmodern capacity individuals have not only to 'present' differently by audience and context, a capacity sensitively and exhaustively analysed by Goffman (1971), but to 'be' different. Increasingly, people in sport, including elite professionals, can accommodate to what (modernist) psychologists used to refer to as cognitive dissonance: they can live comfortably with the *contradictory* images of themselves as both law-abiding citizens deserving of respect and trust *and* illicit drug users bent on fame and fortune. They can simultaneously *be* both moral and immoral. They do not merely present as but *are* multiple selves. Differently expressed, relativistic *petit* narratives have displaced universalistic *grand* narratives as rationales for identity-formation and sense of self.

This bears on doping in sport in a number of ways. Elite athletes, most conspicuously in heavily professional and commercialized sports, find it easier in disorganized capitalism than previously to 'rewrite' cheating as maximizing earning potential. But this is a product of a deeper structural transition, a point that goes missing in journalistic reports. Is is, above all, an expression of reinvigorated *objective* class relations, paradoxically in societies in which *subjective* class relations have come to play a diminishing role in constructions of identity and self. Sports stars, as we shall see in Chapter 6, can gain, if not 'earn', tremendous incomes; but their value and return to others, that is, members of the rapidly globalizing capitalist-executive and their closest allies in the new middle class, is far higher. Compare, for example, the wealth and incomes of members of the IOC with those of athletes who win gold medals. The chairman of Manchester United was worth a good deal more at the time of Beckham's departure to Real Madrid than was his former captain.

Sports are being colonized at a growing rate and most notably by the subsystem of the economy operating through the steering media of money. Drug use in sport emerges out of an ongoing dialectic between the logic of capital accumulation and relations of class and what, after Weber, might be termed the logic of honour and relations of status or − increasingly in our postmodern culture – celebrity. If class allows for or fosters status and celebrity, status and celebrity lead not only to high paid labour but, more significantly, to enhanced profits on the part of members of the capitalist-executive. Class and status or celebrity feed on and off each other. Drug use by those in sport cannot be explained sociologically without reference to such logics and relations. These are themes to be revisited later.

It will be instructive, finally, to return to and reflect on the common-sense assertions that doping is unfair, harms athletes and undermines the integrity of sport. The charge of unfairness presumes a compelling distinction between fair and unfair advantage. It is clear, however, that athletes enter competition with different physiological and psychological attributes and that this is *not* deemed unfair, perhaps because these differences are 'natural'. Although some sports, like boxing or judo, specify weight categories, most do not. If natural advantages derived from birth and/or training are acceptable, what about 'unnatural' ones, like ultra-low resistance swimsuits, ultra-light cycles or innovative Formula One engines? Like drugs, these are external to the athlete; but unlike drugs, they are accepted across most sports. Maybe the telling criterion is whether the advantage is secret or restricted: new designs for more aerodynamic javelins tend to be accepted after a while if they are made widely available. Would drug use be fair if all athletes had equivalent access? Few, it seems, would be willing to accept such a rationalization of drug use. A further possibility is that what matters is not whether an advantage is natural or unnatural, or whether it is differentially available, but the perception of how it is acquired. Compare, for example, an athlete who trains at altitude, thereby acquiring a greater oxygen-carrying capacity of his or her blood, with an athlete who achieves the same effect by using synthetic erythroprotein (EPO). But then the former might enjoy state sponsorship for training while the latter is from a developing country with no such schemes.

The notion that doping is bad for athletes' health is susceptible to similar interrogation. Often there remains a dearth of evidence: because of the quantities of drugs, especially steroids, that some athletes take, it would be not ethical to replicate their pattern of usage in clinical trials. Another complicating factor is that there are a number of sports in which participants are pushed to their physical and psychological limits in training and in which risk of injury is normal (see the earlier account of rugby). Most elite sports carry risks. And what of athletes who routinely take analgesics or anti-inflammatory drugs? It has been argued too that risks associated with the use of performance-enhancing drugs are exacerbated by driving the practice underground. And is it not paternalistic to deny an athlete the right to decide for him- or herself?

What of the contention that doping undermines sport's integrity? The presupposition here is that sport *per se* prescribes a set of core values that are threatened by drug use: blood doping in the Tour de France is as inimical to the essence of sport as adding a motor to a cycle would be. Drug use, others argue, is unacceptable merely because the rules of sports prohibit it, as they do handling the ball in football. Houlihan (2003: 220–22), whose analysis has been closely followed here, suggests that in practice opponents of doping typically rely on hybrids of these three propositions, and policy-makers on a mix of principle and public support. As if in anticipation of the potential of gene doping, Cashmore (2000: 217) adds that by 2010 'it is possible that there will be no way of preventing competitors from taking drugs which does not involve prison-like supervision in training as well as competition: inspection, invigilation, regulation, and punishment would become features of sport'.

To sum up, it has been argued in this chapter that it is certain forms of exercise and not sport *per se* that are health-bestowing. Indeed, many sports, especially at elite levels, are positively injurious to health. Moreover, disorganized capitalism has hastened processes of lifeworld colonization via the hyper-commodification of professional elite sport, establishing new risks. Meanwhile rates of participation in healthy exercise and sport in childhood have stalled, and remain unimpressive throughout the life-course, notwithstanding New Labour's re-discovered enthusiasm for sport as a counter to growing problems of obesity. Generalized recreational drug use in general, and doping in elite sport in particular, have, it seems, grown exponentially during this same period. It has been argued that these phe-nomena can only be understood sociologically within the figuration of nation-states like Britain against the framework of the logics of the regime of capital accumulation of the economy, of the mode of regulation of the state, and of honour, and their respective relations of class, command and status or celebrity. Government policy on health and sport in disorganized capitalism has grown more responsive to class pressure, with the result that policies are designed as much to secure public legitimation as to be effective. Thus policy directives and exhortations to exercise coexist with the continued selling off of school playing fields, reforms of curricula marginalizing sport, and a benign attitude towards the fast-food industry and patterns of consumption promoting sedentary lifestyles, while the 'third-way' doctrine of personal responsibility requires the *irresponsible* who *fail* to exercise to acknowledge their *guilt* and accept all *blame*. As we shall see in the next chapter, disorganized capitalism's excessive system ration-alization, together with its corollary, the colonization of the lifeworld, may have precipitated a new attitude to violence in and around sport, possibly even occasioning a 'de-civilizing spurt'.

5

Sport and Violence:
A 'De-Civilizing Spurt'?

As we shall see, Elias and his colleagues have made a strong case for an historical 'civilizing process' in the occident, not least in relation to sport. Paradoxically, the robust accusations of violence levelled against sports people and, especially, spectators in the high modernity of disorganized capitalism might be interpreted as evidence *for* rather than against Elias' thesis: do such accusations not, after all, speak of acute sensitivity and concern? Yet there remains much more to be said about both the persistence and the contemporary nature of linkages between sport and violence. The representation and mediation of sporting violence have attracted attention of late, far less so, Elias and his progeny apart, its social structural substrates. Violence is not merely a property of the hyperreal. Sociological explanations of violence in and around sporting events, and often too its representation and mediation, need to be anchored in social structures.

This chapter starts with a few reflections on the influential figurational analysis of sport and violence in general, and of rugby in particular. This is followed by a wider assessment of the phenomenon of football hooliganism that draws on a range of empirical studies. This assessment points not so much to the inadequacy of the figurational perspective *per se* as to its weight-bearing limits. For the figurationalists it seems as if football hooliganism – in all its multifarious forms – comprises a *single* figuration that can be explained sociologically with reference to a *single* logic and its *single* concomitant set of relations. In fact, football hooliganism, like all social phenomena, can occur across a variety of figurations and can be revisited and re-analysed with benefit according to different logics and relations.

The third section draws mostly on the logic of honour and its relations of status and, in disorganized capitalism, celebrity, to consider and account for how perpetrators of sporting and spectator violence (villains) have been recast – and recommodified – as celebrities (heroes). In the fourth section violent combat sports are directly discussed and putative similarities between the *pankration* of the ancient Greek Olympic Games and today's modes of 'extreme fighting' evaluated. This is succeeded by a consideration of women's growing interest and participation in violent, including combat, sport. The chapter ends with an assessment of the notion that disorganized capitalism is witnessing something of a 'de-civilizing spurt'.

The Figurational Approach to Sporting Violence

For Elias the civilizing process was the unforeseen outcome of protracted power struggles between monarchs and feudal barons. External constraint eventually yielded to self-restraint with the emergence of (a) a state monopoly on the right to use force, and (b) a correlative lengthening of interdependency chains or, more simply expressed, a growth in the division of labour. The sportization of pastimes was linked in particular to the 'parliamentarization of political conflict'. The more civilized habits acquired by the aristocracy for governing came to inform and promote the organization of less violent and more civilized forms of enjoyment. In nineteenth-century England the cult of the public schools turned these 'forms of enjoyment', or sports, into a secular religion. In the twentieth century a mix of commercialization and professionalization lent a new seriousness to athletic activity, with the result that the strategic use of 'illegitimate' violence became more common. This, it was argued, did not contradict core figurational theses since such violence was rational and controlled rather than pleasurable. With regard to the violence associated with football hooliganism, most notably since the 1960s, Dunning has made the case that football violence is far from new, even though the mobility of fans and inter-national and inter-club rivalries have refashioned it. For him, it remains largely a gendered, class phenomenon that is facilitated – worldwide – by the social composition of football crowds.

Importantly, civilization and violence are not antitheses in Elias' sociology. They have a relationship of interdependency. Dunning (1986) has offered a helpful general typology of human violence drawing on eight distinctions:

1) whether the violence is actual (e.g. a physical assault) or symbolic (e.g. involving verbal and/or non-verbal gestures);
2) whether or not weapons are used;
3) where weapons are used, whether or not assailants come directly into contact;
4) whether the violence is intentional or the accidental product of an action-sequence that was non-violent at its outset;
5) whether the violence is initiated without provocation or a retaliatory response to an intentionally or unintentionally violent act;

6) whether the violence takes a mock or play form (i.e. ritualistic) or is serious or real (i.e. non-ritualistic);
7) whether the violence is legitimate (i.e. in accordance with socially prescribed norms) or illegitimate (i.e. in contravention of accepted standards);
8) whether the violence assumes a rational (instrumental) or affective (expressive) form.

Dunning recognizes that the different forms of violence found in sport and elsewhere overlap and can be transformed into one another:

> verbal or non-verbal gesturing often precede hand-to-hand fighting in war situations and find their sporting counterparts in professional wrestling, for example, and ceremonial battle dances such as that of the Maori rugby team. Similarly, a fast bowler in cricket may bowl a bouncer with the intention of merely intimidating a batsman but may strike him accidentally with the ball. Or, an act of instrumental violence in rugby, soccer, or American football, perhaps engaged in on the instruction of a manager or coach with the aim of neutralizing a key opponent or 'taking him out of the game', may provoke retaliation, leading to a fight in which the emotion level rises. (Dunning, 1986: 47)

Using a developmental, processual or figurational perspective, Dunning re-articulates Elias' arguments. The latter's civilizing process reflects the displacement of *segmental by functional bonding*. Segmental bonding divides society into blocks that are internally more or less homogeneous and that maintain boundaries vis-à-vis outsiders. Functional bonds grow out of the interdependency implicit in a complex division of labour. Segmental bonding lends itself to a high rate of violence in social relations, and this violence typically has a high emotional or affective content. Functional bonding, by contrast, lends itself to a high degree of individual and social control over violence, with any violence tending to be of a rational or instrumental kind.

Dunning illustrates this transition from segmental to functional bonding with a discussion of rugby union arising out of his study with Sheard (Dunning and Sheard, 1979). The folk antecedents of modern rugby involved matches played by variable and 'formally unrestricted' numbers of people, sometimes in excess of 1000. The boundaries of the playing area were defined only loosely by custom. Matches typically took place either in open countryside or through the streets of towns. The rules were oral and locally specific. Matches shared a single common feature: 'they were all play-struggles that involved the customary toleration of a level of physical violence considerably higher than is normatively permitted in rugby and comparable games today' (Dunning, 1986: 49). In fact, rugby matches were 'ritualized expressions of the gang warfare' congruent with segmental bonding. A folk pastime in these circumstances constituted 'an institutionalized test of the relative strengths of particular communities', growing out of, and existing side by side with, 'the perpetual and more serious struggles between local groups' (Dunning, 1986: 53).

Modern rugby, on the other hand, exemplifies a 'civilized' game-form, distinguished from its ancestral forms in at least four respects. First, an intricate and formal set of written rules insists on strict control over the use of physical force, specifically prohibiting interventions like stiff-arm tackling and hacking. Second, clearly defined sanctions or penalties are brought to bear on offenders, and these are backed up by the threat of exclusion from the game. Third, the role of the referee, as it were 'outside and above the game', is institutionalized. And fourthly, a national, centralized rule-making and rule-enforcing body, the Rugby Football Union, is created. Dunning contends that the civilization of rugby occurred over a long timeframe. However, he draws attention, first, to the institution of the first written rules at Rugby School in 1845, which outlawed hacking and other forms of physical violence as well as the use of *navvies*, that is, the iron-tipped boots long worn at Rugby and some other mid-nineteenth-century schools; and second, to the formation in 1871 of the Rugby Football Union, which, among other things, instigated an absolute taboo on hacking. Dunning (1986: 49) summarizes:

> What happened at each of these moments was that the standards of violence-control applied in the game advanced in the sense, first, of demanding from players the exercise of a stricter and more comprehensive measure of self-control over the use of physical force, and, second, of attempting to secure compliance with this demand by means of externally imposed sanctions.

Rugby, in short, has always been and remains a hard physical sport, replete, some would say necessarily and appropriately, with 'tasty' incidents (Johnson, 2003). Revisiting Dunning's typology, today's rugby violence is frequently actual (1), intentional (4), without provocation (5), serious or real (6) and illegitimate (7). However, the risk of injury has been exacerbated by processes of professionalization and commodification, which have transformed players' physical bulk, prowess, intensity and mental edge. These colonizing processes are the circuitous issue of system imperatives, most notably those originating in the economic subsystem – especially television – and imposing themselves through the steering media of money. While it is difficult at one level to resist Elias' documented insistence on a gradual civilizing process in sport, it should be remembered that he took pains not to rule out de-civilizing spurts in the future. As we have seen, he had no truck with either simple linear or teleological models of historical development. Might it be that violence on the rugby pitch, epitomized in the *prima facie* rational, instrumental phenomenon of 'the hit', is recovering something of its past emotional and affective content? Kitson (2004) cites England captain, Lawrence Dallaglio: 'before you play any kind of rugby you have to assert yourself, dominate the physical battles, the rucks and the collisions'. He expressed confidence that second-rows Borthwick and Kay could assume the 'enforcer' mantle previously shouldered by (retired) Johnson and (injured) Grewcock. Is violence more *pleasurable* for this generation of participants and spectators than for the last? Possibly not, at least yet; but would the same answer be forthcoming in relation to football hooliganism or combative sport?

Understanding Football Hooliganism

The figurational characterization of football hooliganism has its critics. It has been claimed, for example, that the research programme it generated was designed to confirm rather than confront Elias' theories (e.g. Taylor, 1987). Indeed, the 'Leicester School's' chief researcher, John Williams (1991), left in the late 1980s because he found Elias' influence too stifling. Critics have maintained that the figurationalists have proferred all-embracing and untestable theories; fallen back on the expedient of de-civilizing spurts to refute counter-evidence; and failed to adopt appropriately challenging methodological strategies (e.g. ethnographic studies with *non*-working-class clubs) (Giulianotti, 1999). They have insisted too that historical and contemporary data are telling against them. Armstrong (1998: 305) is unsparing:

> The Eliasian construct ultimately proposes that those who commit violence at football matches are an uncivilized throwback in social evolution. Yet the latter half of the twentieth century has seen 130 wars with 27 million dead, whilst the first eight decades of the century saw 99 million die in warfare – a figure twelve times greater than that for the previous century and twenty two times that of the eighteenth century (Sivard, 1989; Hobsbaum, 1994). In the last decade further millions have died in wars waged against non–combatants by powerful regimes that have used everything from the euphemistic 'ethnic cleansing' to indiscriminate bombing and shelling of food markets and civilian housing. In the same years of the hooligan headlines we have read accounts and watched TV newsreels showing children starved to death, shot dead by soldiers and hacked to pieces in internecine disputes ... Meanwhile we are one of the largest exporters of weapons and tools of torture to many brutal regimes and silently accept the imprisonment of political dissidents and mass rape as a natural by-product of these conflicts. Yet our politicians, police and many commentators rage against the comparatively innocuous activities of football hooligans.

And Armstrong was writing prior to the invasion of Afghanistan, let alone Iraq! Armstrong may be misrepresenting Elias, but it will be argued here that the figurational approach prompts as many questions as it answers. While its principal tenets retain empirical as well as theoretical credibility, the generality of their pitch leaves much work to be done. As so often, relations of class and command go missing.

Counter-posed to the Leicester School is the social-psychological stance of the so-called 'Oxford School'. The work of the latter arose out of observational studies of Oxford United FC in the 1970s. Marsh (1982) and colleagues (1978) wrote of the cathartic 'ritual' of football violence: football crowd violence was viewed as a

> unique cultural adaptation to the lower working-class environment, which manifests itself in terms of aggressive but largely symbolic and harmless rituals in soccer stadia, and thus facilitates the release of aggressive impulses for young working-class adolescents.

One message to the authorities seemed to be that this kind of ritualized aggression should be tolerated in order to avert more 'serious' violence elsewhere in society (Young, 2000: 385). Critics have maintained that the Oxford School's empirical focus on hand-to-hand combat between fans during matches blinded them to more serious and organized forms of violence outside stadia before and after games. While there is undoubtedly a ritualistic dimension to football hooliganism – many of the songs, chants and profanities as well as some aspects of inter-group fighting testify to this – too little is said of the more serious and occasionally fatal hooligan encounters (Young, 2000).

In his early contributions, Taylor (1971) argued from a Marxist perspective that the football *subculture* in working-class communities comprised working men bound together by a concern – or *consciousness* – for the game in general and their local team in particular. At the start of the twentieth century rank-and-file supporters considered themselves members of a 'collective and democratically structured enterprise' in which players, managers, owners and fans were all engaged in a form of working-class 'participatory democracy' (Taylor, 1971: 145). The postwar commercialization of the people's game, however, fundamentally changed this. In particular, members of the working-class football subculture became alienated from the clubs that had traditionally supplied their cultural *raison d'être*. It was from this 'subcultural rump' that rowdy behaviour spiralled. Such behaviour represented an attempt on the part of a working-class subculture to reclaim 'their game'. In similar vein, Edgell and Jary (1973: 227) characterized this behaviour as 'a highly specific protest against football's loss of class exclusivity'.

In the 1980s Taylor (1982, 1982a, 1987) modified this thesis somewhat, linking manifestations of football hooliganism with ongoing crises of the British state. He argued that industrial and residential dislocations in working-class experience led to new differentiations within the working class: for instance, a growing upper working-class jingoism (a 'Little Englanderism') emerged during Thatcher's period of office and exacerbated Britain's hooliganism problem. As Young (2000) notes, this locates hooliganism in a different segment of the working class than was the case in his earlier work. Taylor's contributions have undoubtedly challenged colleagues to 'contextualize' explanations of football hooliganism; it has been objected, however, that he failed to anchor his case empirically.

Another distinctive approach is associated with the Centre for Contemporary Cultural Studies at Birmingham. Its representatives argued that hooliganism is a product of the way in which the traditional forms of football encounter the professionalization and 'spectacularizaton' of the game. In other words, hooliganism is one of the consequences of the changing relationship of the audience to the game (Clarke, 1978). This analysis again puts the accent on working-class reaction to the commercialization of the people's game; but it is an analysis that allows for the transition from organized to disorganized capitalism: 'into the hiatus between the traditional supporter and the modern consumer stepped the football hooligan' (Critcher, 1979: 171). As with the work of Marsh and colleagues and of Taylor, however, little attempt appears to have been made to subject the theses of Clarke and Critcher to empirical interrogation.

Figurationalism and the three of its rival schools or approaches remarked on here do not, of course, exhaust British contributions to understanding what was once, but no longer, defined as the 'British disease' of football hooliganism. From the 1980s onwards there have been regular studies too of hooliganism overseas. Indeed, some of the more infamous incidents of crowd disorder or stadium crushes in both organized and disorganized capitalism have not involved British fans at all: for example, as early as 1964 over 300 fans were killed in a riot erupting in the National Stadium in Lima, and in 1969 a one-week 'soccer war' was waged between Honduras and El Salvador following a game between the two national sides in a neutral stadium in Mexico (Young, 2000: 389). Enough has been said, however, for a number of conclusions to be firmly drawn. First, it should be apparent that just as no single theoretical perspective is able to demonstrate a monopolistic grasp of the truth of this, as of other, sports and sports-related phenomena, so each has something to offer. Second, there are overlaps between the descriptions and explanations of football hooliganism proffered on behalf of the different perspectives: there is a widespread consensus, for example, that football hooliganism is a heavily classed and gendered phenomenon.

The third conclusion invites a fuller treatment. The salience for understanding football hooliganism of the logics of the regime of capital accumulation (and class relations), of its mode of regulation (and command relations), and also of patriarchy (and gender relations), is widely accepted. To these must be appended the logic of tribalism (and ethnic relations) for matches, domestic or national, involving (often post-nationalist) ethnonationalist rivalries. Football hooliganism must be understood against the background of further system rationalization or colonization – through the commodification and, in disorganized capitalism, hyper-commodification – of the people's game, driven, typically outside football, by significant players in the capitalist-executive and sanctioned by the weakened power elite of the state (see Chapter 6). It must take account of mobilizations of ethno-nationalist sentiments and aspirations. It must be appreciated too as a product of the sport's long history and nurturance of, and appeal to, a masculine ethos. But the salience of these logics and relations to the sociological explanation of *events* of football hooliganism may nevertheless vary from figuration to figuration. This is one reason for doubting any *single* – as it were, overarching – theory of football hooliganism. It may be, for example, that, for all the contextual or background relevance of relations of class, command, gender and/or ethnicity, it is quite some other social structure or set of relations that is decisive. Hence there is a requirement to revisit particular figurations according to different logics and relations, and to maintain an ongoing dialectic between such empirical visitations and the overall picture. None of this, of course, is to suggest either that sociological explanations of football hooliganism – that is, explanations in terms of social structures – are the only explanations relevant or available, or that they can somehow allow – as it were, in advance – for the omnipresence of contingency in social phenomena. Sociology can and must be explanatory, but cannot be predictive.

This point may need illustration. Consider an interesting social-psychological account of football crowd violence involving England fans at the 1990 World Cup ('Italia 90') by Stott and Reicher (1998). Undoubtedly the logics and relations mentioned above would contribute to an adequate sociological explanation of events occurring at this particular figuration. But Stott and Reicher show the significance of both non-sociological explanations and of contingency. What they found was that a durable presumption on the part of the Italian *Caribineri* that all English fans were potentially dangerous, and their subsequent treatment of fans as such, precipitated a situation in which fans initially eschewed violence but later came into conflict with the police. The authors posit a model of developmental inter-group dynamics showing, in essence, how the assumption that fans spell danger may become a self-fulfilling prophecy. In other words, notwithstanding the explanatory pertinence of social structures such as those comprising relations of class, command, gender and ethnicity for the violence involving English supporters at Italia 90, what also mattered, explanatorily, was the developmental inter-group dynamic uncovered by Stott and Reicher; and, one might add, the contingent 'spark' that set off the actual conflagration.

A final conclusion returns to the notion of a de-civilizing spurt. While advocates of the figurational perspective may be justified in emphasizing modernity's civilizing impact on sport, a *prima facie* case exists for a 'postmodern' de-civilizing spurt. However, just as, for example, 'the hit' in professional rugby union bears inconclusive testimony to such a process, so too do the *moral panics* associated with football hooliganism: if Armstrong misunderstands Elias' concept of a civilizing process (dropping napalm from the anonymity of 30,000 feet *is* – sociologically, if not morally –

different from casting babies onto pyres), he is right to draw attention to the ideological impetus behind power elites' condemnation of football hooliganism (i.e. the violence *they* sponsor, is, *by contrast*, civilized). An argument in favour of a de-civilizing spurt might take the following form. As modern *grand* narratives give way to postmodern *petit* narratives, so norms proscribing violence become relativized. Violence, in a nutshell, no longer offends against more or less ubiquitous norms derived from the moral universals of *grand* narratives. Rather, not least with *grand* narratives themselves transmuting to *petit* narratives, norms lose their ubiquity along with their grounding in moral universals. As a result, recalling the concept of self-turnover introduced in Chapter 4, individuals find it easier in disorganized capitalism – that is, less incongruent or self-contradictory than was the case in organized capitalism – to be violent in one status/role/ identity and non-violent in another. This contention will be elaborated in the next section on 'villains' as 'heroes'.

Villains as Heroes

It has been suggested that in our rapidly individualizing and post-modernized culture, that privileges and lends new urgency, volatility and precariousness to identity formation, individuals, whether athletes or spectators, can opt simultaneously for and manage identities that would once have been deemed incompatible: they can *be* both violent *and* non-violent. Moreover, this 'cultural shift' must be interpreted as part and parcel of a culture-ideology of consumerism that must, in turn, be viewed as a non-necessary but sufficient product of the resurgence of – objective, if not subjective, but undoubtedly colonizing – relations of class with the transition from organized to global or disorganized capitalism. Self-turnover cannot be explained without reference to the class-induced hyper-commodification associated with disorganized capitalism; yet it cannot be 'explained away', that is, reduced to, class relations.

The logic of honour and its relations of status and celebrity are pertinent at this point. As Marx insisted, and Weber admitted typically occurs, status relations are derivative of those of class in most figurations. It is characteristic of disorganized capitalism, however, both that relations of status can afford opportunities for attaining celebrity and that the special status of celebrity can assume a life of its own. This is not to deny celebrity's transparent links to hyper-commodification, but rather to assert, once again, that it does not reduce unproblematically to relations of class. In his *Illusions of Immortality*, Giles (2000: 110–16) adduces a typology of fame. He distinguishes between 'public figures', 'meritocratic fame', 'showbusiness "stars"' and 'accidental fame'. The fame of public figures is in large part a function of their social roles (e.g. prime minister); meritocratic fame flows from individuals' exceptional qualities in their chosen fields; showbusiness stars attain their celebrity because they work in fields directly in the public eye; and accidental stars become famous mainly as a result of forces beyond their control (e.g. winning the lottery). Giles allows too for fame or celebrity to be domain-specific, community-based, national or international. Following Braudy's (1997) 'ideal of fame', he contends that the qualification for meritocratic fame is that an individual has earned fame through merit, and that it is athletes who most readily meet this criterion.

> One reason for the modern eminence of sport is that its rewards, unlike those of other public activities, are highly visible and *quantifiable*. Linford Christie at his peak was the fastest runner in the world. He had the medals, the record times and the videotapes to prove it. You cannot be a famous footballer without being good at football. Sports such as cricket, which are saturated with statistics, are even more unambiguous; if you score enough runs or take enough wickets you will eventually be picked to represent your country. If you don't you will never rise beyond the ranks of club or county and your opportunities for fame are extremely limited. (Giles, 2000: 113)

So, in principle if not always in practice (e.g. if drugs are used), athletic feats represent meritocratic or achieved, as opposed to ascribed, status or celebrity. But of course not all high sports achievers become celebrities. Consider the England Rugby World Cup conquerors in 2003. Whatever pains coach Clive Woodward has taken to be inclusive, not only of the 'starting XV' and substitutes in the final against Australia but of the full squad, it is Jonny Wilkinson who stands out as raw material for celebrity, the David Beckham of rugby union. Rugby union, a traditionally middle-class preserve, at least in England (Dunning and Sheard, 1979), is not a contender for the people's game, so Wilkinson's (hyper-)commodification cannot match Beckham's, but he, rather than, say, Martin Johnson or Richard Hill, is the media's selection for celebrity. As Wilkinson would be the first to confess, merit is not enough: celebrity is mediated, and Wilkinson is adjudged the optimum product. Wilkinson's natural reticence should not disguise either his earning potential from his celebrity or, in this age of 'reflexive modernization' (Beck et al., 1994), his awareness of it. As Stead (2003: 191) writes:

> The elite performers in a number of sports have become all to aware of their marketability as part of the media sport package and also of the vast amounts of media money that have flowed into sport. Aided by the emergence of agents working on their behalf, an increasing number of elite athletes have sought and obtained very high salaries or substantial prize money.

This process, Stead adds, tends not only to alienate them from their publics but can lead to their own uncomfortable entrapment in the media sport spectacle: 'the media creates sporting personalities to help sell their programmes and newspapers and this involves athletes being media commodities in situations that extend way beyond the direct sporting context' (Stead, 2003: 191).

So a select few elite sports people may qualify for an increasingly reflexive or self-conscious meritocratic fame, and a few of these may wittingly or unwittingly be dealt the enriching and alienating card of hyper-commodification. Reflexive decisions about dyed hair, idiosyncratic boots and even bold and conspicuous plays, like big hits in international matches, can advance the process of hyper-commodification. But in an individualized, relativized culture, permissive of self-turnover, hyper-commodified and mediated identities can also metamorphose villains into heroes. An obvious example from English football is Vinnie Jones. Jones is remembered less for his skills and solidity than for his dirty play: he was the archetypical 'hard man'. What better qualification for hyper-commodification through a career in gangster movies? Violence, off as well as on the pitch and after as well as during a long professional career, has been amply rewarded, even celebrated through the conferring of celebrity. Before we turn to the paradigmatic case of fighters as elite athletes, it will be instructive to revisit football hooliganism, because in this context too violent thugs or villains have been recast as heroes and discovered fame, even fortune.

A brave investigative literature on off-the-pitch thuggery, sociological as well as journalistic, has been succeeded by a plethora of popular books openly promoting violent offenders as heroes. Some of these are of dubious provenance. Armstrong (1998: 19) is unsparing in his castigation of Buford's (1991) often-cited *Among the Thugs*. He refers to Bill Buford's putative ethnography as a

> self-aggrandizing journey amongst fans who obviously wondered why this 40-year old American was in their midst. The author in pursuit of fitting in with his subjects admits to pushing two pensioners down a railway station staircase whilst abusing them, such was his supposed method acting. This confused man produced a book that was more fictional than a novel.

Nevertheless, Buford's story of 'thugs', apparently representative of a 'country of little shits', was translated into 40 languages. But the vivid portraits in Buford's bestseller, fictitious or otherwise, have been trumped since by a series of (auto-)biographies of violent youths and men masquerading as fans of football. Many of these present as bravado demonstrations of individual and collective brutality designed to secure the fearsome reputations of gangs affiliated to various Premiership, Nationwide and other league clubs. There is mediated celebrity and capital, it seems, even in remorseless violence dealt to strangers who happen to be in the wrong place or colours at the wrong time. But, as has often been asserted, there are strong antipathies between football fans and the hooligans or 'fighters' who attach themselves to the game.

The *Pankration* and 'Extreme Fighting'

Fighting has been omnipresent on the sporting landscape, figuring in premodern, modern and, some would say, postmodern eras. It is instructive and appropriate to recall the main properties of combat, and especially of the *pankration*, in the ancient games at Olympia before turning to contemporary Western forms of sporting combat. What the Greeks termed the 'heavy' events comprised boxing, wrestling and the *pankration*. There were no rounds in the boxing, matches continuing until one party held up his hand to acknowledge defeat. Hitting with the open hand was permitted and effective. Matches could last a long time and evasive tactics, like those deployed centuries later by the young Mohammed Ali, were common. Boys as well as men boxed at Olympia, and both wore leather thongs around hands and forearms. In the earliest games, vase paintings suggest that a single thong approximately 15 feet long was wrapped around each hand to keep the fingers together, protect the knuckles and possibly stiffen the wrists. Later the wrapping became more elaborate, as the bronze statue of a seated boxer in the Terme Museum indicates:

> On his forearm at the upper end of the wrapping is a sheepskin pad (like a tennis player's) for wiping off the sweat and blood. Around his knuckles, over the thongs, are wound three broad, thick leather bands ... whereas Roman boxing gloves were loaded with jagged hunks of metal, the Greeks never allowed such barbarous devices. (Robertson, 1988: 21)

In wrestling, three falls signalled defeat, with any part of the body touching the ground, including the knee, counting as a fall. Initial holds were vital, and many illustrations in Greek art, often representing Heracles or Theseus, testify to the range of effective body holds.

But the *pankration* was unquestionably the most 'exciting' and punishing of the 'heavy' events. Described by Plato as 'a contest combining imperfect wrestling with imperfect boxing', it was introduced at the thirty-third Olympiad in 648 BC, in part as a preparation for warfare (the Spartans were specialists). The first winner was Lygdamis of Syracuse, but the most celebrated exponent was Arrichion of Phigaleia, who won three successive crowns in 572, 568 and 564 BC. In the last of these Arrichion was in a strangle hold and on the verge of defeat when he managed to grip his opponent's foot, dislocate his ankle and win a sign of submission; but the last-gasp victory cost him his life and he was awarded the wild olive branch posthumously. Less ritualistic and rule-bound than boxing or wrestling, this form of fighting would today be called 'all-in' or 'no-holds-barred'. It permitted blows such as elbows to the face or knees to the groin, although eye, mouth and nose gouging and biting were prohibited. As in boxing, the struggle continued until one contestant raised his arm. Protagonists bore their scars, and more of them than boxers or wrestlers, with honour. It took one of two forms: *kato pankration*, in which the contest continued after opponents fell to the ground, or *ano* or *orthostanden pankration*, in which opponents had to remain standing. The former was the type used in the Olympic Games (Palaeologos, 1976).

As we shall see, there are modern reincarnations of the Greek *pankration*; but these, such as they are, remain well outside of the modern Olympiad, and indeed on the periphery of sport itself. What, then, of the sportization of combat? It is boxing rather than wrestling or judo or other 'martial arts' that has made the most compelling impact on occidental sport. Unsurprisingly, fighting did not disappear on the demise of the ancient games. Not only did it feature, as cruel theatre, in Roman sequelae, it survived without much interruption throughout post-Roman Europe. It was, however, in Elias and Dunning's (1986) first phase of sportization, in seventeenth- and eighteenth-century England, that 'pugilism', or boxing, assumed its modern form. This transition is brought to life by Gee's (1998) *Up to Scratch: Bareknuckle Fighting and Heroes of the Prize-Ring* (1988). Gee names James Figg as boxing's first champion. No less skilled with sword and quarterstaff, Figg was a master of the 'noble science of defence'. He was depicted in several of the works of Hogarth, who also painted 'The March to Finchley', in the background of which is one of the earliest representations of a bareknuckle mill. When Figg was proclaimed English champion in 1719 there were few rules associated with pugilism: 'in addition to punching, kicking was tolerated and wrestling holds were permitted, as was the practice of gouging – inserting fingers and thumbs into the opponent's eye sockets' (Sugden, 1996: 15). However, the more prize fighting developed as a public spectacle and a forum for gambling, the stronger the necessity to introduce rules to ensure that all contests were governed by the same principles. It was Jack Broughton who laid down prize-fighting's initial set of rules in 1743. These were known as the London Prize Ring Rules and are reproduced in Figure 5.1. This early codification did little to reduce the naked brutality of the prize ring, since there were no weight classifications and fighters with markedly different physiques, styles and experience were pitted against each other, often for fifty or more rounds. Deaths at the conclusions of fights, or shortly after, were not uncommon.

Why did men take part in such contests? Sugden's (1996: 17) answer, in brief, is the 'prevailing social and economic conditions'. Recruits typically came from an itinerant, unskilled, pre-industrial pool in which members of ethnic minority groups – immigrant Irish, diaspora Jews and a smaller number of Africans and Afro-Americans – were over-represented. This trend was, of course, to dominate the social stratification of boxing throughout the twentieth century, most vividly perhaps in the USA. Boxers were the more or less desperate issue of the lower echelons of the working class. To adopt the terminology of Hobbes, life for the urban poor was nasty, brutish and short. In this context boxing would not have struck as especially uncivilized: 'the bloodiness in the ring and the pit paralleled the bloodiness of society' (Gorn, 1986: 27). Moreover, the rewards from boxing could be considerable: when Jack Broughton died in 1789 his legacy amounted to seven thousand pounds, the equivalent of half a million pounds 200 years later (Brailsford, 1988). There was celebrity too for successful fighters, and opportunities to rub shoulders with the gentry.

Figure 5.1 London Prize Ring Rules

That a square of a yard be chalked in the middle of the stage; and on every fresh set-to after a fall, or being parted from the rails, each second is to bring his man to the side of the square, and place him opposite to the other; and till they are fairly set to at the lines, it shall not be lawful for one to strike the other.

That in order to prevent any disputes as to the time a man lies after a fall, if the second does not bring his man to the side of the square within the space of half a minute, he shall be deemed a beaten man.

That in every main battle, no person whatever shall be upon the stage except the principles and the second. The same rule to be observed in bye-battles, except that in the latter, Mr Broughton is allowed to be on the stage to keep decorum and to assist gentlemen to get to their places; provided always that he does not interfere in the battle; and whoever pretends to infringe these rules, to be turned immediately out of the house. Everybody is to quit the stage as soon as the champions are stripped, before they set-to.

That no champion be deemed beaten unless he fails coming up to the line within the limited time, or that his own second declares him beaten. No second is to be allowed to ask his man's adversary any questions, or advise him to give out.

That in bye-battles the winning man to have two thirds of the money given which shall be publicly divided upon the stage, notwithstanding any private agreement to the contrary.

That to prevent disputes in every main battle, the principals shall, on coming on the stage, choose from the gentlemen present, two umpires, who shall absolutely decide all disputes that may arise in the battle; and if the two umpires cannot agree, the said umpires to choose a third, who is to determine it.

That no person is to hit his adversary when down or seize him by the hair, the breeches, or any part below the waist; a man on his knees to be reckoned down.

Sugden (1996)

Prize fighting peaked in the early years of the nineteenth century but soon after fell into decline, inimical to the ethics of both Protestantism and industrializing capitalism; and, like pedestrianism, discussed in Chapter 2, increasingly susceptible to corruption. As the century wore on 'uncivilized' practices such as public hangings, floggings, dog-fighting, cock-fighting, bear-baiting and, of course, prize fighting were opposed and subsequently banned by those occupying the moral high ground. By the 1830s prize fighting was being forced underground; by the 1840s it was formally outlawed; by the 1860s it was being pursued by a newly organized and effective police force; and by the 1880s it had all but disappeared.

In the meantime, in 1866, again following a pattern familiar from Chapter 2, John Grantham Chambers teamed up with a fellow Cambridge graduate John Sholto Douglas, the eighth Marquess of Queensbury, to found the Amateur Athletic Club, an initiative dedicated to training young gentlemen to box. They suggested 14 modifications to Broughton's rules, hence the Marquess of Queensbury rules that have, with only minor adjustments, governed amateur and professional boxing ever since. Again, it is simplistic to claim that boxing immediately became more civilized. 'On the surface', as Sugden (1996: 26) observes, 'the introduction of gloves, a limited number of three-minute rounds, weight equilibrium and a standardized system for refereeing and judging gave the appearance of a safer sport.' But Gorn's (1986: 204) research suggests 'no diminution of violence'. In fact, paradoxically, boxing may even have become more dangerous. The gloves that protected fighters' hands enabled them to throw more and harder punches to opponents' heads. Under Broughton's rules, if fighters were tired they could drop to one knee and take a breather for a full minute before being required to 'come up to scratch' to start another round. The new rules obliged contestants to fight full three-minute rounds until the bell went, they were knocked down or the towel was thrown in (Sugden, 1996).

If amateur boxing began as a diversion for gentlemen, like football in Britain and baseball in the USA, it spread rapidly to the working class, where, with the demise of prize fighting, it immediately proved popular (Shipley, 1989). The Amateur Boxing Association (ABA) was established in England in 1880. The ABA went on to organize championship meetings every spring (excepting only the years 1940–43). The International Amateur Boxing Federation was formed in 1920, and boxing featured prominently in the Paris Olympic Games of 1924 (having made its first appearance in the London Games in 1908). The English team remained undefeated in England until losing 6:4 to the USA in 1951. Ten years later a huge television audience watched England 'whitewash' the USA 10:0.

But if amateur boxing has retained many of its original properties, professional boxing has undergone considerable change. And nor did English dominance last so long. Professional boxing, especially in the pre-eminent heavyweight category, rapidly became an American rather than British preserve, at least until the emergence of the Canadian-born British fighter Lennox Lewis. The watershed contest took place in New Orleans on 7 September 1892 between Yankee Sullivan and Gentleman Jim Corbett. This was the first 'world championship' to be fought under the Marquess of Queensbury rules, and it was staged openly, was socially inclusive and attracted interest well beyond New Orleans. In the event it proved a mismatch, the older and heavier Sullivan being dispatched at leisure by the agile Corbett. In the build-up to the First World War Theodore Roosevelt commended boxing as a means of military training, and more than one commander linked American prowess in boxing with its military might. After the War, however, the pre-eminence of black boxers – investing their all in an alternative route to material and social well-being – incited a predictable racist response. The all-conquering black heavyweight, Jack Johnson, was hounded out of the sport and the country. His eventual return to Cuba and to defeat by the white Texan boxer Jess Willard was greeted with enthusiasm and relief by the white American community. When Jack Dempsey won the title from Willard in 1919 he made it clear he would not accept challenges from blacks. White domination, predictably, hastened the legitimation of professional boxing in US law. The 1920s proved a golden era. More than 80,000 paying fans watched Dempsey knock out the Frenchman Carpentier in 1921, with millions more listening on radio (Sammonds, 1990). The colour bar was only relaxed when American contenders began to fare less well. It was in these circumstances that mild, inoffensive yet brave and skilful black boxer Joe Louis endeared himself to American audiences. Louis, the 'Brown Bomber', eventually defeated James Braddock for the world heavyweight title in 1937; almost single-handedly Louis had cast the colour bar out of boxing. He kept his title until retiring in 1948 (although he ventured an unsuccessful comeback later) (Sugden, 1996). The white boxer Rocky Marciano was the next dominant figure, and he remains the only fighter in history to win all his professional contests (from 1953 to 1956), earning an estimated $2,000,000 (Andre and Fleischer, 1993: 151). In the post-Marciano era, however, black boxers again dominated. With the brief exception of the Swede Ingemar Johansson (1959–60), no Caucasian has since seriously threatened black supremacy in the heavyweight division.

'It may be', Sugden (1996: 40) ponders, 'that black men make better boxers than whites. It is much more likely that the social position of blacks relative to whites in the United States and corresponding societies helps to determine their over-representation in professional boxing. Boxing was and continues to be the product of urban poverty.' It is not necessary here to parade the succession of black title-holders, but it would be remiss to neglect the hero and celebrity Cassius Clay/Muhammad Ali and the villain-as-hero and celebrity Mike Tyson. When Floyd Patterson was twice easily beaten by Sonny Liston, the 'Bad Negro' had defeated the 'Good Negro' and 'black White Man's Hope'. The 22-year-old Clay was given next to no chance against Liston in 1964 but won in six rounds, his characteristic victory celebrations prefiguring his growing commitment to the Nation of Islam: 'I am the greatest! . . . I don't have a mark on my face . . . I upset Sonny Liston . . . I just turned 22-years old . . . I must be the greatest . . . I showed the world . . . Tell the world . . . I talk to God every day . . . the real God . . . I'm the King of the world . . . I shook up the world . . . I am the prettiest thing that ever lived' (see Lemert, 2003: 73). But if Patterson was the Good Negro hero and Liston the Bad Negro villain-as-hero, what was Clay, or, as he became after dispatching Liston, Ali? And if Paterson and Liston were celebrities of sorts, what, especially after the legendary 'Thriller in Manila' and 'Rumble in the Jungle', was Ali? Maybe he was ahead of his time, earnest and playful, issue and parody of the logic of tribalism and relations of ethnicity in the figuration of Civil Rights America: 'I don't have to be what you want me to be.' Lemert (2003) cleverly calls Ali a 'trickster in the culture of irony'.

Ali, the trickster-celebrity, displayed a honed – if in his youth opportunistic – reflexivity almost totally lacking in Don King's no less hyper-commodified and globalized Mike Tyson. Revealingly, Tyson v Hollyfield II, during which Tyson twice bit off and spat out bits of Hollyfield's ear, is featured in Hotten's (1998) *Unlicensed,* a strong but sober account of the raw flipside of boxing. Tyson, as representative of the 'black' underside of disorganized capitalism as Liston was of organized capitalism, was scripted, mediated and marketed as the 'Baddest Man on the Planet'. Tyson in particular was villain-as-hero, a celebrity who no less conveniently than lucratively confirmed popular white stereotypes of Afro-Americans.

Unlicensed boxing, illicit offspring of nineteenth-century English prize fighting, never died out, although it has now been relegated to out-of-the-way car parks and disused warehouses. Gorman and Walsh (2002) trace the gypsy tradition of bareknuckle fighting back to 'Prince Boswell' in the early 1700s prior to charting Gorman's 'championship' fights from the late 1950s to the 1990s. Closely allied to this tradition have been more recent fights involving the likes of Donny 'The Bull' Adams, Roy 'Pretty Boy' Shaw and Lenny 'The Governor' McLean. Hotten (1998: 41–2) graphically describes a 1970s tape of unlicensed fights, two of which involved Shaw:

> The first fight on the tape was a fable of the underground – 'Pretty Boy' Shaw versus Donny 'The Bull' Adams. It was put on in front of a large audience in a circus tent. Shaw looked far more like a bull than Adams, who was an ageing gypsy fighter. Shaw was short, squat and muscular. On the bell he threw a straight right into the face of Adams and put him down. Adams slumped into a corner. Shaw walloped him twice more and then attempted to lift him up so that he could continue to fight. The referee was yelling, 'He's gone, Roy, he's dead'.
>
> Shaw dragged Adams up and then flattened him again with some powerful punches and threw in a couple of stomping kicks for good measure. On the tape, the knockdown was shown again in slow motion, as the piano chords of 'Jungle-land' echoed gently. Roy cuddled and kissed his girl in the ring . . .
>
> . . . The final bout matched Pretty Boy with Lenny McLean. As the crowd began to file in and take their seats, the camera focused on a trainer's bucket in the center of the ring that was stuffed full of old green banknotes. A man in a suit was pulling out handfuls of them and counting them out on to the mat.
>
> McLean was a huge man. His head was almost shaved, his nose crooked. He had vast, thick shoulders and a neck wider than his head. He was muscular but not defined. The real menace was not in his size but in his attitude. He was savage beyond any compromise, he was wild and he didn't know when to stop. To Lenny a fight wasn't over when the other man went down. Roy Shaw seemed much smaller than McLean, but his own reputation was high. McLean ran at him immediately on the bell. It was like a cartoon fight. Lenny smashed Shaw's head from side to side, left, right, left, right. Only the punches kept Shaw up. Lenny stamped on him when he finally went down.

Both Shaw and McLean went on to publish best-selling (auto-)biographies, while McLean joined Vinnie Jones in the film industry. In other words, even unlicensed fighters, surely paradigmatic villains-as-heroes, can accomplish and cash in on the status of celebrity in disorganized capitalism.

Mention should be made, finally, of what Gentry (2002) terms no-holds-barred or mixed martial arts, a form of combat directly descended, he claims, from the Greek *pankration*. He goes on to define this type of fighting, one might say sympathetically, as 'any competitive contest whereby the participants can punch with a closed fist, kick, wrestle, and perform submission techniques under strict guidelines in a professionally supervised setting' (Gentry, 2002: 16). Around for a long time and represented in many cultures, no-holds-barred fighting surfaced as a cult and media phenomenon in the USA in the 1990s. The first major commercial event, the Ultimate Fighting Championship (UFC), was staged in 1993. Political opposition on behalf of the 'moral majority' rapidly caused the UFC to be dropped by major pay-per-view television companies, although to a degree the Internet picked up the slack. Subsequently displaced by a revamped World Wrestling Federation, no-holds-barred combat has had to dig in to survive. At the end of the decade, however, Japan hosted ReMix World Cup 2000, a 16-woman tournament with fighters from Japan, Russia, the USA and Holland. In the UK, where no-holds-barred competition has remained fairly parochial, fighters like Mark Weir and Ian Freeman are among the few to make an international impact. There are even lobbies to 'return the *pankration*' to the modern Olympiad, although it is widely acknowledged that clearer, more 'civilized' rules would have to be agreed and implemented.

What these few paragraphs have established is that professional boxing, and unlicensed forms of combat extending to more or less rigorously supervised varieties of extreme fighting, have, in the postmodernized culture of disorganized capitalism, come to provide avenues for the achievement – admittedly through raw skill, nerve and heart – of celebrity. The logic of honour and its issue, relations of status, have been reworked. Arguably, 'uncivilized' behaviour is beginning to pay and to be acceptable once more.

Women in Contact and Combat Sports

Women's football in England was attracting an increasing number of participants into the 1990s. The Football Association assumed responsibility for the women's game in 1993, since when there has been a near-tenfold increase in women's teams (from 500 to 4500) (Leighton, 2001). More pertinent to this chapter, however, is the growth of women's rugby. Women's rugby was first played 'seriously' in Britain in the 1970s. The Women's Rugby Football Union was founded in 1983 with 12 founder teams, most of which were associated with universities (including UCL). In

1994 the Rugby Football Union for Women (RFUW) was formed. The RFUW currently has over 350 clubs, comprising 170 senior clubs, 85 student sides, 15 under-18 sides, 60 under-16 sides and 22 schools. Leading men's clubs with women's teams include Wasps, Saracens, Worcester, Rosslyn Park, London Welsh, Blackheath and Harlequins. The first women's international took place in 1986 (France defeating Britain 14:8) and the pioneering Women's World Rugby Cup in 1991 (the USA defeating England 19:6 in the final).

Liberal feminists might welcome women's growing participation in 'masculine' sports such as rugby: after all, opportunities long available to men should not be denied to women. Radical feminists, however, question the very masculinity of sports such as rugby (see Chapter 7): is it *necessarily* either liberating or empowering for women to occupy traditional, and sometimes violent, male sporting roles? And there is no doubting the masculinity of rugby: it is expressed through uncompromising physical engagement and oblivion to pain, epitomized in what Pringle (2001: 431) calls 'perverse pleasures in the tackle'. Moreover, the recent professionalization of men's rugby union, as we saw in Chapter 4, has lent a new and harder edge to the game's tradition of 'manliness'.

Howe (2003) has complemented his study of Pontypridd Rugby Football Club with a study of women's rugby in Wales. If football has conventionally been considered 'a game for rough girls' (Williams, 2003), what of the contact sport of rugby? Howe emphasizes the role rugby has played as a vehicle for national identity in Wales: if football became the people's game in England, rugby, never the preserve of 'upper-middle-class schoolboys', became the people's game in Wales (although paradoxically his sample club was dominated by middle-class graduates) (Andrews, 1991; Andrews and Howells, 1993). The body, he begins by noting, is the fundamental tool a sports person has to work with. However, sporting bodies are idealized in the media as part of disorganized capitalism's culture-ideology of consumerism (Hargreaves, 1986); and, as Hargreaves (1994) has compellingly demonstrated, the pressure for social conformity of the body has a greater impact on women than men.

> Women who participate in contact sports have difficulty in achieving acceptance of their bodies. 'Because I am a prop, people outside the club will struggle to see the value of me being as big and strong as I am. My size and the strength that in part is related to it is one of the major reasons that I have played for Wales. On the pitch I am valued for my physique ... off it I am not.' (Howe, 2003: 231)

Women who play rugby challenge norms for which, across most if not all figurations, gender relations reflecting the logic of patriarchy are categorical. Only if women's rugby is professionalized and commercialized are gender relations likely to become, in more if not all figurations, derivative of those of class.

So associated with masculinity are contact sports such as rugby that resistance to women's involvement has often been expressed through homophobia. Specifically discussing rugby, White and Vagi (1990: 77) advocate a feminist psychoanalytic perspective to expose such sports because they 'promulgate sexism and homophobia'. 'Nowhere', Burton-Nelson (1996: 88) attests, 'are masculinity and misogyny so entwined as on the rugby field.' Potter (1999: 84) suggests that the conventional patriarchal view of women's rugby is a function of the fact that the game is 'diametrically opposed in its style and purpose to everything that traditional society has encouraged women to be'. Howe (2003: 232) reports of the women he studied, however, that it is 'precisely this contradiction that attracts them to the game'. In short, they accepted the need and had the will to challenge hegemonic masculinity.

The minority of women who play rugby, then, can be seen as offering an active, female physicality in contradistinction to the gender order (Hargreaves, 1994). The social construction of femininity generally commends and rewards sportswomen who mirror female heterosexuality in the community at large. 'The "problem" for sportswomen has long been defined as "masculinization" through the display of muscle, active physicality, aggression and competition, attributes traditionally associated with both masculinity and sport' (Fasting and Scraton, 1997: 2). Howe (2003: 235) makes the point too that women who play contact sports such as rugby and boxing wear attire designed for men, going on to suggest – with supporting quotations from participants – that this feeds public perceptions that rugby is a game for lesbians ('we look like a bunch of dykes'). This 'image problem' can affect recruitment to the game and commercial sponsorship. Interestingly, it may also be the case that the entry of (amateur, albeit elite and committed) women rugby players into quintessentially male domains and activities – for example, profanity, drinking habits and absence of modesty ('We train real hard. We play hard and we drink hard. The men have been doing it for years') (Wheatley, 1994) – is serving to deconstruct masculine practices *even as such activities are (required to be) abandoned by (professional) male rugby players* (Howe, 2003). Elite women rugby players, in short, are becoming more like men as elite male rugby players become less like men (at least in the presence of sponsors and reporters).

What of women now training for combat sports, the martial arts? I have recorded that combat sports like boxing, wrestling and the *pankration* became integral to the Greek Olympiad. In Greek society, however, the division between men and women was stark, even among 'freer' Spartan women – Pausanias: 'the male is larger and stronger than the female, and the extremities of his body are stronger, sleeker and better conditioned and better in respect to everything worth doing' – rendering women all but invisible; women had no reason to excel at sport. Surviving references to fighting women tend to be either mythological, like the ready accounts of Atalanta, or transparently erotic, like Lucian's narrative of Palaestra's 'tactical advice' to a young wrestler even as he penetrates her (Golden, 1998: 124).

In English sport boxing and wrestling were long deemed 'low-life' sports for women. There is continuity to the logic of patriarchy and gender relations here: as late as the 1920s and 1930s women wrestlers were popular, with 'gimmick' matches including mud-wrestling attracting large crowds. Both wrestling and boxing remained 'underground' sports for women, 'characterized as disreputable and dangerous, and self-contained in working-class venues' (Hargreaves, 1994: 183). As far as wrestling is concerned, little seems to have changed in some nations, with women keen to compete afforded opportunities to do so only to satisfy the erotic demands of male spectators (that is, outside of the 'theatre' of American-style professional wrestling) (Scambler and Jennings, 1998). In other nations this is not the case. In fact, almost 80 nations have sanctioned women's wrestling and World Championships have been held since 1987, with Japan (74 medals), France (44 medals) and Norway (40 medals) providing the most top-three places. In the USA, fourth in the World Championship list, wrestling is an increasingly popular sport for girls and women in schools and colleges. Women's wrestling made its Olympic debut in Athens in 2004.

Women's boxing may perhaps feature for the first time at the modern Olympiad in Beijing in 2008. It too is showing signs of new appeal in the USA. The ban on professional women's boxing in America was not lifted 'officially' – there had been earlier state-sanctioned bouts – until 1977; and it was 1993 before female amateur boxing was incorporated into USA Boxing's formal programme: there are currently 763 registered participants in the USA, up from 340 in 1996, the year in which the English Amateur Boxing Association lifted its 116-year ban against women boxing. For many commentators the *de facto* birth of women's professional boxing occurred when Christy Martin fought Diedre Gogarty on the undercard of the 16 March 1996, Tyson–Bruno fight in Las Vegas. Disappointed by Tyson's comfortable dispatch of Bruno in three rounds, 1.1 million pay-per-view fans lapped up the 'bloody six round slugfest' between Martin and Gogarty. The first professional boxing bout in Britain took place between Jane Crouch and Simona Lukic from Yugoslavia in 1998. Supported by the Equal Opportunities Commission, Crouch had overturned the British Boxing Board of Control's farcical but far from unpredictable insistence that pre-menstrual tension made women too unstable to box. Women's boxing, like women's wrestling, is experiencing unanticipated expansion. There are innovations too, as intimated earlier, in extreme or no-holds-barred combat, with women entering the ultimate, one is tempted to say Spartan, masculine domains of unarmed combat.

What is to be made of this female intrusion into archetypical male territory? To many, women's football and rugby seem tame compared to female/female – let alone more experimental forms of female/male – combat, whether in the form of wrestling, boxing or indeed the other combined martial arts. According to the logic of patriarchy and relations of gender, they have long represented a blatant affront to norms of respectability. If liberal feminism offers grounds for celebrating the opening of exclusive male sporting enclaves to women, more radical feminists reject as irretrievably flawed *not* the gendered norms that have denied them opportunity for so long *but* the gendered norms that continue to permit brutality in the name of sport. For some there is no contradiction here. If men are permitted to fight, women must be; but this is not to say that fighting *per se* should be permitted or colonized – that is, commodified, in line with the logic of capital accumulation and relations of class, or juridified/legitimated, in line with the logic of the mode of regulation and relations of command – *either inside or outside sport.* And as Hargreaves (1994) has observed, it is all too easy to treat sporting and societal violence as separate phenomena.

The final section of this chapter makes a provisional case for a de-civilizing spurt in relation to sport in disorganized capitalism. The last two sections have afforded evidence of (a) the increasingly injurious properties of post-1995 men's professional rugby union; (b) the newfound expediency of violence (in rugby, but more conspicuously in combat sports) as a form of entertainment in its own right and as a qualification for enhanced status/celebrity; and (c) the – belated, overdue, questionable – extension of the 'pay-offs' and 'privileges' of sporting violence to female sports stars as they participate in what Snyder and Spreitzer (1989) term 'categorically unacceptable' combat/body contact sports.

A De-Civilizing Spurt?

Even allowing for an understandable but imprudent over-allegiance to the figurational sociology of Elias, it would be foolish to deny an historical 'civilizing process' in occidental sport. Rugby, wrestling, boxing and assorted martial arts all bear general witness to a Weberian tendency to civilizing rationalization. Nor has the focus on violence in contemporary sports in this chapter yielded conclusive evidence of a de-civilizing spurt. What it has done, however, is provide a rationale for anticipating and a manner of detecting such a shift. At the core of the figurational stance are the propositions that, following eighteenth- and nineteenth-century processes of sportization, sporting violence has become increasingly disciplined and instrumental rather than pleasurable, and that pleasurable violence in sport and elsewhere survives most efficiently among men with a particular (lower-) class habitus. In general these propositions continue to hold, but they require qualification (beyond figurationalists, admissions of empirical anomalies and calls for further research).

A number of commentators have made a distinction between aggression and violence in sport. In his *The Anatomy of Human Destructiveness*, Fromm (1973) distinguished between aggression only to facilitate the pursuit of a goal and aggression with the intention to damage. Thing (2001: 279) draws on Fromm to define aggression in sport as 'a playful phenomenon ... a ritual of moving in offence'. Aggression in sport is a metaphor for commitment. Violence in sport, on the other hand, is 'an intended action to injure the opponent'. According to such criteria the big hit in professional rugby would seem to constitute an act of both aggression and violence. Jonny Wilkinson, England's fly-half and linchpin in the World Cup in 2003, has had to learn how to deal with aggressive/violent acts calculated by opponents – not all of them South African – to intimidate or remove him altogether from the firing line. Wrestling, boxing and many, if not all, martial arts, would seem necessarily to call for a mixture of aggression *and* *violence*. In many other contact sports, aggression that leads directly to the injury or incapacitation of opponents is deemed a bonus, not least by coaches. Sports bureaucrats are of course aware of this dynamic (The Seville Statement on Violence, 1997).

There is nothing new here. Contact and combat sports did not lack this reliance on violence as well as aggression in liberal or organized capitalism. What *is* novel, this chapter suggests, is the potential in disorganized capitalism – characterized by a resurgence of relations of class (relative to those of command), and therefore of (hyper-)commodification, since the 'logical' end-product of *any* logic of capital accumulation and its class relations is the optimally efficient commodification of everything – to deliver a 'postmodern' cultural formation that allows for a newfound toleration, and therefore marketing, of violence as entertainment. Class relations, it needs to be reiterated, constitute a necessary but insufficient condition for the displacement of a modern by a postmodern culture: no argument is being advanced for any form of economic determinism. The new virulence of class could have led to a non-postmodern culture; but it would, *ceteris paribus*, have precipitated an alternative no less functional for its requirements.

Postmodern culture in its guise as the culture-ideology of consumerism fulfils the criteria for disorganized capitalism's regime of capital accumulation in general, and its capitalist-executive in particular. It *will* exploit violence, and therefore villains-as-heroes, as commodified – increasingly mediated and hyperreal – entertainment; that is, *unless* constrained by Habermas' civil society/public sphere. And there is currently little indication that the steering media of 'influence', deriving from the public sphere, is likely to resist or arrest 'money', deriving from the economy, backed by 'power', deriving from nation-states. The historian David Landes (1998: 520) has presciently observed that 'men' of wealth buy men of power. Those I have elsewhere dubbed 'greedy bastards', personifying relations of class operating beneath-the-surface and behind our backs, have in disorganized capitalism gained presidence over sporting celebrity and iconography. And profit knows no limits: do lower working-class black men who fight (each other) to escape disadvantage primarily afford (white, masculine) entertainment (Wacquant, 2001)? And are those 'hard' women who join the ranks of such men 'winners' or 'losers' (Mennesson, 2000)?

6

The Colonization and Mediation of Sport

In Chapters 4 and 5 it was claimed that the speed with which exercise and sport have been colonized has increased of late, and especially in the era of disorganized capitalism. This theme is explored further in this chapter, which focuses mainly on changes in the organization and appeal of football in England over the same time period. The first section sets the scene historically and examines the emergence and unfolding of the Premiership against the background of the newly state-sanctioned business ambitions of media personnel such as Rupert Murdoch, and its product, the hyper-commodification of football. The second section considers in more detail the ramifications of football's newfound 'mediation': 'actual' audiences have been in part displaced by 'virtual' audiences. In the third section the notion of celebrity is revisited. Building on the discussion in the last chapter, the nature of the development of celebrity in English football is addressed via a comparison of the lots of modern 'Gazza' with postmodern 'Becks'.

The Hyper-Commodification of Football

Like many other sports, association football, or soccer, has declined in schools during the era of disorganized capitalism. Dunning (1999: 121) cites the Football Association's (FA) estimate of a 70 per cent decline in opportunities to play soccer in English schools. He notes, however, that, correlatively with this, there has occurred a fivefold increase in the number of independent, non-school-affiliated clubs catering for the 9–16 age range. Indeed, in many respects the people's game would seem quite healthy in England. In 1991, for example, around 45,000 football clubs were affiliated to County Football Associations, fielding between them approximately 60,000 teams (giving, Dunning estimates, between 780,000 and 900,000 players of organized FA-affiliated football clubs in England at that time). Moreover, a sixfold increase in affiliated clubs for girls and women took place between 1971 and 1991, only one in ten of which were associated with pre-existing male clubs (FA, 1991).

To arrive at a better and more sociological understanding of the present-day dynamics of football – in schools and in amateur as well as in pro-fessional clubs – I shall trace in some detail the changes that have occurred, especially in the upper echelons of the game, since the mid–1970s. Maguire's (1999) five-phase model of the emergence and diffusion of modern sport will serve as a point of historical reference, and we shall see that the genesis of modern football differs considerably from that of track-and-field athletics recounted in Chapter 2.

The premodern forerunners of football or soccer had long ancestries. It may be that China has prior claim, with stone balls manufactured to be kicked around in games in Shan Xi province during Neolithic times (Walvin, 1994). There is evidence of early forms too in Europe and the Americas. Football in England had its origins in folk pastimes, where it often took violent forms (Elias and Dunning, 1986). Birley (1993: 32) notes that daggers were frequently carried – and drawn – by players in the thirteenth and fourteenth centuries. 'Hacking, punching and general fighting were commonplace as old scores were settled by rival players; broken bones, serious injuries and deaths were not unexpected outcomes' (Giulanotti, 1999: 2–3; see also Elias and Dunning, 1970). By the sixteenth century, folk football was most likely to be played on religious days, like Shrovetide, when the 'carnivalesque' predominated and the symbolism and figures of the ruling elite were ritually parodied (Birley, 1993). Matches between rival villages, towns or guilds took place alongside rustic pastimes like cock-fighting and dog-tossing. For Durkheimians at least, football functioned both to maintain local social order – 'by giving youth its head' and thereby publicly consecrating *rites de passage* from adolescence to manhood – and to foster a strong sense of social solidarity (Giulanotti, 1999).

But folk football proved incompatible with expanding industrial com-munities and, relatedly, increasingly middle-class mores. Delves (1981) has charted its decline in Derby, arguing that many such forms of 'popular recreation' were deemed antithetical to the thrust of a rapidly indus-trializing economy; corrosive of moral and social standards; and undesirable agents of the reproduction of a dysfunctional working-class culture. Opposition to folk football was far from new (Brailsford, 1992), but it undoubtedly became more intense in the evolving urban context of nineteenth-century England. But even as middle-class resistance to football grew in towns like Derby, novel football codes were being promulgated in the public schools. Mason (1980) documents this process of codification as occurring between 1845 and 1862 at seven public schools. It involved a redefinition of the limits of acceptable physicality, what Mason (1980: 14) refers to as 'a process of reconciliation . . . between spontaneity and vigour on the one hand and control and moderation on the other'. Former public schoolboys who went on the Universities of Cambridge and Oxford continued to experiment their way towards a formal body of rules. The FA, formed in 1861, was the by-product of ex-public school and university players working in London (Mason, 1989). By 1871 there was sufficient of a consensus on rules to permit a match between the southern-based FA and the Sheffield Football Club, founded in 1857 and the product of former pupils of the Sheffield Collegiate School. In 1871 too, however, the Rugby Football Union (RFU) was founded, marking the formal separation of the association and rugby codes of football. By 1877 a single set of rules or laws for association football was finally accomplished, the London FA having recognized and accepted some of Sheffield's innovations. The FA began to emerge as the game's leading authority (see Horne et al., 1999).

Amateurism versus professionalism was an issue for football as for other sports.

> The professional game reflected English society in the critical area of labour relations. Working-class fans could follow both on-the-field heroics and the player-director struggles of their favourite teams . . . (the introduction of) admission fees at matches revolutionized numerous aspects of football. The sport became less a gentleman's pastime and more a commercial enterprise when played at its highest levels. Relationships among teams increasingly came to resemble the relationships among ordinary competitive business firms. Indeed, the debate over professionalism was a by-product of the commercialization of football. (Tischler, 1981: 36 and 41)

Amateur traditionalists lamented the changes, maintaining that professionalism was in general corrupting of sport and would serve to undermine all but the largest, wealthiest clubs. But they could not stay the tide. The FA legalized professionalism in 1885. The professional Football League was founded in 1888, with 12 participating clubs: Accrington, Aston Villa, Blackburn Rovers, Bolton Wanderers, Burnley, Derby County, Everton, Notts County, Preston North End, Stoke, West Bromwich Albion and Wolverhampton Wanderers. Transparently, and unlike the London-based FA, 'the roots of this professional League lay in the emergent industrial communities of the nineteenth century, in the quintessential expanding industrial regions of the North-West and the Midlands' (Horne et al., 1999: 42). Many clubs had their roots in the church or chapel, while others were formed from the workplace and local pubs and neighbourhoods, even streets. The dozen clubs comprising the first professional League owed much of their commercial viability to the increase in purchasing power consequent upon a rise in real wages estimated at approximately one-third between 1875 and 1900 (Russell, 1997: 14). A Second Division was added in 1892, a Third Division (South) in 1920, and a Third Division (North) in 1921 (the regionalized Third

Divisions gave way to national Third and Fourth Divisions in 1958, a system which remained virtually intact until the creation of the Premier Division in 1992).

It was only a matter of time before the FA Cup, first competed for in England in 1871–2 (and rapidly imitated in Scotland in 1874, Wales in 1877 and Ireland in 1881), headed northwards: in fact, Blackburn Rovers reached the final in 1882, then the following year their local rivals, Blackburn Olympic, 'toppled the toffs' (Horne et al., 1999: 42). The supporters of amateur values fought on. The Corinthians, a representative team comprising the best – if mainly London-based – amateur players, initially held their own against the professionals, defeating the FA Cup holders, Bury, 10–3 in 1904. When the penalty kick was introduced in 1891 the gentlemen of the Corinthians, who of course did not deliberately commit fouls, 'would neither attempt to score with a penalty nor attempt to prevent their opponents scoring should the referee decide that the Corinthians had conceded one' (Mason, 1989: 147) (the main developments in the laws of the game are summarized in Table 6.1). A special knockout cup was established for amateurs in 1894, and in 1907 a group – again, mainly from the south of England – broke away to form the Amateur Football Association. The word 'amateur' was eventually deleted from the FA rules in 1975, and the last FA Amateur Cup was competed for in 1975.

If modern football emerged in Maguire's (and Elias') second phase of sportization, that is, in the early to mid-nineteenth century, its third or 'take-off' phase, involving its diffusion throughout continental Europe and further afield, occurred soon after. Football's properties were ideally suited for it to become the world game:

> It does not require much equipment and is comparatively cheap to play. Its rules – apart perhaps from the offside law – are relatively easy to understand. Above all, these rules regularly make for fast, open and fluid play, and for a game which is finely balanced among a number of interdependent polarities such as force and skill, individual and team play, attack and defence. (Dunning, 1999: 103–4; and see Elias and Dunning, 1986)

The first German football club was founded in Hanover in 1878, in the Netherlands in 1879–80, in Italy in about 1890, and in France in 1892 (Elias, 1986: 128). Experiments further east followed rapidly. The first FAs outside Britain were formed in Denmark and the Netherlands in 1889, in Belgium and Switzerland in 1895, in Germany in 1900, and in Portugal in 1906. La Fédération Internationale de Football Association (FIFA) was founded in Paris in 1904 by delegates from Belgium, Denmark, France, the Netherlands, Spain, Sweden and Switzerland, representatives from Britain being conspicuous by their absence. 'Presumably their reasons for remaining aloof were compounded by a mixture of feelings of superiority over having "invented" a game and fear regarding diminishing control

Table 6.1 Significant developments in Association football laws

Year	Development
1866	Introduction of tapes across the top of goal-posts
1873	Definition of 'offside' as follows: when a player kicks the ball, any one of the same side who, at such a moment of kicking, is nearer to the opponents' goal-line is out of play, and may not touch the ball himself, nor in any way whatever prevent any other player from doing so until the ball has been played, unless there are at least three of his opponents nearer their goal-line. (The number of opponents between the kicker and the opposing goal-line was reduced from three to two in 1925.)
1877	Cross-bars as well as tapes permitted
1880	Referee fist mentioned
1891	Referee patrols the field of play. 'Umpires' become linesmen who patrol the sidelines. Introduction of penalty kick. Introduction of goal nets
1895	Replacement of tapes by cross-bar
1897	Dimensions of the field of play fixed at: length 100–130 yards; breadth 50–100 yards

Downing (1999)

over a "ludic product" which they regarded as peculiarly their own' (Dunning, 1999: 103). The English FA affiliated with FIFA in 1906, withdrew in 1914, rejoined in 1924, withdrew once more in 1928, and only affiliated with a degree of pragmatic conviction in 1945 (Green, 1953). As this long period of English prevarication illustrates only to well, Maguire's fourth phase points to a period of continuing Western hegemony, although one no longer dominated by Britain (in fact, Britain's influence on FIFA was to come to 'a crushing end' in 1974 when Stanley Rous was 'deposed' as president by the Brazilian, Joao Havelange (Murray, 1994: 70)).

Football, professional and largely working-class, was not an imperial game like cricket. It travelled with trade to the further reaches of the formal and informal British Empire, engendering a mixed reception (Russell, 1997). Its impact in the USA was notoriously minimal, although when the Americans celebrated the centenary of their native football code in 1969, the game held to mark its beginnings, between Princeton and Rutgers on 6 November 1869, 'was closer to soccer than any other code' (the ball was round and there was no running with it). But after this 'brief affair' with the round ball, the Americans proceeded to continue

> in their own peculiar progress, making themselves an island in the sporting world, rejecting both soccer and rugby to found 'gridiron' football ... By the 1880s Walter Camp was devising the changes in the rules that resulted in the creation of America's own game, which was then played in the uniquely American circumstances of college football. (Murray, 1994: 75)

The situation in South America was very different. The game first took root there in the large British communities of Argentina and Uruguay in the 1860s. By the turn of the century the first leagues had been formed and the two countries began playing each other in 1901. Argentina and Chile joined FIFA in 1912. It was through the Olympic Games, however, that South American football came to the attention of the wider world: a brilliant Uruguay was victorious in 1924 and 1928 (the latter in a replayed final against Argentina).

Returning to the development and consolidation of the game in England, it has been claimed that by 1914 there were 4740 professional players turning out for 158 clubs (Walvin, 1944). There was certainly no lack of spectator interest. Even before the war, crowds of more than 100,000 regularly attended FA Cup Finals at the Crystal Palace. The minimum price of admission for a League match at this time was sixpence (or 2.5p), rising to an average of one shilling (or 5p) between the wars. Attendances during the interwar period set records that still survive, the peak year being 1948–9, which saw 41.2 million attend League football. Tables 6.2 and 6.3 show average attendance by Division for 1888–1939 and 1946–2002 respectively (see Tabner, 2002). The decline in attendance after the interwar years and remarkable postwar boom is very apparent, especially in the lower divisions.

Moves were made to restrict players' wages early in the professional game: a maximum wage of £4 (still double the wage of a skilled worker) and a ban on match bonuses were introduced for the 1901–2 season. Players organized to resist and some of the more wealthy clubs undoubtedly made clandestine payments. The Association Football Players Union was formed in 1907, led initially by Charlie Roberts from Manchester United, but it struggled and football was to remain a working-class sport, involving hard work – 'Millwall, Derby and Aston Villa played 65, 58 and

Table 6.2 Average Divisional attendances 1888–1939

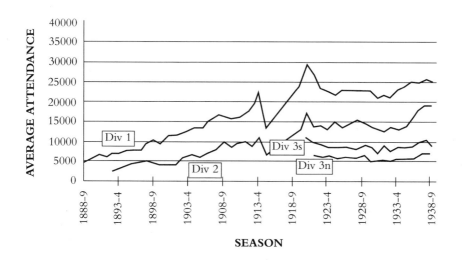

Table 6.3 Average Divisional attendances 1946–2002

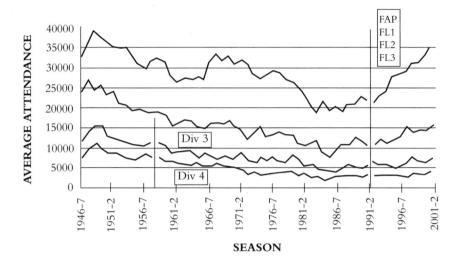

56 matches respectively in 1895–96, while Everton played 17 games in 25 days in April of the same season' (Russell, 1997: 49) – for restricted wages, for many years. The maximum wage was £8 a week for most of the interwar period, gradually rising after 1945 to reach £20 per week during the playing season and £17 in the summer by 1961. Not all players scaled such heights, even in the bigger clubs: between a quarter and a third were on the maximum wage by 1961. It was during the 1960–61 season that the newly elected chair of the (re-named, in 1958) Professional Footballers Association, Jimmy Hill, organized a successful strike ballot to abolish the maximum wage; in the event they succeeded without needing to strike. It was the George Eastham case in 1963, however, which broke management control over the crucial retain and transfer system. By the end of the 1960s, the era of celebrities such as George Best and the members of the victorious England World Cup team of 1966, First Division players' wages had risen to between £3,500 and £5,000 a year. In 1968 FA rules still forbade players to have agents, but by 1978 'no top player was without a financial entourage of agent, accountant and bank manager' (Mason, 1989: 162). By this time too, organized capitalism was giving way to disorganized capitalism.

Kevin Keegan's career in the 1980s epitomized that of the 'modern footballer-business-man'.

He signed contracts to promote Faberge Toiletries, Harry Fenton Suits, Mitre Sports Goods, Patrick UK (Ltd) Boots, Nabisco Shredded Wheat and Heinz Baked Beans. He formed companies registered in tax havens such as the Isle of Man: Kevin Keegan Investments Ltd, and Kevin Keegan Sport and Leisure Ltd. He also had a four-year contact with BBC television worth, it was reported, twenty thousand pounds. (Mason, 1989: 163)

Bryan Robson signed a contract for £25,000 p.a. to wear Balance Boots and Gary Lineker to endorse boots for a 3 per cent royalty on sales that, his accountant estimated, would earn £1 million. In 1951 Stanley Matthews had received £20 a week for endorsing football boots made by the CWS.

Dobson and Goddard (2001: 123) have maintained that, taken in the round, the 1970s and 1980s were a period of economic decline for football:

> Pressures emanating from social and demographic changes, the hooligan phenomenon, and the failure of football clubs themselves to maintain their own physical infrastructure, had taken their toll on attendances over many years, to the extent that the future survival of large numbers of clubs (both large and small) seemed to be in jeopardy.

It was the tragedies of Heysel, Bradford and Hillsborough that precipitated reform. Football's 'rehabilitation' in the 1990s, however, has coincided with a sharp rise in financial and competitive inequality between clubs. As we shall see, and resonating with the account of the changing trajectory of the modern Olympic movement in Chapter 3, the shifting balance of football revenues reflects technological changes in broadcasting and its dual status as spectator sport and television spectacle. If footballers had in its earliest days been 'soccer slaves', they are now, it seems, 'socceratti' (Harding, 2003).

One of the best accounts of these changes is Morrow's *The People's Game? Football, Finance and Society* (2003). Morrow ranges widely over European clubs, although I shall continue to concentrate here on the English scene. Although the English Premier League as a whole continues to have competitive balance, judged in terms of points differential, it is now a small cluster of elite clubs that provides the actual winner. Morrow notes that only eight clubs out of a possible 25 have managed a top-five position in the Premiership in the last five seasons. In fact the last occasion on which the title was won by a club other than Manchester United or Arsenal was in 1994–95.

An expedient way of broaching this emergence of an elite of clubs is via a consideration of the Bosman ruling in 1995:

> The requirement for the payment of compensation to the former club of an out-of-contract player who was signing for a new club was found to be incompatible with provisions in Article 48 of the Treaty of Rome for the freedom of movement of labour. The existing 'three-foreigner' rule, which had the effect of limiting the number of individuals outside the jurisdiction of each national football federation allowed onto the field of play at any one time, also contravened Article 48, by restricting the opportunity for EU nationals to play for clubs located in other EU countries. (Dobson and Goddard, 2001: 95)

This ruling fundamentally changed the players' labour market. The removal of restrictions in relation to players from EU countries, extended to non-EU players of international standing, has prompted an influx of foreign players, especially into the Premier League. The net transfer expenditure outflow of the English League clubs as a whole was underway prior to 1995, with the notable move of Eric Cantona from Nîmes in 1991, first to Leeds United and subsequently to Manchester United, proving a catalyst; but the post-Bosman increase has been spectacular. In his analysis of the nationalities of squad members of England's Premier Division clubs in the summer of 1999, Macias (2000) found that 57 per cent were from England and Wales, 7 per cent from other parts of the UK, 5 per cent from Ireland, 7 per cent from Scandinavia, 16 per cent from the rest of Europe, and 8 per cent from the rest of the world (the pattern of migration to other European first divisions differed considerably).

The Bosman case also altered the balance of power among League clubs, with the richest clubs gaining unfettered access to the best professional labour (Giulanotti, 1999). The experience of Chelsea, or 'Chelski', is paradigmatic. When the Russian oil czar Roman Abramovich spent £111 million – out of total assets of over £8 billion – to purchase ten star recruits in 62 days, he not only set a world record but transformed the club's prospects (Harris, 2003). No less eloquently, in the summer of 2003 the Real Madrid first team was valued at £230 million, with David Beckham registering as only its fifth most expensive acquisition, at £25 million, compared for example with Zinedine Zidane's £46 million. Finally, the Bosman ruling – alongside other factors like players' agents and, pre-potently, television revenues – accelerated wage inflation. By the late 1990s it was far from unusual for the best players at top clubs to be on annual incomes of over £1 million. The average income for a player in the English Premiership, not the optimum European League by any means for those football migrants Maguire and colleagues (2002) term 'mercenaries', currently exceeds £500,000 (Deloitte and Touche, 2002).

The significance of the Bosman ruling *per se* should not be exaggerated; often it was precipitant rather than cause, and in many ways it was symptomatic of deeper (system-driven) processes of globalization and market deregulation (Lanfranchi and Taylor, 2001). Undoubtedly, however, it fuelled the core predicament of English football, to which we now turn.

It has been argued that it is the symbiotic relationship that has developed between television and football that has most powerfully undermined competitive league balance and become the major challenge facing professional football (Brown, 2000). While football has become integral to television's business model, concomitantly the monies from television rights have become a vital income stream for football clubs. Morrow dates this 'dependent relationship' to a fundamental reversal in the economics of broadcasting markets: 'while in the past programme content had to compete for scarce transmission outlets (i.e. television channels), by the early 1990s large numbers of channels were competing for (relatively) scarce content' (Morrow, 2003: 13). This new scenario accounts for the fact that the combined worth of contracts covering Europe's major leagues in 2001–2 was a staggering £1795 billion.

Europe's top clubs were quick to introduce mechanisms to enable them to maximize their incomes from broadcasting. In England this precipitated the formation of the FA Premiership in 1992; and in Europe it led to the metamorphosis of the European Cup into the UEFA Champion's League in 1992–93. In countries such as Spain, where clubs are permitted to negotiate their own deals, television income is unsurprisingly skewed towards the top clubs. Even in leagues where the rights have continued to be negotiated collectively, however, there is evidence of television income becoming polarized. Table 6.4 focuses on the English Premier Division, using selected figures from 1992–93 to 2001–2: it shows that the earnings gap between top and bottom clubs has grown substantially over this period. One important property of television income is that it is effectively cost-less (compared with income received from sources like merchandising). Consequently it is often seen and treated by clubs as a windfall gain, immediately available for player recruitment or pay. 'Current systems are designed for continual strengthening of the strongest teams and clubs; competition is in danger of being replaced by structural self-perpetuation' (Morrow, 2003: 16). Moreover, a predictable consequence of top-heavy financial reward mechanisms prevalent in leagues such as the English Premiership is that clubs have to spend heavily to survive. Rosen and Sanderson (2001) liken it to a military arms race between nations. Pressures on clubs are heightened and encourage 'excessively short-termist behaviour and decision-making by club directors' (Morrow, 2003: 19).

Table 6.4 Distribution of television income – the FA Premier League

	2001/02 (£m)	2000/01 (£m)	1996/97 (£m)	1992/93 (£m)
Top earner	25.7	20.4	6.3	2.4
Median earner	17.3	13.4	4.2	1.6
Lowest earner	10.8	8.4	2.8	1.1
Parachute payment	4.0	3.1	1.0	0.8
Earnings gap★	138%	142%	125%	118%

★ Earnings gap = £(top earner – lowest earner)/lowest earner.
Parachute payments are made to relegated clubs for two seasons after their relegation to cushion them from the financial impact of losing their position in the FA Premier League.
Source: FA Premier League Annual Reports (various years)

Morrow (2003)

If the gap between top and bottom clubs within major leagues has increased, that between top and lower leagues has become a chasm. Only nine of the twenty clubs promoted to the FA Premier League at the end of its first seven seasons (1993 to 1999 inclusive) avoided relegation in the first season after promotion. Things appeared to improve in the two subsequent seasons, with only one club from six, Manchester City, being relegated in its first season following promotion. However, of the other five, Ipswich Town were relegated at the end of their second season, while Fulham enjoyed the support of Mohammed Al Fayed, and Blackburn Rovers continuing support from the legacy of its former benefactor, Sir Jack Walker. The introduction of so-called 'parachute payments' to cushion clubs relegated from the English Premier League to Division One (Nationwide League), making it easier for them to retain their players, implicitly recognizes the skewed distribution of television revenues in English football. But parachute payments are worth considerably less to clubs than the monies that would have accrued to them had they not been relegated from the Premiership. Moreover, the collapse of the Nationwide League's deal with ITV Digital, the television company set up by Carlton and Granada, has meant that instead of Nationwide League clubs receiving £314 million to be shared over three years, they will now receive only £95 million to be shared over four years (Plunkett, 2002). Several Nationwide League clubs were technically insolvent even before the collapse of ITV Digital. At the close of the 2000–1 season, 10 out of 24 Nationwide League clubs had liabilities greater than their assets, which is not surprising given that the average club in that division had a wages to turnover ratio of 101 per cent (Deloitte and Touche, 2002).

In sum, if professional English football has regained a measure of economic healthiness in the 1990s, it has also assumed novel and worrying properties. Most conspicuously, its relationship with television has become deeply paradoxical. Clubs seek ever more rewards from broadcasting companies, yet the consequence of those rewards and the manner of their distribution is a competitive imbalance that reduces the attractiveness of the product and leads to lower revenues from rights in the future. And television audience figures are falling, both in terms of domestic competitions and the UEFA Champions League. The *Match of the Day* (highlights) audience declined by 10.4 per cent and Sky Sports (live) audience by 21.8 per cent from 2000 to 2001 (Clarke, 2002). As for the UEFA Champions League, while 9.6 million viewers aged 4+ in the UK (41.9 per cent of those homes with television sets turned on) watched Champions League in 1997–98, this was down to 7.1 million viewers (31.2 per cent of those homes with television sets turned on) in 2001–2 (Morrow, 2003: 30). Furthermore, the same short time-span has witnessed a fall of approximately 5 per cent in the global advertising market and a reduction in the number of satellite broadcasters, arising either from mergers and takeovers (e.g. Sogecable and Via Digital in Spain) or company collapse (e.g. KirchMedia and ITV Digital). Nor has Pay-TV, or pay-per-view, proved the success that many anticipated. According to Sky's Rupert Murdoch, the sports rights market has peaked.

What next for English football? Football clubs, particularly the super clubs, are now mature businesses; but they are businesses with limited opportunities to expand, either by horizontal integration (that is, by taking over other companies in the same line of business) or by vertical integration (that is, by expanding backwards towards sources of supply or forwards towards consumers) because of football's regulatory structures. For example, BSkyB's attempted takeover of Manchester United, an instance of vertical integration, was prohibited by the UK Monopolies and Mergers Commission, which feared it would gain undue influence or control within English football. Much greater integration of sports franchises into large media and entertainment conglomerates is found in the USA. The FA and UEFA also proscribe an array of options generally available to directors of companies. At the time of writing, it seems most likely that we will see a hermetic European Super League, akin to Major League Baseball or the National Football League in the USA (Morrow, 2003).

In what ways does this rapid commercialization, or hyper-commodification, of English – and European, even world – football represent a lifeworld-to-system colonization of the people's game? Undoubtedly certain members of the capitalist-executive, much more globally oriented and predatory in disorganized than in organized capitalism, and almost as likely to be non-British as British, have been key players in English football's 'economic revival'. But the contention that it is the new owners and directors of clubs – together with a new coterie of advisers, namely, 'accountants, brokers, lawyers schooled in the nihilism of "market forces" ' (Conn, 1997) – who are responsible, or culpable, is a partial truth. Only a few top clubs have generated significant returns. While some owners/ directors engage with football exclusively in pursuit of profit, entirely obedient to the logic of the regime of capital accumulation, for others it is, for example, the logic of honour that is categorical: in short, for some it is relations of status – and increasingly in our postmodern culture, of celebrity – rather than those of class that take precedence.

However, we should not neglect the causal influence of those representatives of the capitalist-executive *located outside of both football and sport*, characterized elsewhere by the technical term *greedy bastards* due to their visceral dedication to personal riches and influence secured for the most part on the backs of the working class and its displaced segment, the 'new poor', in an era of rank and deepening intra- and inter-national inequality (Scambler, 2002). For these figures, profit undoubtedly remains the single or overriding goal. Rupert Murdoch affords us a pertinent example (see Page, 2003). Murdoch's interests are astonishingly diverse and defy easy summary, although Lanchester (2004: 3) has had a go and is worth citing:

> We in Britain know about the *Sun* and the *News of the World*, *The Times* and the *Times Educational, Higher Education* and *Literary Supplements*; we know about HarperCollins, and hence about Jack Higgins, and about Fourth Estate, and hence about *The Connections*; we

know about the BSkyB network in Britain, about its role in pioneering multi-channel TV, and about its ownership of the rights to transmit Premier League Football, which have just been diluted by the European Commissioner for competition, Mario Monti. (His requirement was that Sky sell eight games a season to other networks. Golly, what a fearsome sanction.) If we think about it for a moment we remember that he owns the Fox network in America, and 20th Century Fox the film studio, and Fox News the toxic right-wing news channel, the Star satellite network in Asia, and the LA Dodgers baseball team, and part of Ansett airlines until it went broke, and the US *TV Guide*. Some of us may be aware that he owns 70% of Australia's newspaper industry, and one of its main TV channels. He is the unmoved mover behind *The Simpsons, That 70s Show, Married with Children, Fight Club, The Full Monty, Ally McBeal, Buffy the Vampire Slayer, King of the Hill, Titanic.*

In fact, as Dobson and Goddard (2001) argue, television in general, and Murdoch in particular, have been the primary agencies of the colonization of English football via the steering media of money. The impact of television was minimal through the 1960s and 1970s because the fees paid for broadcasting rights were parsimonious. Televised football bore the hallmarks of a public good. Even at this time, however, coverage was skewed towards the larger clubs, gaining them a following at the price of smaller clubs. Thus when the long-term decline in attendances accelerated rapidly in the late 1970s and early 1980s, the smaller clubs were disproportionately hit. Under growing commercial and political pressure to increase viewing figures, the BBC-ITV cartel disintegrated, fees rose sharply, as did the coverage devoted to big-market teams. But it was the arrival on the scene of Murdoch's BSkyB and pay-television at the end of the decade that marked the turning point. Dobson and Goddard (2001: 424) take up the story:

> Unprecedented expansion of the potential audience concentrated disproportionately on a handful of big-market clubs, achieved at almost zero incremental cost to the clubs and players, combined with acute scarcity in the supply of the very best talent, created ideal conditions for massive wage inflation, and for the employment of the most talented players to become increasingly concentrated with those same big-market clubs. So while it is undoubtedly true that the big-market clubs are the only ones able to afford to pay the most talented players, the ultimate reason for this lies in the changing level and composition of effective demand, which in turn has been driven mainly by technological innovation in broadcasting.

And, one might add, by a lust for profit on the part of greedy bastards whose only mode of accountability to the lifeworld is via football supporters *qua consumers*; and of course the comprehensive transmutation of supporters into consumers is itself an aspect of football's colonization.

It is not of course necessary to posit a conspiracy comprising, minimally, the owners and directors of big-market clubs, their financial and legal advisers, and television entrepreneurs like Murdoch, to colonize the people's game. It is enough to point, first, to the forward march of class interests vis-à-vis those of command over the last generation (giving Murdoch and kin a telling advantage over government and the public-sector guardians of the BBC-ITV cartel), and, second, class habitus. It is not that significant players in the capitalist-executive are beyond or incapable of conspiracy, far from it (Scott, 1991), rather that the resurgence of class relations and a capitalist-executive habitus fully amenable to the logic of the regime of capital accumulation almost always render it unnecessary.

Notes on the Mediation of Sport

If the pivotal role of television in the colonization of English football is clear, there is much more that needs to be said about its dynamic new role in the 'representation' or 'mediation' of sport. It is congruent with the last section to suggest that in the 1990s in England the structural nexus of football and the working class has been strongly undermined.

> Football clubs and the police are less tolerant of expressive forms of support. Ground redevelopment has replaced the old terraces with more expensive, family-friendly stands. Those locked out must forfeit a hefty subscription fee to watch on television. Merchandizing and share issues mean that clubs pursue wealthier, national fan groups rather than satisfy local supporters. On the park, the local one-club heroes have become peripatetic national or international 'celebrities', drawn increasingly from affluent suburbs rather than poor housing estates. (Giulianotti, 1999: 147)

Concomitantly, the working class itself has undergone major structural changes in disorganized capitalism. De-industrialization and the rise of the service sector have led to a reduction in the industrial working class and an expansion in white-collar employment. What has variously been called the underclass, the new poor, or more precisely the displaced segment of the working class (Scambler and Higgs, 2001), has become sedimented at the base of the hierarchy of class. This displaced segment of the working class, together with the class strata 'just above', comprise those supporters most conspicuously excluded from football's 'brave new world'. Football's targeted audiences have increasingly become family groups, the first-generation middle classes and the young metropolitan elite; and these new constituencies have played an important part in the game's new fashionability from the 1990s (Giulianotti, 1999).

Most professional football is now consumed through television rather than *in situ*. Many fans never attend live matches, and even those who attend regularly also engage in what Sandvoss (2003: 137) terms 'extensive televisual consumption'. It is an opportune moment to reflect both on declining rates of participation in exercise and sport amongst younger people, arguably in favour of passive televisual fandom, and on the roots of this change in excessive system rationalization giving rise to further colonization of the lifeworld. At the beginning of the decade of the 1990s, if people wanted to watch sport on television they paid a licence fee and tuned in to four publicly regulated terrestial channels which together provided 2800 hours of sport a year. Ten years later, football alone received 5000 hours' coverage per annum, with total sports television output closer to 25,000 a year.

> You can watch sport on the five – substantially less regulated – terrestial channels or invest in a satellite or cable delivery system, pay various subscription fees and watch three additional all-sports channels aimed at a UK audience and a host of others carrying sport from around the globe. Most of the major sporting events you can watch live from the comfort of your armchair. For those willing to pay, there has never been a better time to be a television fan. (Boyle and Haynes, 2000: ix)

It is no less apparent that fans watching football on television do so 'in line with the cultural and social framing of televisual consumption' (Sandvoss, 2003: 138). In other words, football has come to meet the expectations and needs of an audience familiar with other forms of televisual entertainment. Football is in this respect home-centred and compatible with the rhythm of daily life, embodying an ongoing narrative and sense of drama not dissimilar to that of 'soaps', and is visually pleasing. It even allows for an erotic 'gaze' at competitors (referred to in the terminology of psychoanalytic film critique as 'scopophilic') (Sandvoss, 2003). Moreover, watching football on television is 'efficient': the fan does not have to travel, queue, pay for a seat or endure discomfort. Recalling McLuhan (1964), time and space have 'imploded' in fans' media-bound consumption.

One way of pulling these threads together is to say that the 1990s have witnessed a growing divide between unmediated and mediated football, and indeed sport. Now it is mediated football, and sport, that is 'authentic'. Television football privileges vision, which Baudrillard (1990) has characterized as the most time-efficient form of (inter-)action. The televised game has become one-dimensional. 'Television sport', Bale (1998: 273) observes,

> produces a landscape of sameness. Drawing on the writing of Virilio ... we can note the difference between spectating at a sports event and watching it on television (Virilio, 1991). At a football game no

two people see the same event (because no two people can occupy exactly the same place) whereas the game on television is exactly what the camera saw. Spectators see this wherever they sit. Television replaces the spectator.

Picking up on Bale's analysis, Sandvoss suggests that television football has led to the displacement of an individual perspective in a collective environment (the football stadium) by a collective perspective in an individual environment (the private home).

Baudrillard's (1983) notions of hyperreality and simulation are relevant here. Televisual football in the millennium has become so detailed and all-encompassing − 'with ever more varying shots, angles, positions and the fragmentation of time through replays and slow motions' − that a shift has occurred from representation to simulation, thereby 'eliminating the game as its actual referent': 'the game itself is defined by its own simulation, becoming its shadow rather than point of reference' (Sandvoss, 2003: 146). Sandvoss (2003: 147), to whom this analysis is indebted, sums up as follows: 'today the simulacra of television football rather than the actual *in situ* attendance of football constitute the point of reference to fans. To many fans television has become the "(hyper-)real thing".' It should be noted, however, not only that televisual football (the 'copy' as it were) takes on a 'life' of its own, but that there is resistance: the emergence of a few rich English super-clubs, for example, has led some fans to switch their allegiance to smaller, local teams in the lower divisions, *whose matches they actually attend.*

It was previously argued that the decline in participation in health-bestowing exercise and sport, especially in schools, and the emergence of professional, commercialized forms of sport conspicuously injurious to health, have their tap roots in a resurgence of relations of class in disorganized capitalism, legitimated, in the absence of any threat of a crisis of legitimation, by a (weakly globalized) power elite of the state rendered more deferential to a (strongly globalized) capitalist-executive. Those deemed responsible for enhanced rates of childhood obesity, however, were − deploying the Foucauldian notions of technologies of the self and governmentality, immured in the philosophy of the 'third way' of Clinton and Blair, or 'neo-liberalism Mark II' − the increasingly individualized parents of privatized families (see also Scambler, 2002). The analysis of changes in English football speak no less eloquently of excessive system rationalization and lifeworld colonization, once again with the subsystem of the economy, its logic of the regime of capital accumulation of disorganized capitalism and class relations as categorical.

As Sandvoss contends, fans attending (real) local matches in football stadia have typically been supplanted during the 1990s by fans of (hyper-real) televisual football. Hyperreal televisual football serves as a telling exemplar for our postmodern culture. This postmodern culture, as we have seen, is itself largely a product of disorganized capitalism (social structural analysis is needed to explain Baudrillard's hyperreal). The money of the capitalist–executive of the economic subsystem has held sway over the power of the state's elite, with the result that English football, never fully accountable to the 'people' of the 'people's game', has become further commodified/colonized, principally via the agency of 'greedy bastards' like Rupert Murdoch. The logical end-point of capitalism is the commodification of everything, and it is entirely consistent with this logic that English football supporters have been (re-)invented as consumers. But this is one piece of a complex jigsaw. As we shall see in the closing chapter, there are always other logics/relations/figurations.

Iconography from Ali to Beckham

It has already been intimated that a gap has opened up between the heroes of modern and postmodern culture. Ali, Lemert's (2003) trickster-celebrity, belongs to modern culture for all his unquestionably hard-won global and enduring stature, while Beckham is no less unambiguously the product of its postmodern successor. Michael Jordan and 'Gazza' occupy intermediate points. How and why is this? The 'how' has been more readily addressed by commentators, including sociologists, than the 'why'. Ali differs from Beckham in telling ways. What was distinctive about Ali was not that he won the light-heavyweight 'golden gloves' title in the USA in 1959, took the gold medal in the Rome Olympics of 1960, upset Sonny Liston and the bookies to capture the world heavyweight title in 1964, or even that he went on to recover himself to famously vanquish Foreman in 1974 (in the 'Rumble in the Jungle') and, in his last 'great fight', Frazier in 1975 in their rubber match (in the 'Thriller in Manila'). Love him or hate him, the charismatic Ali served up more than a spectacular and spectacularly hyped and mediated boxing career. In 1964 he had confirmed his association with the Nation of Islam and changed his name from Cassius Clay to Muhammad Ali. In 1966 he requested deferment from military service, claiming conscientious-objector status; denied this request he refused induction into the army, was indicted and had his boxing licence suspended. Only in 1970, when the US Supreme Court decreed conscientious-objector status allowable on religious grounds, was Ali able to return to boxing. He fought for the last time, losing to Berbick, in 1981, and in 1984 he was diagnosed with Parkinson's syndrome (which his doctors in 1987 attributed to his 61-match boxing career). Post-retirement, Ali has conducted a series of high-level humanitarian missions, incorporating meetings with national leaders including Castro. In 1999 numerous sporting bodies outside as well as inside the USA judged him the outstanding athlete of the twentieth century (Lemert, 2003).

Certainly, the relentless and astute marketing of Michael Jordan, the king of basketball players and endorsements alike, made that of Ali seem amateur (see Andrews, 2001; LaFeber, 2002). When he signed his endorsement deal with Nike in 1985 Jordan was already an Olympic gold medallist and had left the University of North Carolina in his third (junior) year to sign with the Chicago Bulls in an arrangement worth $3 million. This groundbreaking 'arrangement' gave Jordan a guaranteed income plus a percentage of every piece of endorsed clothing or pair of shoes sold. Cashmore (2002: 141) takes up the story:

> Not just products bearing his name, but all those in Nike's Air range. In the following year, Nike upped its advertising budget from $231 million to $281 million (almost 22%). It seemed like manic profligacy; but the sales justified it. The first year's sales of Nike's Air Jordan range hit $300 million. And, as if to underline the importance of Jordan's TV presence, sales dropped off in the second year, when Jordan missed sixty-two games through injury. Jordan was effectively advertising Nike every time he stepped on to the court.

According to Klein (2001: 52) in *No Logo*, 'it was Nike's commercials that made Jordan a global superstar', a metamorphosis worth more than the money they paid him. Jordan was synonymous with a brand. Jordan became a global icon through Nike, and Nike a market leader through Jordan.

If Ali is truly – as it were, ideal typically – representative of modern sport, Jordan is no less transparently the issue of postmodern sport. He is a natural product of disorganized capitalism. Yet David Beckham seems even more so. Why is this? It is true of course that Jordan plays basketball, of more fascination to Americans than to many others, while Beckham is an outstanding exponent of a sport, football, still claiming to be the people's game and undoubtedly the world game. But this is a far from sufficient condition for postmodern sporting iconography. Probably modern stars like George Best, as well as early 'experimental' postmodern stars like Paul Gascoigne, on whom the British tabloids sharpened their canines, paved the way for and made Beckham possible, as indeed did Eric Cantona. Cashmore's (2002) study is a shrewd if largely journalistic attempt to answer the question why Beckham's rise to postmodern superstardom is without parallel. The context of Beckham's rise is relevant.

Beckham played his first Premier League game for Manchester United in April 1995, a year before Gascoigne was controversially omitted from England's World Cup squad and two years before Cantona announced his retirement (and unusually – and unlike Ali and Jordan – kept his word). Cantona had proved the perfect vehicle for merchandising operations at what became the brand, 'ManU', even his departure providing ManU with good cover (Bose, 2001). In 1996, fully 27 per cent of those aged 7–19 across England who described themselves as football fans identified as ManU supporters (Cashmore, 2002: 47). By this time Beckham had won medals for the Premiership and the FA Cup (the double) and been selected to play for England.

Cashmore chronicles the rise of ManU through the 1990s under the stewardship of Martin Edwards, who replaced his father as chair in 1980, and the marketing guru, Edward Freedman. Focusing on their prompt realization that forging a winning brand requires the creation of emotional as well as instrumental bonds, so that the impress of United might be used to 'sell almost anything', he concludes:

> During Edwards' tenure, Manchester United came to represent about 30% of the net worth of the entire Premiership and almost one-fifth of the league's total turnover. Its annual profits were typically three times those of its nearest rival. Its salary bill was usually the biggest in the league, though, as a percentage of its turnover (usually £118m+), the smallest. In 2001/2 the club generated £24m from television, just £1m short of the total which the Football League's seventy-two clubs received from TV for the whole season and £10m more than the whole turnover of Premiership club Southampton. In two hours on any given match day, 15,000 people spend about £10,000 in the Manchester United megastore. The club has the largest membership of any British football club – 40 to 50 million worldwide – and a tour in Asia was watched by 200 million viewers. United made a revolutionary deal with the New York Yankees baseball team in 2001, forming a 'super-club' which can package itself to potential sponsors and TV networks and increase merchandise sales by stocking each other's souvenirs and kits. In terms of sponsorship, United has few peers: one deal alone, with Nike, is worth £230m to the club. (Cashmore 2002: 58–9)

In March 2004 Deloitte and Touche identified Manchester United as the richest sporting team in the world, worth £167.9 million in 2002–3, ahead of their 'partners', the Yankees, by £5 million. It is worth adding too that the *Sunday Times Rich List 2004* places Martin Edwards 356=, on £110 million, and David *and Victoria* Beckham 621=, on £65 million (Beresford and Boyd, 2004).

So clearly Beckham joined the right club and made his mark on the game at the right time. But so did others, Ryan Giggs for instance (himself worth an estimated £17 million). In fact Manchester United and other leading Premiership clubs have thrown up an assortment of meritocratic celebrities, such as Alan Shearer at Newcastle United and Michael Owen at Liverpool, but none has shone like Beckham. Pertinent but not decisive are Beckham's skills, notoriously his trade-mark free kicks, and his 'looks'. Of greater salience was his union with Victoria Adams, at the time a member of the Spice Girls. The Spice Girls were launched in 1996, and 'Posh' met 'Becks' in March 1997 when she attended a Manchester United versus Sheffield Wednesday game at Old Trafford as a VIP guest. The attraction, it transpired, was mutual. Moreover, she shared some of his traits; she was, in Burchill's (2001: 47) vivid prose, 'a lovely bit of state-of-the-art machinery hiding a rather lonesome, driven outsider'. 'Beckham's relationship with Adams soon became a narrative, a saga even; a predatory media monitored each episode and image, so that, individually, Posh and Becks – as they were dubbed – became quarry' (Cashmore, 2002: 23). It was a relationship that changed Beckham. Adams' – at the time, higher – status and celebrity were transferred to Beckham 'as if by osmosis'. Moreover, symbolically, their relationship brought together sport, and football at that, and the popular music and entertainment industries (Boyle and Haynes, 2000).

But these contextual factors, even in combination, seem less than decisive. Perhaps the key to understanding Beckham's popularity is the nature of the dialectic between the man and postmodern fandom. On the face of it, Beckham is missing any singular qualities, apart, that is, from his athletic skills. He has been described as decent, bland and uninteresting, opinionless and disengaged, lacking even the newsworthy vulgarity of a Gascoigne, and the very antithesis of a modern hero like Ali (although, as Burchill (2001) pointedly observes, it is unclear why athletes are required to be intellectuals when intellectuals are not required to be athletes). But is Beckham's 'weakness' his strength? Cashmore (2002: 155) again:

> Can we read Beckham like an open book? Or is he a book that's been slammed shut, fastened with one of those locks used to secure private diaries and hidden under a pillow? Sometimes he seems completely transparent. At other times he's positively inscrutable. That's part of the fascination of course: knowing yet not knowing for certain, reading yet never quite being sure whether you've figured out the right meaning.

Cashmore cites Gamson's thesis in *Claims to Fame* (1994) that we have all now become knowledgeable 'readers', with celebrities and the various stages on which they perform being 'texts' that can be encoded and decoded. Beckham can be all things to all people, or at least enough things to enough people to capture the popular imagination.

The mediated or hyper-real/hyper-commodified texts that are 'Beckham' can be read off a variety of *petit* narratives within the broad compass of the culture-ideology of consumerism reflective of disorganized capitalism. Wondrous or ludicrous though his personal 'earnings' may be, he makes far more for the far less visible greedy bastards who employ, fabricate and exploit 'their Beckham' as expeditious text. This worker/celebrity/ superstar remains for the time being a worker rather than a capitalist, for all his structural (re-)conditioning and enticing new placement, vested interests and opportunity costs. He is a worker who has become a *natural* ally of the capitalist-executive and new middles class. In precisely the same way, of course, elite black athletes are at once workers and have become *natural* allies of the *overwhelmingly white* capitalist-executive and new middle class; and elite female black athletes are workers and have become *natural* allies of the overwhelmingly white and *overwhelmingly masculine* capitalist-executive and new middle class. The structural tendency to weakness rather than freedom of will – conditioned by class, command, gender, ethnic and status relations – sets parameters for elite athletes' sense of what is *natural*. There is more than an echo of the early Marx here.

Back to David Beckham. Beckham, unlike Paul Gascoigne and most of his Premiership consociates, is a post-new-lad man.

> Growing up in an environment in which men's interest in fashion, style, narcissism and the possibility of being objectified have all been nurtured by a decade of the style press ... in a period in which sport and fashion have become more closely linked, in which footballers and pop stars gravitate to one another's glamour, and in which fame has itself become commodified, he is subsumed by his own image. His star persona has become the substance, the marketable object – all that is solid melts into air, or at least, into magazine pages ... Beckham appears rootless: he can be dressed as anything because surface appearance is all. (Whannel, 2001: 148; see also Whannel, 2002)

Cashmore paints a complementary picture and is again worth quoting at length:

> Beckham now captivates a fandom that includes young females who have no obvious interest in sport, gay men for whom Beckham has acquired almost fetishist properties (his hairstyle, accessories and clothes are assigned status as gay symbols), and working-class 'Lads' who proclaim their patriotism through their champion. (I am using the word *fandom* to mean a collective domain in which whole con-gregations of people devote parts of their life to following or just admiring an actor, a rock star, a sports team or virtually anything.) Whether we like it or not, we're all part of this fandom. We may not be consciously aware of it; we may openly despise the inordinate amount of coverage given to Beckham and others of his ilk. But, we watch TV, read newspapers, listen to the radio. We just can't help but be aware of him. We can't escape images of him, stories about him. He's become part of the contemporary cultural landscape. Should we be surprised that someone whose talent extends only as far as the touchlines of a football pitch has been recreated as a symbol of our times? Not really: Beckham is actually perfect for our times. He may be superficial, but who wants depth? He may give us only image, but who wants reality? He may even come across as a bit phony, but who wants authenticity?

Beckham, in short, is a paradigmatic – that is, an almost infinitely mar-ketable – (post-Diana) postmodern text: he is everything to everybody, a perfect malleable resource for the everyday *business* of identity-formation. He has been a multifaceted hero, villain-as-hero (after his sending off against Argentina during the World Cup in 1998), and rejuvenated multi-faceted hero; at the time of writing he retains his front-page tabloid status but is pressurized to re-invent himself as a hyper-commodity, with or without Victoria Adams' expertise, after lucrative accusations of (hyperreal, cell-phone as well as actual) infidelity levelled by the likes of Rebecca Loos (and others).

In Chapter 4, discussions of the alleged health-bestowing properties of exercise and sport, highly topical in light of new evidence of what some are describing as an epidemic of obesity, and of the increasingly injurious and dangerous side those elite professional sports involving contact or combat, were followed by analysis in terms of the logics of the regime of capital accumulation and its mode of regulation, and their respective relations of class and command, in disorganized capitalism. It was argued that this level of social structural analysis is required if sociological sense is to be made of changing behaviours and policies. Particularly salient is the recent reinvigoration of class relations. In Chapter 5 a preliminary case was made for an exacerbation of violence in sport, even for a de-civilizing spurt, over this same time period, again underpinned by the activities of the capitalist-executive, but nurtured by the culture-ideology of consumerism in its guise of postmodern culture. The reflections on the evolving nature of football in the present chapter have given further cause for highlighting aspects of the colonization and hyper-commodification of sport in disorganized capitalism. The seductive cultural power of mediated, even hyperreal, postmodern sporting iconography hides the less conspicuous but more telling economic power of a rapidly globalizing capitalist-executive bent on profit. In the third and final section of the book, the contributions of sociological theory to the understanding of modern sport are addressed more directly.

PART THREE

Social Theory and Sport

7

Sociological Perspectives on Sport

The narratives of three long moments in track-and-field athletic history rehearsed in the opening section, taking us from the ancient games in Greece and Rome, via the rationalization and bureaucratization of modern sport – Elias' 'sportization' – in eighteenth- and nineteenth-century England, to the reconstruction of the modern/postmodern (global*izing*) Olympic movement, were demonstrative of both continuity and change. On the one hand, competing to win a foot-race doubtless carries with it some of the same tensions and emotions independently of time or place. On the other hand, the victory of Koroibos of Elis in the short foot-race at the first Olympiad in 776 BC cannot be understood *in the same way* as even the 'equivalent' victory of Dionysios of Alexandria in the 262nd Olympiad in AD 269, let alone the wins in the 100 metres of Harold Abrahams in Paris in 1924, Jesse Owens in Berlin in 1936 or Maurice Green in Sydney in 2000.

Selected issues in modern or contemporary sport were addressed in Part Two, during which a number of theoretical standpoints and theses were also introduced. The object of Part Three is to systematically review extant theories in the sociology of sport and, drawing on both this material and that in the two previous parts, to promulgate a distinctive perspective and agenda oriented to future contributions. In Chapter 7 summaries, illustrations and provisional evaluations are offered of the principal paradigms within which sociological theorizing about sport has taken place. And in the final chapter the case is made for new initiatives drawing not only on contributions from within these paradigms but also and more specifically on contemporary critical realism and critical theory.

Sociology remains obstinately multi-paradigmatic, although even Kuhn was unsure whether this indicates its independence or its immaturity in relation to the natural sciences. At different times most of its paradigms have provided resources for the theorization of sport. It has been suggested that these paradigms have tended to gravitate towards one or other of Dawe's (1970) 'two sociologies', that is, emphasizing *either* structure ('man on his back') *or* agency ('man fighting back') (Gouldner, 1975); and this can provide a plausible basis for examining their contributions (see Donnelly, 2003). It will serve us better here, however, to adopt a more conventional course and offer a brief critical commentary on six discrete paradigms or perspectives: functionalism, conflict theory, interpretive sociology, feminism, figurational sociology and post-structuralism/postmodernism.

Functionalism

Functionalism has been the most serious contender yet for the status of dominant paradigm or circumscriber of 'normal science' in sociology. Its roots can be traced back to Comte in the early nineteenth century. Durkheim's corpus too is frequently subsumed under the umbrella term of functionalism. Several writers on sport have adopted a Durkheimian perspective to claim that sport can best be understood as a symbolic representation of community and personal identity. Sport can evoke a sense of the 'sacred' and sports teams be created or adopted as 'totems'. Indeed, for some people teams can become concrete symbols of their 'insider' identities. Ashworth (1971) is another who emphasized that sport partakes of the sacred, cut off in time and space from the 'profane' business of everyday life. Jarvie and Maguire (1994: 20) elaborate:

> There are ... many rituals and taboos that surround sport. The opening and closing ceremonies, the medal and award ceremonies, the ritual shaking of hands or bowing towards your opponent, the uniforms, symbols of excellence and trophy rooms celebrating past victories and heroes/heroines all point to the sacredness of sport.

For some Durkheimians then, the rituals and taboos that structure sporting activities both 'reveal' society and the social order to the individual, and shape the individual's narrative of past, present and future.

Functionalism's heyday, however, occurred in the USA in the 1940s and 1950s. It is ironic therefore that it gained its main purchase in the sociology of sport in the 1960s and 1970s, a period of relative decline for functionalism's chief exponents. Loy and Booth (2000) make the general point that 'holist' approaches to the study of society date back well beyond the likes of Comte and Durkheim to the era of the ancient games at Olympia, but it is of course the structural-functionalism associated with the likes of Parsons and Merton that precipitated most modern analyses of sporting activity. Demerath (1967: 506) distinguishes usefully between the structural and the functional within structural-functionalism: 'on the one hand, it is possible to concentrate on the "part", using the "whole" as a kind of backboard off which to bounce effects and consequences. On the other hand, one can concentrate on the whole itself. Here the various parts are constituent elements and only really interesting as they contribute to the entirety.' Merton's approach might be said to reflect the first (structural) element, Parsons the second (functional) element. It is expedient to focus here on selected aspects of Parsons' highly formal and system-oriented brand of functionalism, most specifically his 'general theory of action'.

Each human *action system*, Parsons argued, must confront and respond to four challenges, namely, adaptation (A), goal-attainment (G), integration (I) and latency (or pattern-maintenance) (L). These challenges, denoted by the acronym AGIL, constitute the 'functional prerequisites' or 'functional imperatives' of action systems. Each action system must:

1) adapt to its environment (A);
2) have a means of mobilizing its resources in order to achieve its goals and obtain gratification (G);
3) maintain the internal coordination of its parts and develop ways of dealing with deviance (I);
4) maintain itself as nearly as possible in a state of equilibrium (L).

All action systems are comprised of four primary *action subsystems*, namely, the *behavioural organism, personality, social system* and *culture* (Parsons, 1966). The action subsystem of the behavioural organism is *specialized* around adaptation; that of personality around goal-attainment; that of social system around integration; and that of culture around latency or pattern maintenance. Another level of complexity is introduced since Parsons contended also that each action subsystem can itself be analysed in terms of the four functions of A, G, I and L. Take the social system, for example. Specific institutional spheres can be said to serve particular functions: the economy is primarily related to adaptation, the polity to goal-attainment, socializing institutions to integration and the community to pattern maintenance. Finally, for present purposes, Parsons held that interaction between the four primary action subsystems relies on a constant exchange of *energy* and *information*. In terms of energy, for example, the behavioural organism supplies the energy required for personality; personality provides the energy for the social system; and the fact that energy flows from personality to the social system allows for the development of culture. And in terms of information, to pick up on a linked example, culture controls the social system, the social system regulates personality, and personality governs the behavioural organism (Loy and Booth, 2000).

How has Parsons' framework, précised or edited in this stark fashion, underwritten sociological analyses of sport? There have in fact been relatively few discrete substantive applications of his framework to sport (Kenyon, 1986). Heinila (1960) is one of a handful to utilize the AGIL scheme in his portrayal of football as a social system. He claimed that the rules of the game fit in with Parsons' functional prerequisites or imperatives neatly enough: training rules serve an adaptive function; the technical rules of football promote goal-attainment; rules of refereeing assist integration; and rules of competition and eligibility meet the requirement of latency or pattern maintenance. Heinila's micro-functionalist study is one of a small cluster to highlight sport groups as social systems.

More significant than individual studies like Heinila's, arguably, is the fact that 'functionalism's holistic approach helped direct early sport sociologists to consider sport as a social institution and to look more closely at sport as a reflection of the total society and its complex relationships with other institutions' (Loy and Booth, 2000: 14). A pioneer in this more general sense was Luschen. In an early paper he outlined the functions and dysfunctions of sport and speculated about evolutionary change. Recalling some of the material in Chapter 1, his principal thesis was that in preliterate cultures sport's function was universal, typically religious, collectivity-oriented, and as far as training and preparation were concerned representative and pertinent to skills for warfare. Modern sport's function, by contrast, is specific for pattern maintenance and integration (Luschen, 1967: 139). Drawing loosely on Luschen's work, Stevenson and Nixon (1972; Stevenson, 1974) discerned five basic functions of modern sport: (1) a socio-emotional function, with sport contributing to the maintenance of socio-psychological stability; (2) socialization, with sport aiding the transmission of cultural beliefs and norms; (3) an integrative function, with sport facilitating the harmonious integration of disparate individuals and groups; (4) a political function, with sport serving ideological needs; and (5) a social mobility function, with sport acting as a source of upward mobility.

Studies such as those of Heinila, Luschen and Stevenson and Nixon betray different levels of indebtedness to Parsonian functionalism. Each too is susceptible to critiques commonly mounted against functionalist projects in sociology. Loy and Booth (2000) collate and assess these critiques under the rubrics of *contemporary bias, consensus bias* and *conservative bias*. The charge of contemporary bias refers to functionalism's alleged ahistorical or non-historical character. It not only fails to account for social change but precludes the very possibility of such an account. The accusation of consensus bias is no less familiar. The basis of this objection is that functionalism both overemphasizes the salience of shared norms and values and exaggerates the 'unity, stability and harmony of social systems' (Zeitlin, 1973: 15). Thus insufficient allowance is made either for social conflict *per se*, paradigmatically between superordinate and subordinate interest groups, or for the role of social conflict in – often irregular or disorderly – social change. The charge of conservative bias focuses on functionalism's stress on structure at the expense of agency. Ritzer (2003), for example, contends that functionalism not only neglects history, conflict and social change, but is deeply oriented to how systems are perpetuated and defines actors as passive dupes of social structures.

Loy and Booth show irritation at these insinuations of bias. They point out in response to the charge of contemporary bias, for example, that Durkheim's functionalism was certainly historical and that Parsons was himself concerned with 'social evolution' among Western societies. Heinila (1969), they add, also deployed Parsons' AGIL to describe the different norms and rules apparent through the transition from amateurism to professionalism in soccer. Reacting to the charges of consensus bias and conservative bias, they likewise find them simplistic and unfairly dismissive, citing later attempts by functionalists to revise and move on from the framework set out by Parsons more than a generation ago. They rightly note the continuing influence of functionalist thinking, first, on mainstream writers such as Luhmann and Habermas as well as American neofunctionalists such as Alexander; and second, if more covertly, on sociologists interested in sport, including a number of conflict theorists and Elias and his network of figurational sociologists.

In truth, all three accusations of bias hold some weight. There is a strong case, however, for revisiting and reappraising Parsonian functionalism rather than, as has tended to occur since the 1960s, abandoning it wholesale. For present purposes, two general comments are indicated. First, the argument in Chapter 8 will be premised on the view that too little emphasis in both the parent discipline and in the sociology of sport has concerned the significance of social structure for how and why people think and behave the way they do. The in-depth examination of social structure is indebted to the functionalist paradigm, if as much to Merton's (1957) structuralist as to Parsons' functionalist input to American structural-functionalism. And second, notwithstanding this commitment to the explication and analysis of social structure, it will not do to neglect agency. Donnelly (2003: 19–20) observes that Parsonian functionalism in particular is often judged to 'flip-flop between agency and structure'. What is required of course is a *synthesis* of agency and structure, and this too will be attempted in the next chapter.

Conflict Theory

It has been conflict theorists who have most regularly and persistently laid the charge of consensus bias against the functionalists. However, space again compels succinct treatment of an expansive and heterogeneous body of work. Brief selective consideration will be given to the pioneering classical works of Marx, after which a preliminary exposition and assessment will be offered of neo–Marxist interpretations of sport. I shall focus here on Marx's sense of human potential and the concept of 'alienation'; his analysis of the capitalist mode of production, incorporating the distinction between 'base' and 'superstructure'; and his development of an 'historical materialist' scientific methodology.

It is difficult to grasp Marx's notion of alienation without first understanding how he conceptualized human potential. Humans, unlike other species, are endowed with consciousness and a facility to link consciousness to action. In premodern and modern societies alike, human action has necessarily incorporated acting on nature to appropriate from it that which is required – by way of raw materials such as water, food and shelter – to survive. People have always needed to work or 'labour', and labour for

Marx is a positive process. However, if people are to achieve their potential there must be a 'natural interconnection' between people and (1) their productive activities, (2) the products of their labour, (3) their fellow workers, and (4) what they are potentially capable of becoming (Ritzer, 2003: 21). Alienation has arisen with the breakdown of these 'natural interconnections' in, successively, liberal, organized and disorganized capitalism.

Under capitalism, work or labour is transmuted into wage-labour. Jarvie and Maguire (1994: 92) conveniently express Marx's core theses on modern capitalism in terms of the sport and leisure industry:

> Within the capitalist labour process the means of production, teams, cartels, leisure organizations, are purchased in the market by the capitalist. So too is labour power. The athletes, the teams, the music star, and the box-office film hero/heroine perform the work under the supervision of the capitalist with the product of that labour remaining the property of the owner of the means of production. The purpose of the capitalist labour process is to produce profit, or at least produce commodities whose value exceeds the sum of the values of labour power and the means of production consumed in the process of production.

I noted earlier the nature of the relationship between those labourers qualifying as sporting stars/celebrities, such as David Beckham, and the representatives of the 'capitalist-executive' who either directly or indirectly pay their wages.

Capitalism, in short, automatically generates a conflict between the 'masters of production' – that is, capitalists or owners of the means of production – and the 'direct producers' – that is, workers or owners of labour power. These two groups can be understood as 'classes' competing for power even as the capitalists exploit the wage-labourers economically, paying them wages less than the economic values produced, and suppress them politically. For Marx, the base refers to economic activities and relations, and the superstructure to all extra-economic social and cultural forms. Moreover,

> from a Marxist perspective it is the economy which has determining effects on the superstructure. One key function of the superstructure is to act as a framework for ideologies that justify and stabilize the modes of production and consumption under capitalism. Due to the dependence of the superstructure on the base there will, eventually, be a relationship of total correspondence between them. Consequently, the superstructure reproduces the key ideologies of the capitalist system and reinforces the social realization of the latter. (Rigauer, 2000: 31)

Marx recognized the relative autonomy of cultural processes but insisted nevertheless that its *de facto* exercise is rare.

Materialism, for Marx, posits a distinctive methodological approach to empirical phenomena. It is materialism that informs his theory of societal development focused on the interdependencies between the economic relations comprising the base and the cultural processes and practices comprising the superstructure. Humans may exercise agency, but they can do so only within the prevailing forms of production and interdependency – that is, structures – that potently shape their biographies. It is of the essence of the historical materialism that Marx espoused that the scientific method be deployed to study ('abstract') structures such as those of class in order to explain the 'concrete realities of social life' (Rigauer, 2000: 33). Marx can reasonably be deemed a precursor of the critical realism fashioned by Bhaskar (1978, 1989), which I will put to strenuous use in Chapter 8.

Of course, this snatch of exposition does no justice to Marx's work. Neither can I give more than a flavour of Marxist analyses of sport. Horne and colleagues (1999: 269) distinguish between early attempts to apply Marx's theories – 'interesting and provocative, whilst also being somewhat one-dimensional and prone to a crude reductionism' – and more sophisticated recent efforts. Brohm's influential *Sport: A Prison of Measured Time* (1978) is slotted by the authors into the first of these categories. Brohm argued, in general, that modern sport can only be understood socially as an expression of the interests of imperialist capital (witness, he says, the Olympic Games); and, in particular, that sport is governed by the principles of competition and by the exact measurement of space, time and output.

> For Brohm, sport is the rational organization of human output, and in a most useful formulation he calls sport the Taylorization of the body; in other words the scientific means for producing maximum output from the human body. This gives him a means of applying the principle of labour power and surplus value to athletic performance. (Horne et al., 1999: 269; see also Brohm's paper published in *Quel Corps?* in 1975 and included in his book)

For Brohm, as for many orthodox Marxists, sport is allied to work. Rigauer argues in similar vein in his *Sport and Work* (1981). He offers his own summary in a later piece:

> [u]nder conditions of industrial capitalism sport as an integral part of the superstructure (culture, ideology) reproduces features of social behaviour that are functionally and normatively ingrained in capitalistically organized processes of working, marketing, rationalization, scientification, communication and socialization. All these social processes are reduced in sport to the quantitative principle of 'ideal' and 'material surplus value' (reification, alienation). On the one hand, the central ideological function of sport consists of transposing its base-related (economic) superstructural relation and interdependence into societal practice. On the other hand, it also has to blur this very structural correspondence ideologically in a way that allows the idea

of sport as a socially autonomous area to be maintained. The main purpose of a Marxist sociology of sport should be to explain the real societal functions of sport with the help of critical analysis focused on culture and ideology. (Rigauer, 2000: 41–2)

A more contemporary volume regarded by Horne and his co-authors as 'sophisticated' is Hargreaves *Sport, Power and Culture* (1986). One of Hargreaves' take-off points – and why his contribution is sometimes seen as part of cultural studies (Hargreaves and McDonald, 2000) – is Gramsci's analysis of *hegemony*. Gramsci was less than enamoured with the distinction between base and superstructure and its implicit determinism. What we have referred to as the capitalist-executive and the new and old middles classes may have material, political and cultural advantages – for example, wealth, information and a capacity to 'set' norms and values – over the working class, secured in the course of processes of production and reproduction; but the working class is also able to translate its material, political and cultural aims into action via its own organizations (e.g. parties and trade unions). Hegemonies can be built by and for more than one class. The superstructure can influence the base as well as the base the superstructure.

Like Gruneau (1983, 1993), Hargreaves applies hegemony theory to sport. The relation between sport and capital, he suggests, can assume different forms and he goes on to delineate five. First, there is profit maximizing, as in professional boxing or horse racing. Many sports, however, cannot realize a profit. Thus a second relation between sport and capital occurs when sports attempt only to remain financially viable, adopting strategies such as local fund raising. Third, sport can stimulate the accumulation of capital indirectly, as when it creates a market for goods and services such as equipment, clothing and gambling. Fourth, sport can also assist capital accumulation indirectly by affording opportunities for advertising and sponsorship. And finally, sport can draw in investment for non-economic reasons, as when directors of soccer clubs pursue prestige, local credibility or facilities for corporate entertainment. Often, of course, economic and non-economic motives overlap and two or more of Hargreaves' five relations between sport and capital can obtain simultaneously, as was apparent in the discussion of English football in Chapter 6 (see Horne et al., 1999: 270).

In Chapter 2, I documented the emergence of a bourgeois hegemony in Victorian England, leading to an ideology of the gentleman amateur that reflected and sustained a masculine ruling-class unity. Epitomizing Hargreaves' analysis, Horne and colleagues (1999: 270) write:

> The growth of spectator sport and a demand for sport as entertainment, fuelled by the greater disposable income and free time workers had in the latter part of the century, provided an impetus for the development of professionalism, and a threat to the amateur-gentleman hegemony. Gentlemanly amateurism saved itself by conceding

fresh ground, restricting the effects of commercialism and retaining control.

In fact, resistance to 'rational recreation' varied and some 'working men's sports', such as football, broke these 'shackles' far more rapidly and decisively than did track-and-field athletics.

How then, according to Hargreaves, did commercial or capital-oriented sport insinuate itself into the national culture? His argument breaks down into four components. First, without the 'cult of athleticism' there would be no organized sport. Second, without rational recreation and missionary endeavours on behalf of athletic activity organized sport would not have penetrated and partially 'colonized' working-class culture. Third, without the popularity of sport in some subcultures, and their shift into some amateur-gentleman controlled sports, the commercial flowering of sport could not have taken place. And fourth, without so-called 'mass sport', the political elite would not have had this 'field' for articulating the 'national interest' (Horne et al., 1999: 270).

Although conflict theory is far from synonymous with Marxism, it is the Marxist strand that has been most telling. Familiar criticisms are that Marxism places too much emphasis on economic forces; assumes that capitalists shape sport in line with their interests; and denies sport the potential to yield genuinely creative and liberating experiences (Coakley, 2001). There is some substance to each of these. It might additionally be objected that Marxism tends to stress the significance of work at the expense of *interaction*, a criticism levelled most insistently by Habermas (1986). Certainly in early accounts some Marxist commentators presented sport crudely as simply mirroring capitalist relations. However, Gruneau, Hargreaves, the neo-Marxist critical theorists from the early and late Frankfurt School, and related theorists like Bourdieu, are less easily dismissed (for an overview, see Morgan, 1994).

Interpretive Sociology

Functionalism has long been associated with the elucidation of structure at the expense of agency, notwithstanding Parsons' early determination to supply a theory of action. Conflict theory too, whether in Marxist or other guise, has been linked with structure more than agency. Interpretive sociology, on the other hand, seems ineluctably wedded to agency. It has its origins in the thought of Weber rather than Marx or Durkheim, let alone Parsons or Merton. Rooted in the neo-Kantian philosophy of Rickert, the aim of sociology for Weber was to accomplish an *interpretive understanding* of subjectively meaningful human action that exposed the actors' motives, at one level the 'causes' of actions, to open view. Action is *social* if the subjective meaning attached to it by the actor takes account of the behaviour of others and is thereby 'oriented in its course'. There is clear continuity between Weber and Schutz, whose labours to refine the

Weberian project – introducing, for example, a distinction between 'because' and 'in order to' motives – culminated in his phenomenological sociology. In his discussion of interpretive perspectives on sport, Donnelly (2000) includes other 'sociologies of everyday life' beside phenomenological – and its offshoot existential – sociology under the rubric of 'interpretive sociology'. On the grounds that they too (1) treat interpretation as problematic and (2) go beyond actors' own understanding of what they are doing, he lists symbolic interactionism, Goffman's dramaturgical sociology, labelling theory, ethnomethodology and hermeneutics as interpretive sociologies. For good measure Grant and Jarvie (1994) add Simmel to this list. It will not be possible to do any kind of justice here to an interpretive paradigm defined as comprehensively as this. Rather, we shall concentrate on a handful of sport studies deploying Weberian and later more sophisticated frames after the manner of Geertz's (1973) 'thick description'.

Extensive reference was made in Chapter 1 to Guttman's characterization of ancient versus modern sport in his overtly Weberian *From Ritual to Record* (1978). In his conclusion he asserts that:

> one of the great advantages of the Weberian model is that it enables one to see in the microcosm (modern sports) the characteristics of the macrocosm (modern society) – secularism, equality, specialization, rationalism, bureaucratic organization, and quantification. These six characteristics, plus the quest for records which appear even more strikingly in modern sports than in the rest of the social order, are interdependent, systematically related elements of the ideal type of modern society. They derive from the fundamental Weberian notion of the difference between the ascribed status of traditional society and the achieved status of a modern one. (Guttman, 1978: 80–1)

Sporting activities, Guttman (1978: 89) recognizes, originate in the 'spontaneous expression of physical energy' and have their source in 'the irrational'. 'Sports are an alternative to and, simultaneously, a reflection of the modern age. They have their roots in the dark soil of our instinctive lives, but the form they take is that dictated by modern society.' Modern sport is to be understood neither as a product of industrial capitalism, as in early Marxist accounts, nor indeed as a belated expression of the 'Protestant Ethic', but rather as 'the slow development of an empirical, experimental, mathematical *Weltanschauung*' (Guttman, 1978: 85).

For all the inclusiveness of Donnelly's delineation of interpretive sociology, he rightly acknowledges that post-Weberian interpretive studies on sport published between the 1960s and 1980s owed most to symbolic interactionism and Goffman's dramaturgical sociology. Since then, however, the influence of cultural studies has been strong. Two themes, he suggests, have prevailed: *sport subcultures* and *socialization*. Initially, the concept of 'career' – examinations of non-deviant, including sporting, careers being natural successors to pioneering examinations of deviant careers – was pivotal for studies of sport subcultures, for example in Stone's (1972; Stone and Oldenberg, 1967) research on wrestling, Scott's (1968) on horse racing, Polsky's on pool hustlers, and Faulkner's (1974) on hockey players. Sporting careers, of course, are frequently abbreviated: a competitive swimmer active at 6 may retire at 14 and never be in receipt of any 'earnings'. Female athletes such as swimmers and gymnasts may be exceptional, but Ohlsson's study of professional Welsh rugby players shows that careers can compress *development, professional, establishment, maximization* and *pre-retirement* phases into little more than a decade, and all this against the background of a strong and immanent possibility of career termination through injury (Scambler et al., 2004).

Gradually the idea of career was displaced in the sociology of sport subcultures by an emphasis on thick description, on rich and textured representations of social contexts. By the 1980s too, British subcultural theory was beginning to develop a more radical or critical edge. Subcultures were seen not only as meaningful for their participants but as either 'establishment' or 'countercultural' in orientation or effect, as 'constitutively inserted into the struggles, the forms of compliance and opposition, social reproduction and transformation, associated with changing patterns of social development' (Gruneau, 1981: 10). Among the best-known products of this shift are the studies of British soccer hooligans by Williams and his colleagues (1989) and Giulianotti (1995a, 1995b), a topic that was considered in detail in Chapter 5, and a series of French studies inspired by Bourdieu, including Wacquant's (1992, 1995) on boxing.

The second major object of attention for interpretive sociology has been socialization and sport. The processes involved in 'becoming an athlete and becoming an adult person' were addressed in part by subcultural theorists, including those utilizing the notion of sporting careers (Donnelly, 2000: 84). A second phase of studies, however, moved on to document sport's potential, for example, to either re-enforce or counter conventional stereotypical notions of gender. Coakley and White (1992) threw light on how English teenagers decided to continue or halt participation in post-school sport, and Thompson (1992) showed how the involvement of fathers and children in tennis impacted on the lives of wives/mothers. The topic of socialization and sport has been broached too through 'narrative sociology', most commonly using case study and life history techniques.

According to Donnelly (2000: 85), some commentators now regard the interpretive paradigm as predominant within the sociology of sport, and he cites in defence of this claim the fact that all the Presidential Addresses given at the annual conferences of the North American Society for the Sociology of Sport in the 1990s reflected an interpretive approach. Setting aside the inclusiveness of Donnelly's definition of interpretive sociology, and possibly also an American predisposition to extrapolate too readily from putative US to worldwide trends, it is fair to say that the interpretive paradigm has been reinvigorated. Among the benefits has been the flesh it has put on the skeletons of other more structurally oriented perspectives. In its post-Weberian guises, however, it has typically neglected the structural antecedents of the sporting biographies, activities and contexts it has on occasions brought so vividly to life.

Feminism

Feminism for present purposes may be seen as

> a dynamic, continually evolving complex of theories or theoretical traditions that take as their point of departure the analysis of gender as a category of experience in society ... Whatever the sources, what-ever the mix of voices privileged by a particular scholar, feminist theory within the sociology of sport has as its main purpose to the-orize about gender relations within our patriarchal society as they are evidenced by, played out in, and reproduced through sport and other body practices. (Birrell, 2000: 61)

There is a general consensus that feminist theories of sport did not appear in print until around 1980 (Messner and Sabo, 1990). Since then, however, interest has grown apace.

Scraton and Flintoff (2002: 32) analyse feminist theories, which they go on to apply to sport, as 'founded upon' (a) liberal democratic beliefs (*liberal feminism*), (b) structural power relations (*radical feminism, socialist feminism*) and (c) post-structuralist notions of difference and power as plural and productive (*black feminism, post-structural feminism*). The focus of liberal feminism is on equality of access and opportunity. Rejecting biological explanations for women's subordination in sport, liberal feminists see gender as socially constructed and challenge prevailing patterns of sociali-zation and sex-role differentiation. Sport itself has typically not been defined as problematic, thus the emphasis has been on women gaining access to the same opportunities as men. Missing, in other words, is an account of the significance of the underpinning structures of society.

Radical feminism emerged from the radical politics of the 1960s and 1970s. Seeking to make good the neglect of social structure implicit in liberal feminism, the point of departure of radical feminist analyses was the structural power relations resulting from the systematic maintenance of male power through patriarchy, whereby men dominate women 'as a group'. This prompted an analysis of compulsive heterosexuality and les-bian feminism (extended by pro-feminist writers to a discussion of the position of gay men in sport). While liberal feminists argue that women have unequal access to decision-making positions, radical feminists are more interested in how men's power over women was maintained through sport. In the words of Scraton and Flintoff (2002: 34–5):

> Central to men's domination over women is how men's sexuality functions to control women in their work, sport, leisure and schooling. This control operates in both the private and public spheres

and benefits all men regardless of their desires and objectives. Radical feminists working in sport have been interested in the role of sport in the social construction of male sexual dominance and female sexual submission ... Femininity should be viewed as a code name for heterosexuality.

The force of this contention is perhaps most apparent in the sports clothing often 'required' of women competitors. A notorious example is the statement in the rules governing international women's beach volleyball that bikini bottoms must not have a side deeper than 6 cm. Self-evidently this is about the objectification of women's bodies (see Hargreaves, 1993). Increasingly too the ties between men, sport and *violence* have been explored (see again Chapter 5). Marxist feminists define gender inequalities as a product of capitalism, class relations and exploitation. Socialist feminists typically balk at what they see as this economic determinism: for them, women's 'oppression' cannot be reduced to class relations and the sexual division of labour. It is the complex motley of interrelationships between capitalism and patriarchal power relations that interests them. Research in sport has made use of notions like Cornell's (1987) 'hegemonic masculinity'. In this vein Messner (1992) has examined the historical construction of masculinity and muscularity through sport, assessing how it is that men both enjoy privileges and cement their hegemony through sport.

Scraton and Flintoff hesitate before linking black feminism with the post-structural feminisms, partly because black feminists' resistance to dominant white feminist theorizing dates back at least to feminism's second wave. Their rationale for the linkage is black feminists' emphasis on differences between women, black identities and subjectivities, all major themes in postmodern culture. Even contemporary discourse about women and sport is largely ethnocentric and betrays a 'gendered lens' (Dworkin and Messner, 2001). Writings on race, ethnicity and sport, on the other hand, frequently neglect gender relations. Carrington (2001) is an exception that proves the rule: his investigation of race, racism and cricket in the UK leads him to recognize not only that sport can be a site of black cultural resistance to racism, but that this is black *male* resistance, often itself dependent on gendered power relations. Post-structural feminists

> reject the view that it is a lack of equal access or opportunity (liberal), patriarchy (radical), capitalism (Marxist) or a combination of patriarchy and capitalism (socialist) that explains women's oppression. Rather they focus on difference and diversity and argue that the very term 'women' has little significance in the fragmented and changing world we live in today ... Sport has been analyzed in relation to its role in the maintenance of binary oppositions such as man/woman; heterosexual/homosexual; white/other; healthy/sick, and also for its potential to transgress gender, and deconstruct these binaries. (Scraton and Flintoff, 2002: 40; see Caudwell, 1999)

These are themes I shall consider below, in the final section of the chapter.

It is axiomatic that feminist sociologies of sport ask questions largely left unasked by advocates of the other paradigms we have so far commented on. They have varied in their allegiances to agency and structure. Birrell (2000) detects two trends pertinent to the future. The first anticipates a move towards synthetic theories drawing on the insights of feminist work as 'one thread to weave into more complex theories of power and the interrelationships of gender, race and class' (Birrell, 2000: 71). The second involves a traversing of disciplinary boundaries in response to post-struc-turalist innovation. There are gains to be had from both, but the con-cluding arguments of Chapter 8 might reasonably be said to illustrate the former rather than the latter.

Figurational Sociology

Figurational sociology, encountered in earlier chapters, is associated with the innovative theorizing of Norbert Elias and his Leicester disciples. The notion of figurations was developed by Elias to help overcome the long-standing proposition that 'individual' and 'society' refer to independently existing objects. Rather, sociology is concerned with *homo aperti*, that is, with people bonded together in dynamic constellations.

> The network of interdependencies among human beings is what binds them together. Such dependencies are the nexus of ... the figuration, a structure of mutually oriented and dependent people. Since people are more or less dependent on each other first by nature and then through social learning, through education, socialization, and socially generated reciprocal needs, they exist ... only as plural-ities, only in figurations. (Elias, 1978: 261)

Sociologists should think 'processually' by studying social relations as emerging and contingent processes. Against Marxists, Elias insisted that the importance of economic relations tends to vary from one situation to another. Power, moreover, always involves relative balances that are dynamic and constantly in flux (Murphy et al., 2000).

As we have seen, Elias (1978a, 1982) is most celebrated for his analysis of the 'civilizing process', his central thesis being that Western Europe between the Middle Ages and the early years of the twentieth century witnessed a refinement of social manners and standards, as well as a new social pressure on individuals to exercise self-control over their feelings and behaviour. External constraint gave ground to self-constraint and 'con-science' became a more important regulator of behaviour: '... social standards came to be internalized more deeply and to operate, not only consciously, but also beneath the level of rationality and conscious control, for example by means of the arousal of feelings of shame, guilt and anxiety' (Murphy et al., 2000: 93). Importantly for present purposes, people's 'threshold of repugnance' regarding direct and symbolic manifestations of physical violence has lowered; and relatedly, people have internalized a stricter taboo on violence than in former times. In fact, violence now is routinely associated with psychopathology.

This civilizing process in Western Europe should not be seen as planned but as the unforeseen outcome of violent 'hegemonial' or 'elimination' struggles between monarchs and feudal lords. Rather than being straightforward antitheses, civilization and violence are characterized by specific forms of interdependence. Civilizing processes are associated with

> the lengthening of interdependency chains (in more conventional sociological language, the growth in the division of labour); the growing monetarization of social relationships; functional democratization (the gradual historical tendency towards more equal – though not wholly equal – power balances between different groups and subgroups in society); and lastly, the decreasing privatization of the force and tax monopolies and their increasing public control. (Murphy et al., 2000: 94)

Sociological activity, like almost all other human activity, is a balance of emotional involvement and detachment (Elias, 1987). Sociologists are not *either* objective *or* subjective, rather it is a matter of degree. 'The problem for sociologists ... is not how to be completely detached, for that is impossible, but rather how to maintain an appropriate balance between being an everyday participant and a scientific enquirer and, as a professional group, to establish in their work the undisputed dominance of the latter' (Murphy et al., 2000: 94). Moreover, they can only aspire to explanations with greater 'object-adequacy' or, latterly, 'reality-congruence', than preceding explanations.

The application of figurational sociology to sport is now quite extensive (Dunning, 2002). It was noted in passing in Chapter 2 that for Elias a two-wave process of 'sportization' – that is, the ever more efficient application of the rules associated with modern sport – got underway in eighteenth-century England. Why England, and at this juncture? Elias emphasizes differences between various European societies in, first, processes of state formation and, second, balances of power between ruling groups. For example, while Germany and Italy remained substantially disunited until well into the nineteenth century, France and England were united by the close of the seventeenth century. France, however, was highly centralized, its people subject to a form of 'absolute rule', while the English Civil War in the seventeenth century had restricted the power of its monarchy, effective government being shared by the monarch and the landed classes through the medium of Parliament. According to Elias, the sportization of pastimes occurred simultaneously with the 'parliamentarization of political conflict'. The more civilized habits developed by the aristocracy and gentry for governing were translated into the organization of less violent, more civilized forms of enjoyment (Murphy et al., 2000; see Elias and Dunning, 1986).

One early and paradigmatic study to emerge out of Elias's figurational approach was Dunning and Sheard's *Barbarians, Gentlemen and Players* (1979), an account of the salience of the English public schools for the second-wave sportization of the nineteenth century. Their relative autonomy from the state 'facilitated competition among and innovation within the public schools' which, according to the authors, was 'one precondition for the sportization of football and the emergence of soccer and rugby as modern sports' (Murphy et al., 2000: 96). Dunning (2002) himself summarizes the argument from this point. The cult of the public schools, he and Sheard argued, represented an early stage in the growing socio-cultural and political significance of sport. Sport was becoming a secular, non-theological 'religion', in a Durkheimian sense. Subsequent processes of commercialization and professionalization led inexorably to the institutionalization of sport as a 'serious' phenomenon.

No longer 'fun', at high performance levels at least, sport underwent processes of 'de-amateurization'. This was not just a consequence of the capitalist mode of production, as Marxists have stressed, but also of what Elias (1978) termed 'functional democratization', namely, 'the reciprocal pressures and controls to which people become increasingly subject as chains of inter-dependence grow longer and denser' (Dunning, 2002: 227). Elite competitors could no longer play to please themselves. Success at the highest levels required conscious striving. Moreover, elite competitors were coming to 'represent' communities, counties and nations: there were patrons, 'owners' and supporters to be kept satisfied. Unsurprisingly in this context, Dunning and Sheard contend, the calculated use of 'illegitimate violence' to achieve success became more common. This does not, they claim, contradict Elias' theory of the civilizing process: 'the deliberate, "rational" use of violence to secure advantage or victory in a game is consistent with the personality and habitus of people today who consider themselves to be "civilized" because it involves a high degree of control, relatively little pleasure from directly inflicting pain and is utilized in the achievement of specific ends' (Dunning, 2002: 227).

Dunning also pioneered a figurational approach to football hooliganism, a topic I dealt with in some detail in Chapter 5. In a seminal study conducted with Leicester colleagues (1988), he argued that, contrary to popular conviction, football hooliganism is not a novel phenomenon, a by-product of the 'permissive' 1960s (see also Williams et al., 1989). Although not labelled as such until the 1950s/1960s, 'hooligan-like crowd disorders' had been recorded in British football since the 1870s/1880s, the period of emergence of the modern professional game. The balance of football hooliganism changed, however, after World War II, when improved transport and growing affluence allowed for fan travel to away matches. Whereas before World War I attacks on match officials and opposition players featured, fights between opposing fan groups have predominated since the 1960s.

It was also claimed that although football hooligans came from all social classes, the overwhelming majority (80–85 per cent) came from the 'rougher' elements of the working class. The authors associated the regular production/reproduction of fighting/street gangs and aggressive masculinity with an array of socio-demographic and neighbourhood characteristics in addition to low-skilled manual work: relative poverty, mother–centred families, high levels of sex/gender and age-group segregation, male dominance, and a tendency to socialization on the streets by age-peers and older children. People in these constellations of circumstance, 'segmentally-bonded males', develop strong positive levels of attachment to 'we-groups' and correspondingly strong negative feelings towards 'they-groups' or 'outsiders' (Elias, 1978). Football is a propitious venue for acting out masculinity rituals for three principal reasons: first, football, 'the people's game', is culturally important in working-class communities; second, the game itself is a kind of play-fight with a stress on masculinity; and third, football regularly produces opponents to fight and opportunities to invade the territories of others as well as to defend one's own (Dunning, 2002). Dunning (1999) has recently extended this analysis to the global arena, emphasizing that, although football hooliganism is not simply a function of class stratification, it occurs worldwide mainly due to the social composition of football crowds.

Figurational sociology is not without its critics. One general criticism is that Elias's contribution is less innovative than he and his disciples presume: it merely comprises an elaboration of what are longstanding classical sociological positions. Bauman (1979: 121) is among those who reject this line, arguing that Elias demonstrated, 'with merciless logic and overwhelming empirical evidence', that 'long term changes in what is normally classified as "personality structure" and in what is normally considered under a separate heading of "socio-political structure" were aspects of the same historical process; not only intertwined, but mutually instrumental in each other's occurrence'. Another general criticism is that figurational sociology is a concealed form of Durkheimian functionalism. Rojek (1992) counters that Elias and colleagues neither uncover ready compensatory functions in sport or leisure nor neglect conflict and contradiction. A third objection is that Elias locates the civilizing process in a theory of unilinear progress. Demonstrably, however, Elias's notion of a civilizing process allows for counter-civilizing as well as civilizing movements, an idea utilized in Chapter 5, in the course of which a de-civilizing spurt in disorganized capitalism was mooted (Murphy et al., 2000). What is of enduring value in the work of Elias is his insistence that we recognize the relevance of slow, unfolding processes of history for understanding the present.

Post-structuralism/Postmodernism

Ironically, the difficulties commentators have experienced defining or characterizing post-structuralism and postmodernism seem appropriate enough given the alleged demise of the *Zeitgeist* of the modern era. Both terms are associated with the displacement of the totalizing (*grand*) narratives harking back to the European Enlightenment of the late eighteenth century by the fragmented, relativized (*petit*) narratives of the last generation (Lyotard, 1984). The label 'post-structuralism' reflects the prominent focus on language and text over this period, while postmodernism has broader and more inclusive connotations. There have been numerous attempts to catch the flavour of postmodernism, but as Rail (2002: 180) rightly suggests, it is properly conceived as 'an amalgam of often purposively ambiguous and fluid ideas'. The portrayal of these ideas here will necessarily be selective and economical (see Scambler, 2002).

According to Lyotard (1984), a crisis has arisen in the legitimating of knowledge in the post-industrial era dating from the early 1970s, in short, a collapse of the grand theories or 'metanarratives' that have since the Enlightenment legitimated the 'truth' of history. In particular, the notion that secular, rational – and archetypically, scientific – progress is possible and desirable and will lead ineluctably to humanity's advancement must be, and is being, abandoned. Postmodernists

> refute the existence of a reality characterized by structure, patterns, and causal relationships; a reality that can be studied objectively and usefully represented by theories ... (they) dismiss large stories about history and the world as products of an era wherein European and North Americans mistakenly believed in their own superiority and invincibility. Metanarratives are no longer seen as truth, but rather as privileged discourses that deny and silence competing and dissident voices. (Rail, 2002: 182)

Postmodernism, Lyotard insists, offers and maintains incredulity toward metanarratives.

Foucault (1972, 1973, 1979) is no less scathing than Lyotard of metanarratives, characterizing reason as a fiction and truth as a partial, localized version of reality. Discourse, for him, is the site where meanings are contested and relations of power determined. He asserts the 'false' power of hegemonic knowledge, which is always open to challenge by counter-hegemonic discourses offering alternative versions of reality. Foucault's work has encouraged a (post-structuralist) focus on language, and especially on the way meanings are constructed and deployed. Baudrillard (1983), whose work was cited in the discussion of the mediation of football in Chapter 6, has argued that reality is increasingly 'simulated' for people, constructed in effect by the mass media and other cultural institutions (leading to what he calls 'hyperreality'). It is the work of Derrida (1976), however, that is most frequently associated with the postmodern fascination with language. He calls for a critical deconstruction of (especially written) texts, with special attention paid to the way modern binaries have been produced and maintained – for example, truth/falsity, normal/pathological, man/woman – where the first term is seen as both superior to and dependent on the second. Ultimately, however, every text is 'undecidable' because it conceals conflicts between the text and its 'sub-text': 'what every text appears to say on the surface cannot be understood without reference to the assumptions it makes in presuming that it will be understood' (Rail, 2002: 184). Further, language itself is undecidable. Derrida invents the word *differance*, pronounced the same way in French as *difference* (i.e. the fiction of the former cannot be detected orally, only in writing). He argues that language produces meaning only via reference to other – different – meanings. Thus, *differance* corresponds to the 'dual production of meaning through difference and deferral ... we cannot arrive at a fixed meaning as long as we use a necessarily differing as well as deferring language: every definition needs to be clarified and meaning always lies in the future' (Rail, 2002: 184). For most postmodernists, in fact, reality is based on language and can be thought of as text; and any text is 'interextual' in that 'it is inflected by other texts and therefore any text that attempts to represent anything is necessarily incomplete and biased' (Rail, 2002: 185). Clearly postmodernism, thus understood, challenges each of the paradigms discussed above; indeed, it threatens the very 'territoriality' of modern sociology.

Cole and Andrews (1996: 154) have drawn on Derrida's thought to show how the mediated identities of two US basketball stars, Magic Johnson and Michael Jordan, became sites for the reinvention of the '*what* and *who* categories which organize the racial imagination'. As painstakingly constructed African-American superstars, these two athletes occupied discursive spaces that distanced them from, and in doing so reinforced, stereotypical images and embodiments of the kind of menacing black masculinity that inhabits the popular American imagination. However, the identities of Johnson and Jordan were 'never simply self-identical or self-contained', but rather dependent on the absent other (Cole and Andrews, 1996: 152). Moreover, both athletes subsequently transgressed the racial boundaries denied in their previously inscribed 'virtuousness', Johnson via his HIV seropositivity and Jordan via his gambling exploits: these 'flaws' rendered visible that from which they were previously distanced – 'the pathologized and demonized bodies of African American racial others' (Andrews, 2000: 121). In a further contribution Andrews (1996) has drawn on Derrida to interrogate Michael Jordan's blackness. He presents Jordan as a '*floating* and unstable racial signifier' that seductively reproduces 'the violent racial hierarchy of the evolving American cultural formation' (Andrews, 2000: 121). Derrida is not Andrews' only inspiration, however. In his analysis of the Atlanta Olympics of 1996, for example, he purports to demonstrate, this time after the manner of Baudrillard, how NBC's television coverage manufactured a simulated model of Olympic reality explicitly designed to constitute, and therefore seduce, the female viewer.

Rail (1998: 155–6) advances three general theses in relation to postmodernism and sport. She refers first to the 'implosion of art and sport'. Postmodern art, she suggests, has become fragmentary and ironic as well as inclusive of 'high' and 'low' culture. It has come to envelop the 'kaleidoscopic mosaics of television, publicity images, and the various symbols of consumer capitalism'. Sport, together with its signs and symbols, is thereby aestheticized. At the same time, sport appropriates and reproduces postmodern artistic and aesthetic forms in order to constitute itself as an object of hyper-consumption for postmodern clients. Second, Rail refers to the 'implosion of the body and sport', contending that while the self, 'lost in the culture and structures of the modern era', is re-emerging, the body is disappearing 'under the weight of social power'. The body parts of athletes, mere extensions of self and identity, 'undergo alienation and commodification to excess'. Her third thesis is expressed in terms of the 'implosion of images and sport'. She argues that the contemporary model used to mediate sport contributes to a culture that has been characterized as *excremental* 'by being anti-mediatory, by eliciting fetishism, and by fostering the aesthetic populism, fragmentation, depthlessness, and effacing of history found in postmodern culture'.

Rail's theses testify to the promise and the flaws of postmodernism. Undoubtedly postmodern approaches promote a fresh and innovative questioning of stances long taken for granted in the − occidentalist, bourgeois, masculine and white − modern era, as filtered through the lenses of liberal and organized capitalism. Proclamations of a novel emancipation of relativized *petit* narratives, however, surely imply a 'meta-narrative at the end of meta-narratives'. I have referred elsewhere to a paradox of disinhibition in this connection (Scambler, 2002). Postmodern orientations may serve to disinhibit, but they betray a deeper and more abiding neo-conservatism. Relativism, in postmodern as in other guises, is self-refuting: a statement such as Lyotard's celebration of relativized *petit* narratives not only entails yet another metanarrative but is itself necessarily non-relativistic. No more do Foucault's espousal of discourse, Baudrillard's of the hyperreal or Derrida's of the undecidability of text escape from either metanarrative or the self-refuting character of relativism. There is, as Habermas (1987) has put it, 'performative contradiction' here. It follows that while postmodernism can and does allow for and encourage disinhibited analyses, not least in the sociology of sport, any gains remain fortuitous to the extent to which they necessarily lack any basis in a universal, and therefore compelling, rationality (Scambler, 1996). The argument advanced in the next chapter profits from disinhibited postmodern comment on sport but firmly eschews the inherently contradictory notion of a postmodern sociology of sport.

Eclecticism versus Synthesis

It will hopefully be apparent that each of the paradigms or research programmes described in this chapter, its flaws nothwithstanding, has something potent to offer the sociological description and explanation of sporting processes. There is no simple choice to be made between them. However, there is a crucial distinction to be drawn between two modes of learning from them, *eclecticism* and *synthesis*. The eclectic, like the jackdaw, takes bits and pieces from rival paradigms because they sparkle, then sits back and admires them. The synthesist is a different creature: he or she seeks to fashion a convincing and internally consistent theoretical account of sport, or a sports phenomenon, that is (1) cognizant of the varied, partial and sometimes contradictory contributions of predecessors, and (2) a novel contribution in its own right. In the final chapter of this short volume, the basis of a neo-Marxist synthesis is laid via a detailed consideration of critical realism and critical theory.

There is one final point to be made at the conclusion of this sketch of theoretical positions. At the core of the critical theory of the Frankfurt School, early and late, is an emphasis on human emancipation through the exposure and countering of structured patterns of domination; and this volume falls into this category. It is in this spirit that Sugden and Tomlinson (1999) have written of 'retrieving the investigative tradition for a critical sociology of sport'. In Chapter 3, passing reference was made to the work of Simson and Jennings (1992) on some of the dubious exploits of Samaranch's International Olympic Committee (IOC), serving to locate institutions like the IOC at the apex of a multi-billion dollar global sports political economy (see also Jennings, 1996). Jennings (1994) is critical of 'tame' fellow journalists and academics whose accounts fail to penetrate beneath the surface and rhetoric of international sport. In this vein Sugden and Tomlinson call not for a standpoint epistemology but for the revival of a properly critical and investigative sociology. Their slogan is: 'digging the dirt but staying clean'. It is a slogan given substance in their research on the Fédération Internationale de Football Association (FIFA) (Sugden and Tomlinson, 1998; see also their 'Badfellas', 2003). As we shall see, it is an injunction that defies current trends towards the taming or 'colonization' of academic sociology (Scambler, 1996, 2002). And it is an injunction seconded here.

8

Towards a Critical Sociology of Sport

In this final chapter foundations are tentatively laid for a new orientation to the sociology of sport. In the opening paragraphs the philosophy of critical realism is introduced via some general reflections on the concept of social structure. Based on the pioneering work of Bhaskar, critical realism takes seriously not only the epistemology but the *ontology* of social structures. In fact, it is the pronouncement of the 'epistemic fallacy' – that is, the commonplace conflation of our knowledge of what exists with what exists – that provides Bhaskar with his starting point. The second section draws on the wide-ranging theory of communicative action of Habermas to outline a critical theoretical framework for understanding and empirically investigating the dynamics of society in disorganized or global capitalism, together with the changing role of sporting phenomena. In the third section the *jigsaw model* is introduced and its potential for the sociology of sport explored. The closing section offers a summary statement of the 'overall picture' of sport in disorganized capitalism, leading to an agenda for future research.

Agency and the Ontology of Social Structures

Almost independently of the aspirations of their founders and proponents, some of the paradigms summarized in Chapter 7 seemed to emerge from or lend themselves to a focus on agency (e.g. interpretive sociology and possibly feminism and post-structuralism/postmodernism), while others seemed to favour structure (e.g. functionalism, conflict theory and possibly figurational sociology). Acceptance of agency is crucial and possible, but requires qualification. Rational action presupposes freedom of will, but it will be suggested here that 'weakness of will', not freedom of will, is the rule rather than the exception (see Searle, 2001).

The opportunities, contexts and scope humans have for the exercise of agency are fashioned by what Archer (1995: 196) refers to as 'structural conditioning'. Structural conditioning is a mediating process best grasped as an 'objective influence which conditions action patterns and supplies agents with strategic directional guidance'. This influence is exercised through the definition of the situational logics in which agents find themselves or enter into during the lifecourse. Thus Archer (1995: 201) writes: 'it is the situations to which people respond which are mediatory because they condition (without determining) different courses of action for those differently placed, by supplying different reasons to them'. I will return to Archer's notion of structural conditioning a little later.

Even when we act freely and rationally, the sequelae are rarely quite those we plan or would predict. This applies not only at the level of the individual but also in relation to mobilizations leading to collective action. Bhasker (1989: 35) pertinently observes that although we neither work in order to reproduce capitalism nor marry to reproduce the nuclear family, 'it is nevertheless the unintended consequence (and inexorable result of), as it is also a necessary condition for, their activity. Moreover, when social forms change, the explanation will not normally lie in the desires of agents to change them that way, *though as a very important theoretical and practical political limit, it may do*' (emphasis added). We carry the potential, in short, to act freely and rationally, individually and collectively; but in fact we seldom do, and when we do we typically fail to allow for our structural conditioning, the unintended consequences of our actions and the dynamism and complexity of the social world we inhabit.

Agency survives but is: mitigated by weakness of will; framed by structural conditioning; generally ineffective in shaping and controlling change; and – in our postmodern culture – increasingly protean. Each of these properties of agency suggests the need for further analysis of social structures, to which we now turn. Drawing more explicitly on premises from Bhaskar's critical realism, it will be suggested that social structures should be seen as *real*, *intransitive* and possessed of *causal powers* which, when *exercised*, become *generative mechanisms* giving rise to *tendencies* in *open systems*. This requires decoding.

Bhaskar (1978, 1989) distinguishes between three ontological strata, maintaining that the natural and social worlds consist not only of events (the *actual*) and experiences (the *empirical*), but also of underlying mechanisms (the *real*) that are intransitive (that is, they exist whether or not they are detected) and that govern or facilitate events. Social structures, real and intransitive, also have causal powers that may or may not in any given context be triggered or exercised. When they are exercised, they become generative mechanisms issuing in tendencies. Tendencies here do not refer to consequences or outcomes, that is, a pattern of events. Rather, they denote, as it were, 'the force itself' (Fleetwood, 2002: 7). Moreover, generative mechanisms and their tendencies, or forces, impact in open systems. In other words, while objects of sociological interest, such as social structures, are, like many of the objects of the natural sciences, unperceivable and therefore theoretical, unlike many of the objects of the natural sciences, they only manifest themselves in open systems, that is, in systems where 'invariant empirical realities' do not obtain. In short, sociology, due to an absence of spontaneously occurring 'closures', and the impossibility of creating them, for example through laboratory experiments, is denied, in principle, decisive test situations for its theories. It follows that the criteria for the rational confirmation and rejection of its theories cannot be predictive, but must instead be 'exclusively explanatory' (Bhaskar, 1989a).

This is an opportune time to return to Archer's notion of structural conditioning. She specifies three aspects to structural conditioning: *involuntary placement, vested interests,* and *opportunity costs.* In order to appreciate the notion of involuntary placement we need to remind ourselves that the social environment is 'pre-structured' by 'material and cultural emergents' prior to our engagement with it. These emergents account for 'the nature of the extant role-array, the proportions of positions available at any given time and the advantages/disadvantages associated with them' (Archer, 1995: 201). People find themselves inserted at birth, in other words, into social structural or relational axes that influence their resources and therefore their life chances.

Involuntary placement distributes vested interests to those differently placed. Vested interests refer to those modes of praxis or behaviour which, given an individual's involuntary placement, are 'appropriate' to the furtherance of his or her life chances or well-being. 'One of the main antecedent effects of structures', Archer (1995: 203) summarizes, 'consists in dividing the population ... into those with vested interests in maintenance and change respectively, according to the positions in which they find themselves involuntaristically.' People's vested interests, then, are not subjectivist phenomena but objective features of situations.

Of course, people do not always either recognize or act in accordance with their involuntary placement and attendant vested interests. They may find their wants or desires more compelling than their objective vested interests. Opportunity costs, the last of Archer's triad, provides a mediatory mechanism by means of which the vested interests associated with structural situations in society become more efficacious in explaining the consciousness and conduct of agents. Creaven (2000: 211) elaborates:

> Opportunity costs are attached to the various modes of social praxis or activity by which individuals may pursue their human needs and culturally constructed wants, meaning that particular action-responses to structurally determined agential circumstances are likely to induce either rewards (in terms of greater societal enfranchisement or improved life-chances) or costs (in terms of reduced autonomy or freedom of action and stagnant or declining life-chances) – or a different balance between the two – and indeed to induce these effects differentially for members of different agential groupings.

There is no 'hydraulic determination' of consciousness and conduct here. We have our free will; we are 'sovereign artificers'. But most of us for most of the time find those reasons (typically, reasons as *rationalizations*) for pursuing vested interests (which issue in 'rewards') more compelling than those reasons that recommend alternatives (which issue in 'costs').

Enough has been said to ground one of the abiding themes of this book, namely, that it is a central task for sociologists to study and publicly disseminate the role of social structures in tempting, exhorting and occasionally cajoling us to think and act as we do. As we have seen, following Bhaskar's ontology, this entails the identification of those real structures that, as generative mechanisms issuing in tendencies, manifest themselves in events, as well as in our experiences of them: it entails looking beneath-the-surface in order to explain occurrences on-the-surface.

Critical Theory, Habermas and an Analytic Framework

Habermas has long been sensitive to the complexities of the agency/structure dichotomy. Sitton (1996) not unreasonably suggests that the overriding goal of his theoretical endeavours has been to discover a way of synthesizing those sociological paradigms strong on agency (that analyse society – on-the-surface – as a meaningful for its members) and those paradigms strong on structure (that analyse society – beneath-the-surface – as a system that is stabilized behind the backs of its members). He has sought such a synthesis through a reconstruction of Marx's historical materialism, although some commentators have expressed scepticism over the extent of his continuing commitment to a Marxist perspective (Rockmore, 1989).

One of Habermas's clear points of departure from Marx, and for that matter from Weber and his Frankfurt mentors Horkheimer and Adorno, concerns their putative fixation on *labour* and neglect of *interaction*. With reference to Marxist theory, he rejects what he takes to be the reduction of interaction to labour, arguing that this not only inhibits the sociology of contemporary society but removes any possibility of reconstructing a project of human emancipation. This argument can be clarified and elaborated sufficiently for present purposes by considerations of Habermas's (1984, 1987) distinctions between *communicative* and *strategic action* and *lifeworld* and *system*, and his notions of the *uncoupling* of lifeworld and system and the *colonization* of the former by the latter (for critical expositions, see Eriksen and Weigard, 2003; Sitton, 2003).

Habermas has long defended the notion of universal reason. This defence has given rise to a formal or procedural concept of rationality owing much to the linguistic turn in twentieth-century Anglo-Saxon philosophy. Reason, Habermas insists, can no longer be seen as the issue of the subject–object relations of the philosophy of consciousness, whether in its Kantian, Hegelian or Marxian forms. It issues instead from the subject–

subject relations of communicative action. People's use of language implies a common endeavour to achieve understanding and consensus, and in a context in which all participants are free to contribute and have equal opportunities to do so. Language use, in the terminology of Habermas's earlier work, presupposes commitment to the 'ideal speech situation', in which discourse can realize its full potential. This is not to say that the ideal speech situation is readily attained; but it is to say that communicative action, although always reflective of the contexts of time and place, rests also on an *ahistorical* factor. This factor, in the summary of Brand (1990: 11–12),

> is found in the claim for the validity of the reasons which induce people to take their particular share in communicative action. In such claims no historical limitation is recognized since they are based on the (implicit) view that their validity should be accepted by anyone capable of judgement who is free to use it, whether in the past, present or future. The idea of rationally motivated shared understanding – and rational motivation implies the total lack of compulsion or manipulation – is built into the very reproduction of social life ... The symbolic reproduction of society is based on the 'counterfactual' ideal of the 'ideal speech situation', which is characterized by 'communicative symmetry' and a compulsion-free consensus. (see Scambler, 1996, 2001)

Communicative action is necessarily prior and stands in contrast to strategic action. While the former is action oriented to understanding, the latter, heir to Weber's instrumental action, is action oriented to success. In terms of strategic action, achieving success is foremost: 'everything else is simply a means to be used in a purely calculating manner. The actor treats others' resistance as facts to be changed, obstacles to be overcome, thereby assimilating social relations – including moral relations – to 'things' in the objective world rather than relations maintained through intersubjective agreement' (Sitton, 2003: 52). In terms of speech act theory, the actor deploys 'perlocutionary' rather than 'illocutionary' speech acts, that is, forms of words calculated to produce an effect on the hearer. Strategic action is the only comprehensible kind for those who believe that instrumental rationality is synonymous with reason.

The distinction between communicative and strategic action is intimately related to that between lifeworld and system. In a sentence, the lifeworld is characterized by communicative action and the system by strategic action. The notion of the lifeworld points to the fact that all thought relies on background assumptions or 'preunderstandings' (Husserl refers presciently to the 'always already'). The lifeworld, defined by Habermas after the manner of the later Wittgenstein, is the 'inescapable context of knowing and acting; as an encompassing whole it cannot be seen and therefore is beyond doubt. We are always standing somewhere' (Sitton, 2003: 63). We only gain partial awareness of the preunderstandings comprising the lifeworld when they become relevant to our goals or projects, in which eventuality they are 'thematized'. Social life is reproduced through communicative action emergent from the background assumptions or preunderstandings of the lifeworld.

But for Habermas the lifeworld refers to more than a set of background assumptions or preunderstandings. It also fulfils discrete functions in reproducing society as a coherent whole. Sitton (2003: 65) lists these succinctly:

> First, the lifeworld sustains the conditions of mutual understanding through the 'transmission and renewal of cultural knowledge'. Second, it enables social action by maintaining the 'solidarity' of individuals with each other; it integrates individuals into social groups that maintain the coherence of the collective, the sense of being one of a 'we'. Third, the lifeworld forms personal identities in that one's sense of self arises from one's interactions with others. The individual's identity is constituted by seeing oneself through the eyes of another, as the 'other' of this other standing across from me. That is, following Mead, Habermas argues that personal identity is fundamentally constructed and stabilized through communicative action with others.

The reproduction of the lifeworld through communicative action is therefore also the reproduction of what Habermas (1987: 137–8) calls 'the structural components of the lifeworld: culture, society, and person'. Culture, society and person or personal identity are symbolic constructions and have no existence prior to or independent of the lifeworld.

Following Parsons, Habermas maintains that society needs to be understood not only as meaningful for its members but also as a self-regulating system consisting of subsystems differentiated according to specific functional processes. There is a requirement for system as well as social integration. In premodern societies the 'lifeworld aspects' (namely, those processes that maintain societies as comprehensible to their members) and the 'system aspects' (namely, the often unintended fulfilment of those functional demands necessary for social life to be sustained) were 'bound together'. It was only with the development of the market economy and a bureaucratic state that these aspects of social organization became 'uncoupled'. There was, then, a point in 'social evolution' for Habermas when the need for a system theory of society emerged. 'If we are to grasp all the ways in which integration of contemporary societies occurs, the analysis of society as a lifeworld must be complemented by a reconceptualization of society as a self-maintaining system' (Sitton, 2003: 71).

Habermas distinguishes between the economy and state, comprising the system, and the private and public spheres of the lifeworld (the institutional core of the private sphere here is the nuclear family, and of the public sphere the culture industry, the press and the media). From the vantage point of a system theory of society, these constitute four interdependent subsystems. Each subsystem is specialized in terms of what it produces but is dependent on the others for what it does not produce. The economy produces *money*, the state *power*, the private sphere *commitment* and the public sphere *influence*. These products or *media* are traded between subsystems. Thus, for example: 'the economy relies on the state to establish such legal economic institutions as private property and contract, on the public lifeworld to influence consumption patterns, and on the private sphere to provide a committed labour force, and itself sends money into each other subsystem' (Crook et al., 1992: 28).

The media of the subsystems are not, however, equivalent in their capacities. With the progressive uncoupling of system and lifeworld, the media of the former, money and power, have come to dominate those of the latter. This process of domination – of the lifeworld by system imperatives – is termed by Habermas the 'colonization of the lifeworld'. While he acknowledges that the institutionalization of 'de-linguistified' media like money and power, allowing for a 'simplification' of interaction across many arenas and contexts by condensing the conditions necessary for co-ordinating action, is necessary in complex and highly differentiated modern societies, as his use of the notion of colonization implies he also insists that the possibilities of communicative action in the lifeworld have *too often* become attenuated 'as social participation becomes hyper-rationalized in terms of immediate returns. Participants encounter each other as legal entities and as parties to contracts rather than as thinking and acting subjects' (Crook et al., 1992: 28). Unlike either Weber or Horkheimer and Adorno, Habermas sees nothing inevitable or ineluctable about this. Indeed, he argues strongly for a reassertion of communicative rationality and power against its strategic equivalents, for a reconstructed Enlightenment project to 'de-colonize' the lifeworld. There is an urgent need to render the *capitalist executive* of the economy and the *power elite* of the state democratically accountable in today's global or disorganized capitalism (Scambler, 2002).

My argument is that it is within the critical realist/critical theoretic framework sketched here that sports phenomena might productively be re-examined. It remains only to indicate *how* this is to be accomplished, hence the focus in the next section on what I shall refer to as the *jigsaw model*.

The Jigsaw Model

Models in the natural as well as the social sciences are expeditious and often unavoidable devices or means to an end, in our case the explanation of certain general and particular sports-related phenomena. The concept of the jigsaw model advocated here can be said to have three aspects. The first is a 'best guess' at an *overall picture* of the dynamic, complex and highly differentiated social world we inhabit. The second is a series of models, articulated in terms of *logics, relations* and *figurations*, each constituting a discrete *piece of the jigsaw*. And the third is a process of *dialectical reasoning* by means of which the sense of the overall picture informs the application of models and the application of models informs the sense of the overall picture.

At the core of the jigsaw model are the notions of logics, relations and figurations. Perhaps the best way of defining these notions is in terms of two of Habermas's subsystems, those of economy and state. The logic of the economy, which we have already met and deployed before, is that of the *regime of capital accumulation*. This logic establishes the parameters for (*real*, in Bhaskar's sense) *relations of class*. Such relations, when exercised, become generative mechanisms and manifest themselves in tendencies, albeit in open systems; they provide sociology with its explanatory thrust. The logic of the regime of capital accumulation and relations of class can be examined within a number of different figurations. Figuration is a term appropriated from Elias (1978), and figurations are defined by him as spatio-temporal interdependency chains or networks that are fluid and diachronically changing. Thus figurations may be local, regional, national or global, or indeed virtual rather than actual.

The logic of the state, also familiar to us, is that of the *mode of regulation*; this logic establishes the parameters for *relations of command*, and these too can be studied in a variety of different figurations. It has been argued here and elsewhere that the transition from organized to disorganized or global capitalism since the mid-1970s has witnessed a shift in the balance between relations of class and command (Scambler, 2002). The emergence of what has frequently been called the neo-liberal regime of capital accumulation in the subsystem of the economy has necessitated a revised mode of regulation in the subsystem of the state. The upshot has been the ceding of ground in many figurations of relations of command to relations of class.

In addition to these logics and relations pertaining to the economy and state, three other compelling logics and relations feature across a variety of figurations in the sociology of sport. These are the *logic of patriarchy* and *relations of gender*; the *logic of tribalism* and *relations of ethnicity*; and the *logic of honour* and *relations of status*. One virtue of the jigsaw model is that the same substantive area, indeed the same figuration, can be revisited with profit under the aegis of more than one model. A model is defined as *categorical* when a dyad of logic and its relations is primarily causally responsible for a phenomenon in a given figuration; *derivative* when its role is secondary to that of another dyad; and *circumstantial* when it plays a primary causal role but fortuitously (for example, due to unique features of a particular figuration). It should be clear that no sociological analysis of the figuration of, say, a modern Olympiad could be considered in any way comprehensive unless broached under – at least – each of the five logics and relations mentioned.

It remains only to afford some preliminary indication of how the jigsaw model might contribute to our grasp of sport as a social phenomenon. As a vehicle for accomplishing this I shall return to a contemporary urban mega-event touched on at the end of Chapter 3, the Sydney Olympic Games of

2000. This affords the opportunity to indicate *how* the core logics and relations introduced earlier might throw additional light on our sociological understanding of events leading up to and culminating in the Games of 2000.

Preuss (2003) has identified four phases in the economic history of the modern Olympiads. The first, lasting for the bulk of the timespan of the modern Games, from 1896 to 1968, was characterized by recurring financial problems and the more or less urgent pursuit of new sources of income. The second, from 1969 to 1980, was a phase of public underwriting of the Games. The third phase, from 1981 to 1996, featured an expanding reliance on private finance. And the fourth and final phase, from 1997 to 2008, has seen mixed financing and the development of long-term relationships between the IOC and sponsors and TV networks. The Games occurring in the era of global or disorganized capitalism, that is, from the second to the fourth of Preuss' economic phases, also reflected different political objectives on the part of host cities and nation-states: the promotion of a revitalized image was important to Munich (1972), Seoul (1988) and Sydney (2000); city redevelopment provided a stimulus to Munich (1972), Montreal (1976), Seoul (1988) and Barcelona (1992); the affirmation of a political system had special salience in respect to Moscow (1980) and Los Angeles (1984); the benefits accruing from tourism help account for the aspirations of Barcelona (1992) and Sydney (2000); and the spur of inward investment inspired the bids of Barcelona (1992) and Atlanta (1996). So, for Preuss, the Sydney Games, made possible by a mix of public and private financing, were a means to promote the city's image and to attract tourists.

Independently of any variation in financial viability/profitability and/or objective in the recent past, however, there is no question either that the Olympics Games now constitute one of the major global 'circuses'. The statistics for Sydney itself testify to the scale of the modern Games. The number of sports represented at Sydney was 28. As far as participation is concerned, there were 10,651 'total starters'. The number of participating NOCs, reaching across all five continents, was 199. 'Accredited' individuals (that is, athletes, team officials, extra officials, broadcasters and press) totalled 37,423. The total number of tickets sold was 6,679,792. And the television coverage reached 220 countries and 3.7 billion people (adding up to 29,600 hours of coverage and 36.1 billion viewer hours). According to the IOC's own figures, the broadcasting revenues for the Sydney Games totalled US$1,332 million. The same source summarized licensing revenues as follows: approximately 100 licences produced in excess of 3000 different product lines sold in more than 2000 retail outlets across Australia. In all, the Sydney licensing programme generated nearly US$500 million in retail sales of Olympic merchandise. Enough Olympic pins were sold in Australia to provide each household with eight pins.

These Sydney statistics are on their own more than suggestive of the salience of the logics of the regime of capital accumulation and mode of

regulation of disorganized capitalism, together with their respective relations of class and command, for the figuration of the Games. Preuss (2003:
259) identifies six 'interest groups' in relation to the modern Olympiad:
IOC members, representing cultural and geographical interests; nation-
states, geared to international relations and to the positive perception of
'others'; city politicians, with interests in tourism, the status of the capital
city, recognition, economic advancement and personal career progression;
the local construction industry; national sponsors; and television networks.
These interest groups represent a dynamic mix of enactments of class and
command relations, although in most figurations the former tend to be
categorical and the latter derivative of the former. For example, although
state and city politicians undoubtedly pursued their own discrete individual
and collective agendas in Sydney, the currency of their realization was
typically economic, that is, enhancements in power were made effective, if
often circuitously, through the steering media of money.

Axiomatically, the role of relations of class was prepotent in the
aspirations and machinations of Sydney's construction industry, of national
sponsors and of the television networks. It was no less so in the clearance of
'undesirables' and ubiquitous engagement of cheap student and voluntary
labour at the main Games sites. A particularly unambiguous instance of the
enactment of class relations around the Olympic industry in Sydney
involved the American television network, NBC. It was NBC that largely
dictated the staging of the Games. For example, it insisted on Bondi Beach
as the optimum venue for a stadium for beach volleyball, overcoming a
lively, committed – if politically 'trivialized' – campaign of protest from
local and environmental groups, with the connivance of state and city
politicians and a sustained and sometimes militant police presence. Lenskyj
(2002: 186) pointedly observes:

> Not surprisingly, many Bondi stadium opponents could not resist
> critiquing beach volleyball as an Olympic sport, as well as the OCA's
> selection of Bondi Beach as an Olympic venue. Some correctly noted
> the sexploitation of female players' bodies, as exemplified by the new
> uniform requirements, while others viewed it as an American import
> that only achieved Olympic status because Atlanta had hosted the
> 1996 Games. It was also argued that international television cameras
> would focus on the sport (or, in a variation of this, the women) rather
> than on the beach; therefore, one could probably hold the event in a
> parking lot without loss of television viewership.

In the event there was beach volleyball on 10 of the 13 days of Olympic
competition. NBC was no less successful in securing the replacement of
overhead powerlines and 48 electrical towers at Homebush Bay by
underground cables solely to improve television images (the New South
Wales politicians pitched in with a contribution of $20 million). The
positioning of the running track at the main Olympic stadium was decided
because the television cameras required a shadow-free area not facing the

afternoon sun, although the resulting winds seriously impeded athletes' levels of performance. NBC's decision to protect its costly purchase of television rights also resulted in the delay of all telecasts until evening prime time, since most of the networks' viewing audience inhabited a time zone 12–15 hours behind Sydney time. The IOC's policy of banning moving images or audio coverage via the Internet should be noted in this connection.

That relations of class and command occasioned an excessive system rationalization in Sydney, amounting in Habermasian terms to an insistent if often temporary colonization of the lifeworld, is unsurprising. There exists a generalized awareness that the modern Olympiad is highly com-modified and juridified, although this is strategically glossed by expedient but erroneous myths of the Olympic spirit. But if the figuration of the Games is revisited in light of the logic of patriarchy and gender relations, a more finely differentiated picture emerges. In Sydney, women's events comprised 73 per cent of men's events (Houlihan, 2003: 42). Of 10,651 starting athletes, 4069 (or 38 per cent) were women. These percentages may have been the 'best yet' in the history of the modern Games (see Table 3.3), but they represent snail-like progress achieved against strong and obdurate masculine odds. Added to these figures should be those indicating the absence as yet of a female president of the IOC, and the existence of a mere smattering of female IOC members, most of these over the last generation (Miller, 2003).

Statistics on participation in Olympic sport and its governance testify to the gendered nature of modern sport, as does the sexploitation of female volleyball players on Bondi Beach, but there is much more to gender relations in Olympic sport than this. While liberal feminist analyses have tended to focus on rates of participation, other more radical forms of feminism have discerned a 'male model of sport' epitomized in the Olympic movement: 'simple equality should not be confused with either equity or social justice' (Lenskyj, 2002: 6). Pierre de Coubertin's words excluding women from the resurrected Games resonate here. In the *Revue Olympique* in 1912 he restated his philosophy that the Games should be about 'the solemn and periodic exaltation of male athleticism, based on internationalism, by means of fairness, in an artistic setting, *with the applause of women as a reward*' (emphasis added). In a speech in 1928 he elaborated:

> The ruggedness of male exertion, the basis of athletic education when prudently but resolutely applied, is much to be dreaded when it comes to the female. That ruggedness is achieved physically only when nerves are stretched beyond their normal capacity, and morally only when the most precious feminine characteristics are nullified . . . Add a female element, and the event becomes monstrous . . . If women want to play football or box, let them, provided that the event takes place without spectators, because the spectators who flock to such competitions are not there to watch a sport. (cited in Brookes, 2002: 136)

The continuity of male hegemony stretching from de Coubertin to the organizers of the women's volleyball competition on Bondi Beach is as stark as it is paradoxical.

Liberal feminism has presented female Olympians as role models, ironically bringing to mind Nike's 'Just Do It' slogan. This individualist exhortation, fitting in well enough with the enhanced pace of individualization characteristic of disorganized capitalism and its postmodernized culture, flies in the face of a body of evidence that girls and women tend to value the social concomitants of sport, like fun and friendship, more than their male counterparts, who typically emphasize winning and defeating their opponents. Of course, this does not mean either that female athletes do not want to win or that male athletes do not value and appreciate sporting camaraderie (Lenskyj, 1994); but there is no doubt which set of motivations is rated more highly. In short, the modern Olympiad has unfolded through liberal, organized and disorganized capitalist eras in which it seemed 'natural' for class and command relations, *qua* generative mechanisms, to impact on events *in line with* an historically prior logic of patriarchy and relations of gender.

But if relations of class and command are typically enacted in gendered form, what of the logic of tribalism and relations of ethnicity? Were the Sydney Games any less racialized than gendered? In Chapter 3 it was suggested that the persistent concentration of medal winners among Europeans and North Americans in the modern Olympiad, up to and including the Sydney Games, might be deemed a form of cultural imperialism. Of course, the phenomenon of cultural imperialism rarely reduces to the logic of tribalism and relations of ethnicity. In fact, in many instances of cultural imperialism across many figurations this dyad of logic and relations is derivative – via the strategic sponsorship of (ethno-)nationalisms – of the logic of the mode of regulation and command relations and/or the logic of the regime of capital accumulation and class relations. However, as Tatz (1995) has shown, there is ample evidence both that Aboriginal athletes in Australia have been held back 'by the same racist systems, practices and stereotypes that restricted other aspects of their lives', and that ethnic relations were typically not derivative of either command or class relations in the figuration of the Sydney Games. Drawing parallels with Afro-Americans, Lenskyj (2002: 67) observes that

> in much the same way as Black actors, musicians and sportspeople in the United States had access to a narrow range of career opportunities, boxing, rugby league, and Australian rules football provided the entry point into sport for many young Indigenous men, while Indigenous women, facing the combined effects of racism and sexism in sport, lacked even an entry point. As recently as 1994–1995, only two of 524 Australian Institute of Sport scholarships were offered to Indigenous athletes – Cathy Freeman and Kyle Van de Kuyp.

Cathy Freeman can be cast in our individualizing postmodern culture as a floating racial signifier. This phrase indicates that 'the meanings of race are not *fixed* – what the same racial signifier means changes at any given moment of time' (Brookes, 2002: 112); as Andrews (1996: 126) puts it: 'racial identity is not stable, essential or consistent; it is dynamic, complex and contradictory'. Cathy Freeman was in some respects 'the perfect symbol' of ethnic reconciliation (captured in her lighting of the cauldron during the opening ceremony). And yet this ritualized engagement was no more an indication of a newfound racial harmony in Australia than Mohammed Ali's lighting of the Atlanta flame fours years earlier had been in the USA. Cathy Freeman went on to win the 400 metres gold medal. However, as one Aboriginal activist had expressed it in the year prior to the Games, whether she were to win or not would be

> completely irrelevant to the ongoing history of oppression and racial persecution of Indigenous people. Nor would it have the slightest effect on the 200 years of old historic struggle for justice in this country. It would not change one hard-core racist attitude and will not create one opportunity for the army of Indigenous unemployed youth. Nor would it free a single one of the thousands of Kooris in Australian jails. (Foley, 1999)

Cathy Freeman was a potential protagonist in numerous alternate and contradictory *petit* narratives. She found herself particularly susceptible to 'hijack' for political and economic projects (themselves typically articulations of relations of command and class respectively). Nor can it have been easy for her to secure a settled self-identity in circumstances notoriously propitious for self-turnover. Moreover, she was not just a woman competitor representing a long-oppressed ethnic minority, she had also become a *celebrity*. The logic of honour and relations of status have a distinguished pedigree in sociology and are most closely associated with Weber's multi-dimensional approach to social stratification. It is a distinctive feature of disorganized capitalism and its postmodern culture, however, that the rewards of athletic status can prompt not only an archetypically destandardized form of paid work but a novel kind of fame or celebrity. As we have seen, Giles (2000) delineates four types of fame and celebrity: that accruing to public figures (e.g. Australian Prime Minister John Howard); that earned 'on merit'; showbusiness (super-)stardom; and the kind of star status bestowed temporarily on the ordinary but notorious. Sports people like Cathy Freeman are cited by Giles as exemplars of meritocratic celebrity. And the celebrity of Olympic victors is global. Celebrity of this kind is not just a function of relations of class and command, although in some figurations these relations can indeed be categorical. It generally generates its own momentum. And while it can be enriching in a multiplicity of ways, it can also reduce celebrities to 'beings-for-others' and suck their lifeblood.

The Overall Picture

This is an expedient point to offer a rough synopsis of the argument that has permeated this volume. Following a fairly detailed exposition of the emergence of modern sport in liberal capitalism, it has been maintained that the most recent period of Western development commencing in the early to mid-1970s, often termed global or disorganized capitalism, has witnessed a pace of sporting change to match that of societal change. It has been suggested that social structures, every bit as *real* (in Bhaskar's sense) as the structures posited by geneticists or biologists, albeit operating as generative mechanisms in open as opposed to closed systems, are crucial to the sociological explanation of current as of past change. Moreover, for all humans' freedom of will, it is weakness of will that most often typifies our behaviour. Our cognitions, values and behaviour are subject to, if not determined by, what Archer calls *structural conditioning* (that is, they typically follow on from our involuntary placements, vested interests and opportunity costs). Rare is the postmodern sporting hero or icon that interrogates or rebels against 'his' hyper-commodification, let alone renounces the rewards and celebrity that ensue.

It would be inaccurate and misleading to suggest that whereas sporting or athletic engagement in eras prior to the present were lifeworld activities, characterized by communicative action and consensus, they have over the last 30 years been entirely colonized by the steering media of money, representing the economy, sanctioned by power, representing the state, and become in the process examples of strategic action and the dissensus associated with system rationalization. It was only with the evolution of more complex modern societies, with what theorists term social differentiation, that lifeworld and system became uncoupled, affording a very different frame for grasping the role of social structures like relations of class, command, gender, ethnicity and status in explaining social phenomena; each of these sets of relations has figured in illustrations, many of them only too brief, of the jigsaw model.

If lifeworld and system were prised apart before disorganized capitalism, this does not mean their interface has remained static. The contention here is that disorganized capitalism has seen accelerated social changes, among which the reinvigoration of relations of class, articulating the logic of a *new* regime of capital accumulation, relative to relations of command, issue of the logic of a mode of regulation functionally adapted to the new logic of capital accumulation, is prominent and a matter of extraordinary and neglected sociological significance. The view that relations of class have diminished in significance, or even 'died' (Pakulski and Waters, 1996), must be rejected. In so many figurations pertinent to sport class relations remain categorical, notwithstanding people's growing – and politically functional – disinclination in our postmodern culture to perceive or acknowledge as much.

It is the resurgence of class which has fostered and hastened, *but not determined* (since other 'shapes' could have met its functional prerequisites), the novel postmodern shape to the culture of the last quarter of the twentieth century. The postmodernization of culture, in other words, is the acceptable face of what Sklair (1998) terms the culture-ideology of consumerism required by class interests in global or disorganized capitalism. *The logical end-point of capitalism, it is worth remembering, is the commodification of everything.* Bourdieu's (1977) notion of class habitus affords us the opportunity to recognize the renewed salience of *objective* class relations while taking on board decisive evidence in favour of a diminution of their *subjective* input into identity-formation: people's class dispositions are not eradicated by their lack of reflexivity, even in an age of reflexive modernization. Moreover there is a natural 'fit' between the potency of class; the deregulation of international markets; the (relative) decline in the self-regulation of nation-states; the de-standardization of work (including sports work); the persistence of class habitus in the face of its neglect, denial and apparent irrelevance to identity-formation; growing individualization; the postmodernization of culture; and the refining or honing of forms of governmentality to substitute for or complement more explicit modes of domination.

In relation to sport, it has been argued that in disorganized capitalism relations of class, through the mechanisms of the marketplace, have led to a rapid increase in the rate and scale of colonization of both exercise and amateur and professional sport. There is no contradiction in asserting that it is the newly freed-up appetite for the creation of profitable markets that has precipitated *both* worrying rates of obesity in children, youths and adults *and* urgent demands that those affected and unaffected owe it to themselves and society to take regular and *expensively fashionable* dietary regimens or precautions and exercise (although there is of course more to obesity than this (see Crossley, 2004)). It is a function of the social structures/generative mechanisms of class and command that the greedy bastards and their disciples and allies in the capitalist-executive and new middle class, together with agents of the state, through an admix of mechanisms of ideology and technologies of the self/governmentality, are able to project on to individuals all causal and moral responsibility for the *personal problem* of obesity.

Not all of the many sports 'modernized' in Elias' first or second phases of sportization in England followed the same trajectory thereafter, as is apparent if Maguire's five-phase model is used as a benchmark (compare, for example, track-and-field, football and rugby). It is possible, however, to discern a distinctive, if staggered, pattern to sporting change in disorganized capitalism, and once again it is the revised logic of the regime of capital accumulation and class relations that are categorical across many figurations. If there are big profits to be made via the hyper-commodification of fast foods, diets and exercise, so there are via the hyper-commodification of elite sports. Furthermore, continuing to deploy the term 'greedy bastards' in its technical sense, that is, as the personification of exploitative class relations, the profits of this hyper-commodification accrue primarily and prepotently to significant players in our strongly globalized capitalist-executive, aided and abetted – in the absence of the threat of a legitimation crisis (Habermas, 1976; Scambler, 2002) – by the weakly globalized power elite of the state. That the handful of elite stars who become celebrities also make millions is, *in terms of the logic of the regime of capital accumulation and relations of class*, secondary. The hyper-commodification of English football has been driven by greedy bastards from outside the sport, by Murdoch, not Beckham. Sports stars may be beneficiaries in their roles *as workers* (and, acknowledging that the logic of honour and relations of status are typically derivative of the logic of the regime of capital accumulation and relations of class, in their roles *as celebrities*). But it should be remembered that they make far more for their various employers than for themselves (Schumaker may make a lot of money in Formula 1, but Bernie (and Slavica) Ecclestone make far more, being worth an estimated £2,323 million in 2004 (Beresford and Boyd, 2004)). Unless they become 'capitalists' *in their own right*, that is, by 'retiring' to live off their capital or by apprenticing themselves to the capitalist-executive, they remain more labourers than capitalists. A number of noted English footballers, however, along with celebrities outside sport, are becoming 'celebrity investors' (Prince, 2004).

Less has been said of the logics of patriarchy and tribalism and their respective relations of gender and ethnicity. It will be apparent that women have painstakingly won higher rates of participation in exercise and most amateur and professional sports, some becoming celebrities in the process, and that black athletes too have broken down longstanding segregationist and other barriers prohibiting elite representation and celebrity. It is no less apparent, however, that the successes of female and black sports persons have been achieved at a cost. Women who play football and rugby and wrestle and box, for example, have typically been judged to have sacrificed their femininity; and elite black athletes and celebrities have been used by 'white media' both to confirm *biologically determinist* stereotypes of 'blacks' – explosive and powerful, but at a loss for strategy and vision – and to suggest, quite erroneously, that racist barriers to achievement and reward *across all sports and society as a whole* have come tumbling down. Revealingly, male, white, Western dominance amongst the greedy bastards who make their money from sport, as well as amongst its managers and administrators, remains secure. There is far more to gender and ethnicity than athletic participation, or even global success and celebrity.

The culture-ideology of consumerism/postmodern culture of disorganized capitalism have led to a raised tolerance threshold for, and therefore enhanced profitability of, violence in sport. Although the figurational case for an historical civilizing process in relation to sport, as for other arenas of life, in general holds, there are indications not only that less restrained modes of violence might again be served up as profitable entertainment, but that a greater facility for individual identity-formation and what was earlier called self-turnover might permit participants in contact and combat sports to become more violent in their sporting roles while remaining strictly, even morally, non-violent in their non-sporting roles. The hypothesis that we are on the cusp of a de-civilizing spurt warrants further empirical investigation.

How does this synopsis, this positing of excessive system rationalization and lifeworld colonization and a possible de-civilizing spurt, sit with Guttman's Weberian sociology of sport summarized at the close of Chapter 1? Guttman (1978: 85), it will be remembered, epitomized modern sport in terms of the properties of secularism, equality, specialization, rationalization, bureaucracy, quantification and records, which he saw as representative of the 'slow development of an empirical, experimental, mathematical *Weltanschauung*'. This is part of the story. What is missing in Guttman is Habermas's – ironically more Weberian than Marxian – notion of the decoupling of system and lifeworld and the colonization of the latter by the former. This text has advanced a neo-Marxist sociology of disorganized capitalism buttressed by critical realism. It attributes more salience to the logic of the regime of capital accumulation and relations of class, certainly than Guttman in his account of the origins of modern sport in liberal capitalism, and probably than Habermas in his accounts of liberal, organized and, most especially, disorganized capitalism. This is not to say that the *Weltanschauung* discerned by Weber and Guttman in society and in sport can be explained away as a function of class. It cannot; but neither can society and sport in either its modern – in liberal and organized capitalism – or postmodern – in disorganized capitalism – forms be adequately explained without a powerful focus on the social structure/generative mechanism of relations of class. This is perhaps most obvious with the emergence of distinctly postmodern sporting *icons*.

A word more needs to be said of the logic of the mode of regulation and relations of command. Until the 1960s, Moran (2003) contends, sport was paradigmatic of the British tradition of self-regulation. It is true enough, as we saw in Chapters 2 and 3 in relation to track-and-field athletics, that

> there was an earlier tradition that closely connected sport both to ideologies of imperialism and to projects for channeling and controlling the energies of potentially disruptive parts of the working class. But the organization of the most important sports, as they crystallized in the later decades of the nineteenth century, were characteristically club-like in nature ... they involved the domination of individual sports by metropolitan oligarchies often – as in the case of cricket and horse-racing – integrated informally with upper-class gentlemanly cultures. (Moran, 2003: 87)

Another and more sociological way of way of saying this is to insist that sport in disorganized capitalism, most ostensibly through the 1990s, has been colonized not only by relations of class but also by relations of command, becoming in the process a less autopoietic or self-referential system.

Historically the rules of even particular sports were *sui generis*, that is, the rules applicable to, say, football only made sense on the football pitch, being arbitrary and irrelevant to any non-sporting world or even to other sports. It is this self referential property that renders the appeal of varieties of sport all-consuming to some and incomprehensible to others. Sports are 'pointless' beyond their own self-referential domains. We have documented the extent of the colonization of sport by the market over the last generation, most conspicuously through television. With growing insistence from the 1990s the British state too has intervened to raise performance at elite level (witness the publication in 1995 of *Sport: Raising the Game* by the Department of National Heritage, and the subsequent creation of Sport England and UK Sport in 1997). New Labour from its election in 1997 not only sought to capitalize on sporting success, in line with prior political convention, but was innovative in using mass sport as an instrument of social and health policy, namely, as a way of combating social exclusion and promoting public health respectively. This is an example of technologies of the self/governmentality *as* (critical theoretical) *domination as well as* (Foucauldian) *power*. Moran rightly points out that the newly centralizing and 'assertive' – as well as 'marketized' – state has in manifold ways taken steps to colonize sports that were once the preserve of what he calls 'civil society'. However, for all that command relations have been categorical for changes in the regulation of sport as well as derivative of those of class, it is the renewed impact of class relations that remain most striking in disorganized capitalism.

An Agenda for a Critical Sociology of Sport

One outcome of the review of various sociological paradigms and theories of sport in Chapter 7 was that none came close to holding a monopoly of explanatory power. The introduction of the jigsaw model, rooted in critical realism and critical theory, favoured sociological explanations of sporting phenomena in terms of social structures *qua* generative mechanisms issuing in tendencies in open systems, not in denial of agency but in recognition that everyday human action typically suggests weakness rather than freedom of will. Applications of the jigsaw model have been yet more focused, calling most on the logic of the regime of capital accumulation and class relations, addressing in some part the logics of the mode of regulation and honour and their respective relations of command and status or celebrity, and having least to say about the logics of patriarchy and tribalism and their respective relations of gender and ethnicity. While lack of space is the main reason that less than justice has been done to gender and ethnicity, which are fortunately well and now uncompromisingly covered in other texts, another is the judgement that too many sports sociologists neglect, even deny, the contemporary relevance of class. The admittedly time-bound Marxist theories of the likes of Brohm and Rigaeur have generally been ritualistically acknowledged and no less ritualistically dismissed. Of diminishing import to people's definitions of their situations and selves, class, it has been argued here, is of growing import to the sociological explanation of these same definitions together with the social environments within which they are formed. Congruent with this shift, relations of command and status or celebrity have tended to become more, if never wholly, derivative of class in disorganized than in organized capitalism.

A robust case has been made elsewhere for a reflexive critical sociology that remains scientific whilst being post-positivistic and, to use Bauman's (1987) terms, post-legislative but yet not merely interpretive (Scambler, 1996, 1998, 2002; Scambler and Martin, 2001). An agenda for such a sociological engagement has also been ventured and warrants brief summary. A reflexive critical sociology, it was argued, should, first, become truly global, not just in its interests and reach but by encouraging the genesis of a transnational community of sociologists; and global does *not* here mean the propagation and spread of Anglo-Saxon perspectives. Second, it should focus increasingly on – an overall picture of – the world capitalist system. Sociologists of sport have made solid progress in this respect (see, for example, the extensive work on the migration of elite athletes and on social aspects of world games and championships across many sports). Third, its practitioners should, in C. Wright Mills' telling phrase, 'do it *big*'; that is, they should forgo mere specialist excursions to link their research to wider societal change (Mills and Mills, 2000: i). Expressed in terms of the jigsaw model, they should view discrete applications of the model of logics/relations/figurations in dialectical relation to the overall picture. The impact of social structural change on sociology within and without universities during disorganized capitalism has unfortunately led to what Ritzer (2001) calls sociology's 'McDonaldization' and a tendency, often well rewarded by career advancement, to neglect the overall picture to 'do it *small*'. Too much sociology is now non-critical, commissioned, applied and driven by system imperatives via the steering media of money and power. Fourth, its descriptive and explanatory power should be transmitted to a reconstituted civil society/public sphere. Sociological endeavour and output should – logically and morally – inform public deliberation. And finally, it should not purport to be value-neutral, since it is logically and morally contiguous with communicative action, premised not only on the public use of reason, that is, the pursuit of an inclusive, informed and 'argued-out' consensus between a freely and equally participating – and increasingly transnational – citizenry, but, it follows, on the pursuit of – increasingly transnational – legal and social institutions capable of securing and underwriting justice and solidarity. In this sense, sociology's search for the best explanations for why social phenomena are as they are across a wide range of figurations is a moral quest: it carries with it a commitment to lifeworld rationalization *and to counter system-driven attempts to subvert this commitment*. A reflexive critical sociology necessarily has its roots in a reconstructed 'project of modernity' (Scambler, 1996, 2002).

What then of a reflexive critical sociology of sport? On the face of it there would seem to be numerous precedents. 'The critical sociology of sport', according to McDonald, 2002: 101–2), 'is a broad term that is made up from a range of theoretical perspectives and research methodologies'. He mentions as specific antecedents: the neo-Marxist multi-disciplinary analysis of culture and ideology emerging from the Frankfurt School; the Weberian-influenced interpretive work of the Chicago School; and the Gramscian inspired analyses of identity and cultural relations of power developed by the Centre of Contemporary Cultural Studies (CCCS) in Birmingham. Other more recent perspectives he mentions include feminism and post-structuralism. 'The critical sociology of sport can therefore be conceptualized as theoretically eclectic, multidisciplinary, and dynamic; it draws on contributions from disciplines ranging from history to psychoanalysis; and it is constantly developing in responses to theoretical, political and social challenges'. The critical sociology of sport as defined by McDonald is indeed a 'broad term'. He goes on to suggest, however, that while a critical sociology of sport necessarily appears committed, as it were 'in the abstract', to a 'radically-transformative' praxis, its exponents write increasingly of resistance, identity and difference, of the politics of consumption and style (Tomlinson, 1990), or of the subversive power of pleasure (Whannel, 1993), reflecting an unacknowledged slippage of ambition, one might think – certainly with much third-wave feminism and post-structuralism – from modern emancipation to postmodern disinhibition. The truth is, of course, that while sport, like many other cultural phenomena, has become increasingly vulnerable to unaccountable system rationalization/lifeworld colonization – *it remaining a logical and moral requirement of a reflexive critical sociology of sport to analyze, expose and disseminate the 'how' and 'why' of this* – sport's potential to mobilize people in the name of radical social transformation remains marginal.

Unquestionably sport can mobilize groups and publics. This is why it is a ready source of both profits and political kudos. Furthermore, the fact that sport can be used strategically to serve system or vested interests via money and power implies the possibility of lifeworld resistance and challenge. But it would surely be foolhardy in light of the overall picture of disorganized capitalism presented here (for which there is strong empirical support) to predict much in the way of modern rather than postmodern sport-based protest, let alone the formation through sport of a radically transformative praxis? Morgan (1994) takes radical or hegemony theorists, such as those writing from the CCCS, to task for failing to deal adequately with the issue of agency. Having lost confidence in class-based Marxist analyses, and in the agentic and solidary potential of the working class, they appear to be at a loss for an alternative. Gramsci commended culture, and therefore sport, as a site for hegemonic struggle. But as Gruneau (1988: 25) points out, 'the historical coincidence' of the privileging of resistance through culture with the neo-liberal successes of Thatcherism and Reaganism in the 1980s is 'discomforting'; and he warns against a 'celebratory optimism about the autonomous nature and oppositional possibilities of almost all forms of "pleasurable" popular cultural practice'. As this text has shown, there is a real risk of the postmodernization of contemporary movements of opposition, that is, of the 'ironic' neutering of organized opposition to lifeworld colonization by its incorporation in a culture-ideology of consumerism consonant with the vested interests of a resurgent and strongly globalized capitalist-executive and its allies in disorganized capitalism. This is why Habermas (1987, 1989) sees most postmodern or post-structuralist perspectives, for all their capacity to disinhibit, as insidious forms of neo-conservatism; and why, relatedly, he seeks to reconstruct and revive the project of modernity, noting its proven capacity, all too seldom realized, to emancipate.

It is certainly premature to write off class-based action to counter aspects of the colonization of the lifeworld, or even persistent cultural resistance; yet no critical, let alone neo-Marxist or socialist, activist could be sanguine in the era of global or disorganized capitalism. But where does this leave our critical sociology of sport? McDonald (2002) usefully delineates two perspectives within what he calls 'critical social research', namely, the *moralistic* and the *radical*. Moralistic research collapses the boundary between research and activism, and in doing so may jeopardize the integrity and tenets of a scientific sociology. The radical approach is best understood as a 'politicized' application of critical social research. 'It is an orientation to the political situation and a desire to provide resources that can empower subordinate and campaigning groups against dominant relations of power that characterizes radical social research. But unlike moralistic social research, the radical approach recognizes the distinction between political intervention and political activism.' A radical sociology of sport, he concludes, 'should be seeking the reconfiguration of the culture of sport by intervening against dominant relations of power. Social researchers working in the privileged spaces of the academy who claim to be radical can be expected to do no more, but no less, than this' (McDonald, 2002: 115).

The position advocated here differs little from McDonald's portrayal of the radical social researcher. A reflexive critical sociology of sport should be empirical, scientific, inform and be informed by theory and be set in a post-positivist and maybe critical realist frame. Weber was not mistaken in insisting either that research necessarily echoes personal and cultural values or in demanding integrity and scholarship, his 'value-neutrality', in the conduct of empirical, scientific social research. What needs to be added is a reflexive critical sociology's *additional* logical and moral commitment to lifeworld rationalization and de-colonization, which translates in practice into an imperative (1) to resist the strategic distortion of researchers' values and research foci, most obviously via the McDonaldization of universities, and (2) to contest strategic obstacles to the dissemination of research in civil society and the public sphere. Finally, for all the intrinsic morality of a reflexive critical sociology of sport, it remains neutral in relation to *ethical* visions of the 'good life'. Ethics are a matter for the public use of reason.

References

Andre, M. and Fleischer, N. (1993) *A Pictorial History of Boxing*. London; Hamlyn.

Andrews, D. (1991) Welsh Indigenous! And British Imperial? – Welsh rugby, culture and society. *Journal of Sport History*, 18: 335–49.

Andrews, D. (1996) The fact(s) of Michael Jordan's blackness: excavating a floating racial signifier. *Sociology of Sport Journal*, 13: 125–58.

Andrews, D. (1998) Feminizing Olympic reality: preliminary from Baudrillard's Atlanta. *International Review for the Sociology of Sport*, 33: 5–18.

Andrews, D. (2000) Posting up: French post-structuralism and the critical analysis of contemporary sporting culture. In Coakley, J. and Dunning, E (eds) *Handbook of Sports Studies*. London; Sage.

Andrews, D. (ed) (2001) *Michael Jordan, Inc: Corporate Sport, Media Culture, and Late Modern America*. New York; State University of New York Press.

Andrews, D. and Howells, J. (1993) Transforming into a tradition: rugby and the making of Imperial Wales, 1890–1914. In Ingham, A. and Loy, J (eds) *Sport in Social Development: Traditions, Transitions, and Transformations*. Leeds; Human Kinetics Press.

Andrews, D., Howells, J. and Thing, L. (2001) The female warrior: meanings of play-aggressive emotions in sport. *International Review for the Sociology of Sport*, 36: 275–88.

Archer, M. (1995) *Realist Social Theory: The Morphogenetic Approach*. Cambridge; Cambridge University Press.

Armstrong, G. (1998) *Football Hooligans: Knowing the Score*. Oxford; Berg.

Ash, R. and Morrison, I. (2002) *Top 10 in Sport*. London; Dorling Kindersley.

Ashworth, C. (1971) Sport as symbolic dialogue. In Dunning, E (ed.) *The Sociology of Sport*. London; Frank Cass.

Baker, W. (1982) *Sports in the Western World*. Totowa; Rowman & Littlefield.

Bale, J. (1998) Virtual fandoms: futurescapes of football. In Brown, A (ed.) *Fanatics: Power, Identity and Fandom in Football*. London; Routledge.

Baudrillard, J. (1983) *Simulations*. New York; Semiotexte.

Baudrillard, J. (1990) *Fatal Strategies*. New York; Semiotexte.

Bauman, Z. (1979) The phenomenon of Norbert Elias. *Sociology*, 13: 117–25.

Bauman, Z. (1987) *Legislators and Interpreters: On Modernity, Postmodernity and Intellectuals*. Cambridge; Cambridge University Press.

Bauman, Z. (2000) *Liquid Modernity*. Cambridge; Polity Press.

Beck, U. (2000) *The Brave New World of Work*. Cambridge; Polity Press.

Beck, U., Giddens, A. and Lash, S. (1994) *Reflexive Modernization: Politics, Tradition and Aesthetics in the Modern Social Order*. Cambridge; Polity Press.

Bendle, M. (2002) The crisis of 'identity' in high modernity. *British Journal of Sociology*, 53: 1–18.

Beresford, P. and Boyd, S. (2004) *Sunday Times Rich List 2004*.

Bhaskar, R. (1978) *A Realist Theory of Science* 2nd edn, Hemel Hempstead; Harvester Wheatsheaf.

Bhaskar, R. (1989) *The Possibility of Naturalism* 2nd edn, Hemel Hempstead; Harvester Wheatsheaf.

Bhaskar, R. (1989a) *Reclaiming Reality: A Critical Introduction to Contemporary Philosophy*. London; Verso.

Birley, D. (1993) *Sport and the Making of Britain*. Manchester; Manchester University Press.

Birrell, S. (2000) Feminist theories for sport. In Coakley, J. and Dunning, E (eds) *Handbook of Sports Studies*. London; Sage.

Bose, M. (2001) *Manchester Unlimited: The Rise and Rise of the World's Premier Football Club*. London; Texere.

Bourdieu, P. (1977) *Outline of a Theory of Practice*. Cambridge; Cambridge University Press.

Boyle, R. and Haynes, R. (2000) *Power Play: Sport, the Media and Popular Culture*. Harlow; Pearson Education.

Brailsford, D. (1969) *Sport and Society: Elizabeth to Anne*. London; Routledge and Kegan Paul.

Brailsford, D. (1988) *Bareknuckles*. Cambridge; Lutterworth Press.

Brailsford, D. (1991) *Sport, Time and Society: The British at Play*. London; Routledge and Kegan Paul.

Brailsford, D. (1992) *British Sport – A Social History*. Cambridge; The Lutterworth Press.

Brand, A. (1990) *The Force of Reason: An Introduction to Habermas's Theory of Communicative Action*. London; Allen & Unwin.

Braudy, L. (1997) *The Frenzy of Renown: Fame and its History* 2nd edn, New York; Vintage Books.

Brohm, J.M. (1978) *Sport: A Prison of Measured Time*. London; Ink Links.

Brookes, R. (2002) *Representing Sport*. London; Arnold.

Brown, A. (2000) European football and the EU: governance, participation and social cohesion – towards a policy research agenda. *Soccer and Society*, 1: 129–50.

Brunet, F. (1993) *Economy of the 1992 Barcelona Olympic Games*. Barcelona; Centre d'Estudis Olímpics.

Buford, W. (1991) *Among the Thugs*. London; Secker & Warburg.

Burbank, M., Andranovich, G. and Heying, C. (2001) *Olympic Dreams: The Impact of Mega-Events on Local Politics*. London; Lynne Reinner Publishers.

Burchill, J. (2001) *Burchill on Beckham*. London; Yellow Jersey Press.

Burton-Nelson, M. (1996) *The Stronger Women Get, the More Men Love Football: Sexism and the Culture of Sport*. London; Women's Press.

Byrne, M. (1987) Nazi festival: the Berlin Olympics. In Falassi, A (ed.) *Time Out of Time: Essays on the Festival*. Albuquerque; University of New Mexico Press.

Campbell, D., Revill, J. and Townsend, M. (2003) Just one in four has a sporting chance. *Observer*, 28 September.

Carlton, E. (1977) *Ideology and Social Order*. London; Routledge and Kegan Paul.

Carrington, B. (2001) Sport, masculinity and black cultural resistance. In Scraton, S. and Flintoff, A (eds) *A Reader in Gender and Sport*. London; Routledge.

Cashmore, E. (2000) *Making Sense of Sports* 3rd edn, London; Routledge.

Cashmore, E. (2002) *Beckham*. Cambridge; Polity Press.

Caudwell, J. (1999) Women's football in the United Kingdom: theorizing gender and unpacking the butch lesbian image. *Journal of Sport and Social Issues*, 23(4): 390–402.

Clarke, J. (1978) Football and working class fans: tradition and change. In Ingham, R (ed.), *Football Hooliganism: The Wider Context*. London; Inter-Action Imprint.

Clarke, R. (2002) *The Future of Sports Broadcasting Rights*. London; Sports Business Group.

Coakley, J. (2001) *Sport in Society: Issues and Controversies* 7th edn, Boston; McGraw-Hill.

Coakley, J. and White, A. (1992) Making decisions: gender and sport participation among British adolescents. *Sociology of Sport Journal*, 9: 20–35.

Cole, C. and Andrews, D. (1996) Look – its NBA showtime: visions of race in the popular imagination. In Denzin, N (ed.) *Cultural Studies: A Research Volume*. Volume 1.

Conn, D. (1997) *The Football Business – Fair Game in the 1990s?* Edinburgh; Mainstream.

Cornell, R. (1987) *Gender and Power*. Stanford, CA; Stanford University Press.

Coubertin, P. de (1951) Olympism and the IOC. *Bulletin du CIO* (Address at the Olympic Congress, Prague, 29 May).

Creaven, S. (2000) *Marxism and Realism: A Materialistic Application of Realism in the Social Sciences*. London; Routledge.

Critcher, C. (1979) Football since the war. In Clarke, J (ed.) *Working Class Culture*. London; Hutchinson.

Crook, S., Paluski, J. and Waters, M. (1992) *Postmodernization: Changes in Advanced Society*. London; Sage.

Crossley, N. (2004) Fat is a sociological issue: obesity rates in late modern, 'body conscious' societies. *Social Theory and Health*, 3: 222–53.

Crowther, N. (2001) Visiting the Olympic Games in ancient Greece: travel and conditions for athletes and spectators. *International Journal of the History of Sport*, 18: 37–52.

Crump, J. (1989) Athletics. In Mason, T (ed.) *Sport in Britain: A Social History*. Cambridge; Cambridge University Press.

Dawe, A. (1970) The two sociologies. *British Journal of Sociology*, 21: 207–18.

Deloitte & Touche (2002) *Deloitte & Touche Annual Review of Football Finance*. Manchester; Deloitte & Touche.

Deloitte & Touche (2002a) *Comparative Review of Sports Finances*. Manchester; Deloitte & Touche.

Delves, A. (1981) Popular recreation and social conflict in Derby, 1800–1850. In Yeo, E. and Yeo, S (eds), *Popular Culture and Class Conflict 1590–1914: Explorations in the History of Labour and Leisure*. Brighton; Harvester.

Demerath, N. (1967) Synecdoche and structural-functionalism. In Demerath, N. and Peterson, R (eds) *System Change and Conflict*. New York; Free Press.

Department for Education and Skills/Department of Culture, Media and Sport (2003) *Learning Through PE and Sport: A Guide to the Physical Education, School Sport and Clubs Links Strategy*. London; HMSO.

Department of Culture, Media and Sport (2003) School playing fields. www.culture.gov.uk.

Derrida, J. (1976) *Of Grammatology*. Baltimore; Johns Hopkins University Press.

Deubner, L. (1936) *Kult und spiel in alten Olympia*. Leipzig; Hoffman.

Dobson, S. and Goddard, J. (2001) *The Economics of Football*. Cambridge; Cambridge University Press.

Donnelly, P. (2000) Interpretive approaches to the sociology of sport. In Coakley, J. and Dunning, E (eds) *Handbook of Sports Studies*. London; Sage.

Donnelly, P. (2003) Sport and social theory. In Houlihan, B (ed.) *Sport and Society*. London; Sage.

Donohoe, T. and Johnson, N. (1986) *Foul Play: Drug Abuse in Sports*. Oxford; Blackwell.

Dunning, E. (1986) The sociology of sport in Europe and the United States: critical observations from an 'Eliasian' perspective. In Rees, C. and Miracle, A (eds) *Sport and Social Theory*. Champaign, Ill.; Human Kinetics Publishing.

Dunning, E. (1999) *Sport Matters: Sociological Studies of Sport, Violence and Civilization*. London; Routledge.

Dunning, E. (2002) Figurational contributions to the sociological study of sport. In Maguire, J. and Young, K (eds) *Theory, Sport and Society*. London; Elsevier.

Dunning, E., Murphy, P. and Williams, J. (1988) *The Roots of Football Hooliganism*. London; Routledge.

Dunning, E. and Sheard, K. (1979) *Barbarians, Gentlemen and Players: A Sociological Study of the Development of Rugby Football*. Oxford; Martin Robertson.

Dworkin, S. and Messner, M. (2001) Just do . . . what? Sport, bodies, gender. In Scraton, S. and Flintoff, A (eds) *A Reader in Gender and Sport*. London; Routledge.

Edgell, S. and Jary, D. (1973) Football: a sociological eulogy. In Smith, M., Parker, S. and Smith, C (eds) *Leisure and Society in Britain*. London; Allen Lane.

Eichberg, H. (1984) Olympic sport: neocolonialism and alternatives. *International Review for the Sociology of Sport*, 19: 97–105.

Elias, N. (1978) *What is Sociology?* London; Hutchinson.

Elias, N. (1978a) *The Civilizing Process. Vol. 1: The History of Manners*. Oxford; Basil Blackwell.

Elias, N. (1982) *The Civilizing Process. Vol. 2: State Formation and Civilization*. Oxford; Basil Blackwell.

Elias, N. (1986) The genesis of sport as a social problem. In Elias, N. and Dunning, E (eds) *Quest for Excitement*. Oxford; Blackwell.

Elias, N. (1987) *Involvement and Detachment*. Oxford; Basil Blackwell.

Elias, N. and Dunning, E. (1970) Folk football in mediaeval and early modern Britain. In Dunning, E (ed.) *The Sociology of Sport*. London; Frank Cass.

Elias, N. and Dunning, E. (1986) *Quest for Excitement: Sport and Leisure in the Civilizing Process*. Oxford; Basil Blackwell.

Eriksen, E. and Weigard, J. (2003) *Understanding Habermas: Communicating Action and Deliberative Democracy*. London; Continuum.

Espy, R. (1981) *The Politics of the Olympic Games*. Berkeley; University of California Press.

Eyquem, M. (1976) The founder of the modern Games. In Killanin, Lord and Rodda, J. (eds) *The Olympic Games*. New York; Macmillan.

Fasting, K. and Scraton, S. (1997) The myth of masculinization of the female athlete: the experiences of European sporting women. Paper presented at NASSS, November, Toronto, Canada.

Faulkner, R. (1974) Making violence by doing work: selves, situations and the world of professional hockey. *Sociology of Work and Occupations* 1: 288–312.

Featherstone, M. (1991) The body in consumer culture. In Featherstone, M., Hepworth, M. and Turner, B (eds) *The Body: Social Processes and Cultural Theory*. London; Sage.

Finley, M. (1983) *Ancient Greeks*. Harmondsworth; Penguin.

Finley, M. and Pleket, H. (1976) *The Olympic Games: The First Thousand Years*. London; Chatto & Windus.

Fleetwood, S. (2002) What kind of 'theory' is Marx's Labour 'theory' of value? A critical realist inquiry. In Brown, A., Fleetwood, S. and Roberts, J. (eds) *Critical Realism and Marxism*. London; Routledge.

Foley, G. (1999) Cathy and the Olympics. < www.vic.uca.org.au/fairwear/cop.htm >.

Football Association (1991) *Blueprint for the Future of Football*. London; FA.

Foucault, M. (1972) *The Archeology of Knowledge and the Discourse on Language*. New York; Tavistock Publications.

Foucault, M. (1973) *The Order of Things: An Archeology of the Human Sciences*. New York; Vintage Books.

Foucault, M. (1979) *Discipline and Punish: The Birth of the Prison*. New York; Vintage Books.

Foucault, M. (1979a) On governmentality. *Ideology and Consciousness*, 6: 5–22.

Foucault, M. (1980) *Power/Knowledge*. Brighton; Harvester.

Gamson, J. (1994) *Claims to Fame: Celebrity in Contemporary America*. Berkeley; University of California Press.

Gardiner, E. (1930) *Athletics of the Ancient World*. Oxford; The Clarendon Press.

Gee, T. (1998) *Up To Scratch: Bareknuckle Fighting and Heroes of the Prize-Ring*. Harpenden; Queen Anne Press.

Geertz, C. (1973) *The Interpretation of Culture*. New York; Basic Books.

Gentry, C. (2002) *No Holds Barred: The Story of Ultimate Fighting*. Ramsbottom; Milo Books Ltd.

Giddens, A. (1990) *Consequences of Modernity*. Cambridge; Polity Press.

Giles, D. (2000) *Illusions of Immortality: A Psychology of Fame and Celebrity*. London; Macmillan.

Giulianotti, R. (1995a) Football and the politics of carnival: an ethnographic study of Scottish fans in Sweden. *International Review for the Sociology of Sport*, 30: 191–224.

Giulianotti, R. (1995b) Participant observation and research into football hooliganism: reflections on the problems of entrée and everyday risks. *Sociology of Sport Journal*, 12: 1–20.

Giulianotti, R. (1999) *Football: A Sociology of the Global Game*. Cambridge; Polity Press.

Glader, E. (1978) *Amateurism and Athletics*. New York; Leisure Press.

Goffman, E. (1971) *The Presentation of Self in Everyday Life*. Harmondsworth; Penguin.

Golden, M. (1998) *Sport and Society in Ancient Greece*. Cambridge; Cambridge University Press.

Gorman, B. and Walsh, P. (2002) *King of the Gypsies*. Lytham; Milo Books.

Gorn, E. (1986) *The Manly Art: Bare-Knuckle Prize Fighting in America*. New York; Cornell University Press.

Gouldner, A. (1975) *For Sociology: Renewal and Critique in Sociology Today*. Harmondsworth; Penguin.

Grandy, R. (1973) Reference, meaning and belief. *Journal of Philosophy*, 70: 439–52.

Grant, T. (ed.) (2000) *Physical Activity and Mental Health: National Consensus Statements and Guidelines for Practice*. London; HEA.

Green, G. (1953) *The History of the Football Association*. London; Naldrett.

Gruneau, R. (1981) Review of 'Surfing Subcultures of Australia and New Zealand'. *ICSS Bulletin*, 21: 8–10.

Gruneau, R. (1983) *Class, Sports and Social Development*. Amherst, MA; The University of Massachusetts Press.

Gruneau, R. (1984) Commercialism and the modern Olympics. In Tomlinson, A. and Whannel, G (eds) *Five Ring Circus: Money, Power and Politics at the Olympic Games*. London; Pluto Press.

Gruneau, R. (1993) The critique of sport in modernity: theorizing power, culture and the politics of the body. In Dunning, E., Maguire, J. and Pearton, R (eds) *The Sports Process: A Comparative and Developmental Approach*. Champaign, Ill; Human Kinetics.

Guttman, A. (1978) *From Ritual to Record: The Nature of Modern Sports*. New York; Columbia University Press.

Guttman, A. (1984) *The Games Must Go On: Avery Brundage and the Olympic Movement*. New York; Columbia University Press.

Guttman, A. (1988) The Nazi Olympics. In Segrave, J. and Chu, D (eds) *The Olympic Games in Transition*. Champaign, Ill; Human Kinetics Books.

Guttman, A. (1994) *Games and Empires*. New York; Columbia University Press.

Guttman, A. (2002) The development of modern sports. In Coakley, J. and Dunning, E (eds) *Handbook of Sports Studies*. London; Sage.

Guttman, A. (2002a) *The Olympics: A History of the Modern Games* 2nd edn, Urbana; University of Illinois Press.

Habermas, J. (1976) *Legitimation Crisis*. London; Heinemann.

Habermas, J. (1984) *The Theory of Communicative Action, Volume One: Reason and the Rationalization of Society*. London; Heinemann.

Habermas, J. (1986) *Theory and Society*. Cambridge; Polity Press.

Habermas, J. (1987) *The Philosophical Discourse of Modernity*. Cambridge; Polity Press.

Habermas, J. (1987a) *The Theory of Communicative Action, Volume Two: Lifeworld and System: A Critique of Functionalist Reason*. Cambridge; Polity Press.

Habermas, J. (1989) *The New Conservatism*. Cambridge; Polity Press.

Hanks, C. (2002) *Refiguring Critical Theory: Jurgen Habermas and the Possibilities of Political Change*. Lanham; University Press of America.

Harding, J. (2003) *Living to Play: From Soccer Slaves to Socceratti – A Social History of the Professionals*. London; Chrysalis Books.

Hargreaves, J. (1986) *Sport, Power and Culture: A Social and Historical Analysis of Popular Sports in Britain*. Cambridge; Polity Press.

Hargreaves, J. (1993) Bodies matter! Images of sport and female sexualization. In Brackenridge, C. (ed.) *Body Matters: Leisure Images and Lifestyles*. LSA; Eastbourne.

Hargreaves, J. (1994) *Sporting Females: Critical Issues in the History and Sociology of Women's Sport*. London; Routledge.

Hargreaves, J. and McDonald, I. (2000) Cultural studies and the sociology of sport. In Coakley, J. and Dunning, E. (eds) *Handbook of Sports Studies*. London; Sage.

Harris, H. (1975) *Sport in Britain: Its Origins and Development*. London; Stanley Paul.

Harris, H. (2003) *The Chelski Revolution*. London; John Blake Publishing.

Hart-Davis, D. (1986) *Hitler's Games: The 1936 Olympics*. London; Century.

Health Education Authority (1996) *Promoting Physical Activity in Primary Health Care: Guidance for the Primary Healthcare Team*. London; HEA.

Heinila, K. (1969) Football at the crossroads. *International Review of Sport Sociology*, 4: 5–30.

Held, D., McGrew, A., Goldblatt, D. and Perraton, J. (1999) *Global Transformations: Politics, Economics and Culture*. Cambridge; Polity Press.

Hill, C. (1996) *Olympic Politics: Athens to Atlanta, 1896–1996* 2nd edn, Manchester; Manchester University Press.

Hobsbaum, E. (1994) *The Age of Extremes: The Short Twentieth Century 1914–1991*. London; Michael Joseph.

Holt, R. (1989) *Sport and the British: A Modern History*. Oxford; Oxford University Press.

Horne, J., Tomlinson, A. and Whannel, G. (1999) *Understanding Sport: An Introduction to the Sociological Analysis of Sport*. London; E. & F. N. Spon.

Hotten, J. (1998) *Unlicensed: Random Notes from Boxing's Underbelly*. Edinburgh; Mainstream Publishing.

Houlihan, B. (2003) Politics, power, policy and sport. In Houlihan, B. (ed.) *Sport and Society*. London; Sage.

Houlihan, B. (2003a) Doping and sport: more problems than solutions? In Houlihan, B. (ed.) *Sport and Society*. London; Sage.

Howe, P. (1999) Professionalism, commercialism and the rugby club: from embryo to infant at Pontypridd RFC. In Chandler, T. and Nauright, J. (eds) *The Rugby World: Race, Gender, Commerce and the Rugby Union*. London; Frank Cass.

Howe, P. (2001) An ethnography of pain and injury in professional rugby union: the case of Pontypridd RFC. *International Review for the Sociology of Sport*, 36: 289–303.

Howe, P. (2003) Kicking stereotypes into touch: an ethnographic account of women's rugby. In Bolin, A. and Granskog, J. (eds) *Athletic Intruders: Ethnographic Research on Women, Culture and Exercise*. New York; State University of New York Press.

Huizinga, J. (1938) *Homo Ludens*. London; Routledge & Kegan Paul.

Hume, P. and Marshall, S. (1994) Sports injuries in New Zealand: exploratory analysis. *New Zealand Journal of Sports Medicine*, 22: 18–22.

Jarvie, G. and Maguire, J (1994) *Sport and Leisure in Social Thought*. London; Routledge.

Jennings, A. (1994) *Address to the North American Society for the Sociology of Sport*. Savannah, Georgia.

Jennings, A. (1996) *The New Lords of the Rings: Olympic Corruption and How to Buy Gold Medals*. London; Simon & Schuster.

Johnson, M. (2003) *Martin Johnson: The Autobiography*. London; Headline Book Publishing.

Kelso, P. (2002) Health problems growing after decades of neglect on the playing fields of Britain, *Guardian*, 16 December.

Kenyon, G. (1986) The significance of social theory in the development of sport sociology. In Rees, C. and Miracle, A. (eds) *Sport and Social Theory*. Champaign, Ill; Human Kinetics.

Killanin, M. (1983) *My Olympic Years*. London; Secker & Warburg.

Kitson, R. (2004) We're no soft touch insists Dallaglio, *Guardian*, 4 March.

Klein, N. (2001) *No Logo*. London; Flamingo.

Korsgaard, R. (1952) *A History of the Amateur Athletic Union of the United States*. Unpublished Ph.D., Columbia University.

Krotee, M. (1988) An organizational analysis of the International Olympic Committee. In Segrave, J. and Chu, D. (eds) *The Olympic Games in Transition*. Champaign, Ill; Human Kinetics Books.

Kruger, A. (1999) The unfinished symphony: a history of the Olympic Games from Coubertin to Samaranch. In Riordan, J. and Kruger, A. (eds) *The International Politics of Sport in the Twentieth Century*. New York; Routledge.

LeFaber, W. (2002) *Michael Jordan and the New Global Capitalism* 2nd edn, New York; W. W. Norton & Co.

Lanchester, J. (2004) Bravo l'artiste. *London Review of Books*, 26: 3–7.

Landes, D. (1998) *The Wealth and Poverty of Nations*. London; Little, Brown & Co.

Lanfranchi, P. and Taylor, M. (2001) *Moving with the Ball: The Migration of Professional Footballers*. Oxford; Berg.

Lawton, W. (1903) The Greek attitude toward athletics and Pindar. *The Sewanee Review*, 11: 131–2.

Leighton, T. (2001) Women's football in the UK. http://footballculture.net/players/feat_women.html

Lemert, C. (2003) *Muhammad Ali: Trickster in the Culture of Irony*. Cambridge; Polity Press.

Lenskyj, H. (1994) Girl friendly sport and female values. *Women in Sport and Physical Activity Journal*, 3: 35–46.

Lenskyj, H. (2000) *Inside the Olympic Industry: Power, Politics, and Activism*. Albany; State University of New York Press.

Lenskyj, H. (2002) *The Best Olympics Ever? Social Impacts of Sydney 2000*. Albany; State University of New York Press.

Lloyd, T. (2001) *Empire: The History of the British Empire*. London; Hambledon.

Lovesey, P. (1979) *The Official Centenary History of the AAA*. London; Guinness Superlatives Ltd.

Loy, J. and Booth, D. (2000) Functionalism, sport and society. In Coakley, J. and Dunning, E. (eds) *Handbook of Sports Studies*. London; Sage.

Lucas, J. (1988) The genesis of the modern Olympic Games. In Segrave, J. and Chu, D. (eds) *The Olympic Games in Transition*. Champaign, Ill; Human Kinetics Books.

Lukes, S. (1982) Relativism in its place. In Hollis, M. and Lukes, S. (eds) *Rationality and Relativism*. Oxford; Basil Blackwell.

Luschen, G. (1967) The interdependence of sport and culture. *International Review of Sport Sociology*, 2: 127–42.

Luschen, G. (2000) Doping in sport as deviant behaviour and its social control. In Coakley, J. and Dunning, E. (eds) *Handbook of Sports Studies*. London; Sage.

Lynch, J. and Carcasona, C. (1994) The team physician. In Ekblom, B. (ed.) *Handbook of Sports Medicine and Science: Football (Soccer)*. Oxford; Blackwell Series.

Lyotard, J.-F. (1984) *The Postmodern Condition*. Manchester; Manchester University Press.

MacAloon, J. (1981) *This Great Symbol: Pierre de Coubertin and the Origin of the Modern Olympic Games*. Chicago; University of Chicago Press.

Macias, P. (2000) *A–Z of European Football*. Caceras; Copegraf, S.L.

Magnusson, S. (1982) *The Flying Scotsman: A Biography*. London; Quartet Books.

Maguire, J. (1999) *Global Sport: Identities, Societies Civilizations*. Cambridge; Polity Press.

Maguire, J., Jarvie, G., Mansfield, L. and Bradley, J. (2002) *Sport Worlds: A Sociological Perspective*. Champaign, Illinois; Human Kinetics.

Mandell, R. (1984) *Sport: A Cultural History*. New York; Columbia University Press.

Mangan, J. (1981) *Athleticism in the Victorian and Edwardian Public School*. Cambridge; Cambridge University Press.

Marsh, P. (1982) *Aggro: The Illusion of Violence*. Oxford; Basil Blackwell.

Marsh, P., Rosser, E. and Harré, R. (1978) *The Rules of Disorder*. London; Routledge & Kegan Paul.

Mason, T. (1980) *Association Football and English Society, 1863–1915*. Brighton; Harvester.

Mason, T. (1988) *Sport in Britain*. London; Faber & Faber.

Mason, T. (1989) Football. In Mason, T. (ed.) *Sport in Britain: A Social History*. Cambridge; Cambridge University Press.

McDonald, I. (2002) Critical social research and political intervention: moralistic versus radical approaches. In Sugden, J. and Tomlinson, A. (eds) *Power Games: A Critical Sociology of Sport*. London; Routledge.

McIntosh, P. (1963) The sociology of sport in the ancient world. In Dunning, E., Maguire, J. and Pearton, R. (eds) *The Sports Process: A Comparative and Developmental Approach*. Champaign, Illinois; Human Kinetics Publishers.

McKenna, J. and Riddoch, C. (2003) (eds) *Perspectives on Health and Exercise*. London; Palgrave.

McLuhan, M. (1964) *Understanding Media: The Extension of Man*. London; Routledge.

McRae, D. (2002) *In Black and White: The Untold Story of Joe Louis and Jesse Owens*. Scribner; New York.

Mehl, J.-M. (1993) *Jeux, Sports et Divertissements au Moyen Age et à l'Age Classique*. Paris; Editions du Comité des Travaux Historiques et Scientifiques.

Mennesson, C. (2000) 'Hard' women and 'soft' women: the social construction of identities among female boxers. *International Review for the Sociology of Sport*, 35: 21–33.

Merton, R. (1957) *Social Theory and Social Structure*. Glencoe, Ill; Free Press.

Messinesi, X. (1973) *A Branch of Wild Olive: The Olympic Movement and the Ancient and Modern Olympic Games*. New York; Exposition Press.

Messner, M. (1993) *Power at Play: Sports and the Problem of Masculinity*. Boston; Beacon Press.

Messner, M. and Sabo, D. (1990) Toward a critical feminist appraisal of sport, men, and the gender order. In Messner, M. and Sabo, D. (eds) *Sport, Men and the Gender Order: Critical Feminist Perspectives*. Champaign, Ill; Human Kinetics Books.

Miller, D. (2003) *Athens to Athens: The Official History of the Olympic Games and the IOC, 1894–2004*. Edinburgh; Mainstream Publishing.

Mills, K. and Mills, P. (2000) (eds) *C. Wright Mills: Letters and Autobiographical Writing*. Berkeley; University of California Press.

Monaghan, L. (2001) *Bodybuilding, Drugs and Risk*. London; Routledge.

Monaghan, L. (2001a) Looking good, feeling good: the embodied pleasures of vibrant physicality. *Sociology of Health and Illness*, 23: 330–56.

Moran, M. (2003) *The British Regulatory State: High Modernism and Hyper-Innovation.* Oxford; Oxford University Press.

Morgan, W. (1994) *Leftist Theories of Sport: A Critique and Reconstruction.* Urbana; University of Illinois Press.

Morris, J., Everitt, M., Pollard, R. and Chave, S. (1980) Vigorous exercise in leisure time: protection against coronary heart disease. *Lancet*, 6 December: 1207–10.

Morrow, S. (2003) *The People's Game? Football, Finance and Society.* Basingstoke; Palgrave-Macmillan.

Murphy, P., Sheard, K. and Waddington, I. (2000) Figurational sociology and its application to sport. In Coackley, J. and Dunning, E. (eds) *Handbook of Sports Studies.* London; Sage.

Murray, B. (1994) *Football: A History of the World Game.* Aldershot; Scholar Press.

Nabokov, P. (1981) *Indian Running: Native American History and Tradition.* Santa Fe; Ancient City Press.

Office of National Statistics (2001) *Social Trends 31.* London; HMSO.

Office of National Statistics (2003) *UK 2000 Time Use Survey.* London; HMSO.

Page, B. (2003) *The Murdoch Archipelago.* Sydney; Simon & Schuster.

Pakulski, J. and Waters, M. (1996) *The Death of Class.* London; Sage.

Palaeologos, K. (1976) The Pankration. In Douskou, I. (ed.) *The Olympic Games in Ancient Greece.* Athens; Ekdotike.

Parkinson, J. (2003) Can school sport be saved? London; BBC News Online.

Parsons, T. (1966) *Societies: Evolutionary and Comparative Perspectives.* Englewood, NJ; Prentice-Hall.

Plunkett, J. (2002) Sky steps into ITV football breach. *Guardian*, 5 July.

Polsky, N. (1969) *Hustlers, Beats and Others.* New York; Anchor.

Potter, J. (1999) Elegant violence. *Inside Rugby*, January.

Preuss, H. (2003) The economics of the Olympic Games: winners and losers. In Houlihan, B. (ed.) *Sport and Society.* London; Sage.

Prince, D. (2004) Bland, boring this office block may be. But its owners are a new breed of player in property – the celebrity investor. *Evening Standard*, 1 April.

Pringle, R. (2001) Competing discourses: narratives of a fragmented self, manliness and rugby union. *International Review for the Sociology of Sport*, 36: 425–39.

Quercetani, R. (1990) *Athletics: A History of Modern Track and Field Athletics (1860–1990): Men and Women.* Milan; Vallardi & Associati.

Rader, B. (1990) *American Sports: From the Age of Folk Games to the Age of Televised Sports* 2nd edn, New York; Prentice-Hall.

Rail, G. (1998) Seismography of the postmodern condition: three theses on the implosion of sport. In Rail, G. (ed.) *Sport and Postmodern Times.* New York; State University of New York Press.

Rail, G. (2002) Postmodernism and sport studies. In Maguire, J. and Young, K. (eds) Theory, Sport and Society. London; Elsevier.

Redmond, G. (1971) *The Caledonian Games in Nineteenth-Century America.* Cranbury, NJ; Associated University Press Inc.

Redmond, G. (1988) Toward modern revival of the Olympic Games: the various 'pseudo-Olympics' of the nineteenth century. In Segrave, J. and Chu, D. (eds) *The Olympic Games in Transition.* Champaign, Ill; Human Kinetics Books.

Rees, P. (2003) Faster, fitter and so often fractured. *Guardian*, 18 March.

Rigauer, B. (1981) *Sport and Work.* New York; Columbia University Press.

Rigauer, B. (2000) Marxist theories. In Coakley, J. and Dunning, E. (eds) *Handbook of Sports Studies.* London; Sage.

Ritzer, G. (2001) The McDonaldization of American sociology: a metasociological analysis.

In Ritzer, G. *Explorations in Social Theory: From Metatheorizing to Rationalization.* London; Sage.

Ritzer, G. (2003) *Contemporary Sociological Theory and its Classical Roots.* London; McGraw-Hill.

Robertson, N. (1988) The ancient Olympics: sport, spectacle and ritual. In Segrave, J. and Chu, D. (eds) *The Olympic Games in Transition.* Champaign, Ill; Human Kinetics Books.

Robertson, R. (1992) *Globalization: Social Theory and Global Culture.* London; Sage.

Robinson, R. (1955) *Sources for the History of Greek Athletics.* Cincinnati; Author.

Roche, M. (2000) *Mega-Events and Modernity: Olympics and Expos in the Growth of Global Culture.* London. Routledge.

Rockmore, T. (1989) *Habermas on Historical Materialism.* Bloomington and Indianapolis; Indiana University Press.

Rojek, C. (1992) The field of play in sport and leisure studies. In Dunning, E. and Rojek, C. (eds) *Sport and Leisure in the Civilizing Process.* Basingstoke; Macmillan.

Rosen, S. and Sanderson, A. (2001) Labour markets in professional sports. *The Economic Journal,* 111: 47–68.

Rostow, W. (1960) *The Stages of Economic Growth: A Non-Communist Manifesto.* Cambridge; Cambridge University Press.

Royal College of Physicians (1991) *Medical Aspects of Exercise.* London; Royal College of Physicians.

Ruhl, J. (1985) The 'Olympic Games' of Robert Dover, 1612–1984. In Muller, N. and Ruhl, J. (eds) *Olympic Scientific Congress 1984 Official Report: Sport History.* Nierderhousen; Schors-Verlag.

Russell, D. (1997) *Football and the English.* Preston; Carnegie Publishing.

Sammonds, J. (1990) *Beyond the Ring. The Role of Boxing in American Society.* Urbana and Chicago; University of Illinois Press.

Sandvoss, C. (2003) *A Game of Two Halves: Football, Television and Globalization.* London; Routledge.

Scambler, G. (1996) The 'project of modernity' and the parameters for a critical sociology: an argument with illustrations from medical sociology. *Sociology,* 30: 567–81.

Scambler, G. (1998) Medical sociology and modernity: reflections on the public sphere and the roles of intellectuals and social critics. In Scambler, G. and Higgs P. (eds) *Modernity, Medicine and Health: Medical Sociology Towards 2000.* London; Routledge.

Scambler, G. (2001) Unfolding themes of an incomplete project. In Scambler, G. (ed.) *Habermas, Critical Theory and Health.* London; Routledge.

Scambler, G. (2001a) Self-turnover, social representations and the culture-ideology of consumerism: a theory for the health domain. Unpublished manuscript. Annual British Sociological Association Medical Sociology Conference, York, 22 September.

Scambler, G. (2002) *Health and Social Change: A Critical Theory.* Buckingham; Open University Press.

Scambler, G. and Higgs, P. (1999) Stratification, class and health: class relations and health inequalities in high modernity. *Sociology,* 33: 275–96.

Scambler, G. and Higgs, P. (2001) 'The dog that didn't bark': taking class seriously in the health inequalities debate. *Social Science and Medicine,* 52: 157–9.

Scambler, G. and Jennings, M. (1998) On the periphery of the sex industry: female combat, male punters and feminist discourse, *Journal of Sport and Social Issues,* 22: 414–27.

Scambler, G. and Martin, L. (2001) Civil society, the public sphere and deliberative democracy. In Scambler, G. (ed.) *Habermas, Critical Theory and Health.* London; Routledge.

Scambler, G., Ohlsson, S. and Griva, K. (2004) Sport, health and identity: social and cultural change in disorganized capitalism. In Kelleher, D. and Leavy, R. (eds) *Identity and Health*. London; Routledge.

Scanlon, T. (1988) The ecumenical Olympics. In Segrave, E. and Chu, T. (eds) *The Olympic Games in Transition*. Champaign, Illinois; Human Kinetics Books.

Scanlon, T. (2002) *Eros and Greek Athletics*. Oxford; Oxford University Press.

Scott, J. (1991) *Who Rules Britain?* Cambridge; Polity Press.

Scott, J. (1997) *Corporate Business and Capitalist Classes*. Oxford; Oxford University Press.

Scott, M. (1968) *The Racing Game*. Chicago; Aldine.

Scraton, S. and Flintoff, A. (2002) Sport feminism: the contribution of feminist thought to our understandings of gender and sport. In Scraton, S. and Flintoff, A. (eds) *Gender and Sports: A Reader*. London; Routledge.

Searle, J. (2001) *Rationality in Action*. Cambridge, Mass; MIT Press.

Sennett, R. (1998) *The Corrosion of Character: The Personal Consequences of Work in the New Capitalism*. New York; W. W. Norton.

Shipley, S. (1989) Boxing. In Mason, T. (ed.) *Sport in Britain: A Social History*. Cambridge; Cambridge University Press.

Shneidman, N. (1979) *The Soviet Road to Olympus: Theory and Practice of Soviet Physical Culture and Sport*. London; Routledge & Kegan Paul.

Simson, V. and Jennings, A. (1992) *The Lords of the Rings: Power, Money and Drugs in the Modern Olympics*. New York; Simon & Schuster.

Sitton, J. (1996) *Recent Marxian Theory: Class Formation and Social Conflict in Contemporary Capitalism*. Aldershot; Edward Elgar.

Sitton, J. (2003) *Habermas and Contemporary Society*. London; Palgrave-Macmillan.

Sivard, R. (1989) *World Military and Social Expenditures*. Washington, DC; World Priorities.

Sklair, L. (1998) The transnational capitalist class. In Carrier, J. and Miller, D. (eds) *Virtualism: A New Political Economy*. Oxford; Berg.

Smith, A. and Jacobson, B. (1988) *The Nation's Health*. London; King Edward's Hospital Fund for London.

Snyder, E. and Spreitzer, E. (1989) *Social Aspects of Sport*. Englewood Cliffs, NJ; Prentice Hall.

Spears, B. and Swanson, R. (1988) *History of Sport and Physical Education in the United States* 3rd edn, Dubuque; Wm C. Brown Publishers.

Sports Council (1991) *Injuries in Sport and Exercise*. London; Sports Council.

Stead, D. (2003) Sport and the media. In Houlihan, B. (ed.) *Sport and Society*. London; Sage.

Stevenson, C. (1974) Sport as a contemporary social phenomenon: a functional explanation. *International Journal of Physical Education*, 11: 8–14.

Stevenson, C. and Nixon, J. (1972) A conceptual scheme of the social functions of sport. *Sportwissenschaft*, 2: 119–32.

Stone, G. and Oldenberg, R. (1967) Wrestling. In Slovenko, R. and Knight, J. (eds) *Motivations in Play, Games and Sports*. Springfield, Ill; Charles C. Thomas.

Stone, G. (1972) Wrestling: the great American passion play. In Dunning, E. (ed.) *Sport: Readings From a Sociological Perspective*. Toronto; University of Toronto Press.

Stott, C. and Reicher, S. (1998) How conflict escalates: the inter-group dynamics of collective football crowd 'violence'. *Sociology*, 32: 353–77.

Struna, N. (2000) Social history and sport. In Coakley, J. and Dunning, E. (eds) *Handbook of Sports Studies*. London; Sage.

Sugden, J. (1996) *Boxing and Society: An International Analysis*. Manchester; Manchester University Press.

Sugden, J. and Tomlinson, A. (1998) *FIFA and the Contest for World Football: Who Rules the People's Game?* Cambridge; Polity Press.

Sugden, J. and Tomlinson, A. (1999) Digging the dirt and staying clean: retrieving the investigative tradition for a critical sociology of sport. *International Review for the Sociology of Sport*, 34: 385–97.

Sugden, J. and Tomlinson, A. (2003) *Badfellas: FIFA Family at War*. Edinburgh; Mainstream Publishing.

Swaddling, J. (1982) *The Ancient Olympic Games*. London; British Museums Publications.

Sweeney, H. (2004) Gene doping. *Scientific American*, July: 37–43.

Tabner, B. (2002) *Football Through the Turnstiles . . . Again, 1888–2002*. Harefield; Yore Publications.

Tatz, C. (1995) *The Obstacle Race*. Sydney; UNSW Press.

Taylor, I. (1971) Soccer consciousness and soccer hooliganism. In Cohen, S. (ed.) *Images of Deviance*. Harmondworth; Penguin.

Taylor, I. (1982) On the sports violence question: soccer hooliganism revisited. In Hargreaves, J. (ed.) *Sport, Culture and Ideology*. London; Routledge & Kegan Paul.

Taylor, I. (1982a) Class, violence and sport: the case of soccer hooliganism in Britain. In Cantelon, H. and Gruneau, R. (eds) *Sport, Culture and the Modern State*. Toronto; University of Toronto Press.

Taylor, I. (1987) Putting the boot into a working-class sport: British soccer after Bradford and Brussels. *Sociology of Sport Journal*, 4: 171–91.

The Seville Statement on Violence (1997) *ISSP Newsletter*, 1: 13–17.

Thing, L. (2001) The female warrior: meanings of play-aggressive emotions in sport. *International Review for the Sociology of Sport*, 36: 275–88.

Thompson, S. (1992) Sport for others, work for women, quality of life for whom? Paper presented at the Olympic Scientific Congress, Malaga, Spain.

Tischler, S. (1981) *Footballers and Businessmen – The Origins of Professional Soccer in England*. New York; Holmes & Meier.

Tomlinson, A. (1990) (ed.) *Consumption, Identity and Style: Marketing, Meanings and the Packaging of Pleasure*. London; Routledge.

Townsend, M. (2003) One billion pounds fails to halt slide in school sport. *Observer*, 21 December.

Turner, B. (1992) *Max Weber: From History to Modernity*. London; Routledge.

UK Sport (2003) *UK Framework: Strategy For Women and Sport*. www.uksport.gov.uk.

Virilio, P. (1991) *The Lost Dimension*. New York; Semiotexte.

Wacquant, L. (1992) The social logic of boxing in black Chicago: toward a sociology of pugilism. *Sociology of Sport Journal*, 9: 221–54.

Wacquant, L. (1995) Pugs at work: body capital and bodily labour among professional boxers. *Body and Society*, 1: 65–93.

Wacquant, L. (2001) Whores, slaves and stallions: languages of exploitation and accommodation among boxers. *Body and Society*, 7: 181–94.

Waddington, I. (2000) Sport and health: a sociological perspective. In Coakley, J. and Dunning, E. (eds) *Handbook of Sports Studies*. London; Sage.

Waddington, I. (2000a) *Sport, Health and Drugs: A Critical Sociological Perspective*. London; E. & F.N. Spon.

Walvin, J. (1994) *The People's Game*, rev. edn, Edinburgh; Mainstream.

Watman, M. (1968) *History of British Athletics*. London; Robert Hale.

Weiss, L. (1999) Managed openness: beyond neoliberal globalism. *New Left Review*, 238: 126–40.

Whannel, G. (1993) Sport and popular culture: the temporary triumph of process over product. *Innovation*, 6: 341–9.

Whannel, G. (2001) Punishment, redemption and celebration in the popular press: the case of David Beckham. In Andrews, D. and Jackson, S. (eds) *Sports Stars: The Cultural Politics of Sporting Celebrity*. London; Routledge.

Whannel, G. (2002) *Media Sports Stars: Masculinities and Moralities*. London; Routledge.

Wheatley, E. (1994) Subcultural subversions: comparing discourses on sexuality in men's and women's rugby songs. In Birrel, S. and Cole, C. (eds) *Women, Sport and Culture*. Leeds; Human Kinetics.

White, P. and Vagi, A. (1990) Rugby in the 19th-century British boarding-school system: a feminist psychoanalytic perspective. In Messner, M. and Sabo, D. (eds) *Sport, Men and the Gender Order: Critical Feminist Perspectives*. Leeds; Human Kinetics.

Williams, J. (1991) Having an away day: English football spectators and the hooligan debate. In Williams, J. and Wagg, S. (eds) *British Football and Social Change*. Leicester; Leicester University Press.

Williams, J. (2003) *A Game for Rough Girls? A History of Women's Football in Britain*. London; Routledge.

Williams, J., Dunning, E. and Murphy, P. (1989) *Hooligans Abroad: The Behaviour and Control of English Fans in Continental Europe*. 2nd edn. London; Routledge.

Wittgenstein, L. (1958) *Philosophical Investigations*. 2nd edn. Oxford; Blackwell.

Wyatt, D. and Herridge, C. (2003) *The Rugby Revolution*. London; Metro.

Young, D. (1984) *The Olympic Myth of Greek Amateur Athletics*. Chicago; Ares.

Young, D. (1988) Professionalism in archaic and classical Greek athletics. In Segrave, E. and Chu, T. (eds) *The Olympic Games in Transition*. Champaign, Ill.; Human Kinetics Books.

Young, K. (1993) Violence, risk and liability in male sports culture. *Sociology of Sports Journal*, 10: 373–96.

Young, K. (2000) Sport and violence. In Coakley, J. and Dunning, E. (eds) *Handbook of Sports Studies*. London; Sage.

Young, K., White, P. and McTeer, W. (1994) Body talk: male athletes reflect on sport, injury and pain. *Sociology of Sport Journal*, 11: 175–94.

Zeitlin, I. (1973) *Rethinking Sociology: A Critique of Contemporary Theory*. New York; Appleton-Century-Crofts.

INDEX

Page references in *italics* refer to figures and tables.